MARK TWAIN: MAN AND LEGEND

MARK TWAIN

A hitherto unpublished photograph, taken in London in 1907

Mark Twain:
Man and Legend

By

John *DeLancey Ferguson*

NEW YORK / RUSSELL & RUSSELL

1965

COPYRIGHT, 1943, THE BOBBS-MERRILL COMPANY

REISSUED, 1966, BY RUSSELL & RUSSELL
A DIVISION OF ATHENEUM HOUSE, INC.
BY ARRANGEMENT WITH DELANCEY FERGUSON
L. C. CATALOG CARD NO: 66—15430

FOR MARION,
WHO PRODDED;
AND FOR JANE,
WHO PROMISES TO READ IT.

PRINTED IN THE UNITED STATES OF AMERICA

CONTENTS

PREFACE

IN THE last article which he wrote for publication in his lifetime Mark Twain said, "To me, the most important feature of my life is its literary feature." Nevertheless, in the generation which has passed since his death, no one has tried to write Mark Twain's life as a man of letters. To be sure, he never called himself a man of letters, but his favorite term, "literary person," means the same thing. He was a professional writer for nearly forty-eight years out of his seventy-four. That he was also a great many other things matters only in so far as the other things helped or hindered his writing.

This book aims to trace in detail Mark Twain's career as a writing man, passing over lightly, or ignoring, his multifarious nonliterary doings. I have tried to examine the forces which made him a writer, to tell how he wrote his books and why he wrote them as he did. Wherever possible I have allowed him to explain things in his own words, and the fact that a passage is familiar or even hackneyed has not deterred me from citing it if it is the most expressive one. On the other hand, I have not been prejudiced against new or unfamiliar material, when I have been able to find it.

DeL. F.

Cleveland, Ohio
February, 1943

MARK TWAIN: MAN AND LEGEND

CHAPTER I

$DAWN$

AMERICAN optimism reached high tide somewhere between 1815 and 1850. What happened in those years had never happened before in the history of civilized man, and could never happen again. The heart of the richest continent on earth was thrown open for pillage at the moment when steamboats, canals and railways made it possible for the advancing hordes swiftly to consolidate and exploit their gains. Resources and opportunities looked inexhaustible. If you were defeated in one community, there was always more and probably better land farther west. In 1798, when John Marshall Clemens was born in Virginia, the United States was still mostly the Atlantic seaboard; only seven years before, Saint Clair's little army had been bloodily cut to pieces by the Indians near the present western boundary of Ohio. Thirty-seven years later, when John Clemens' famous son was born in Missouri, the settled United States extended to the west bank of the Mississippi, and American life had established the rhythm which it held until after the end of the nineteenth century: fifteen to twenty years of exuberant expansion followed by a brief, sharp period of panic, deflation and transient gloom.

A conquering army does hot count its casualties. When men drop out it is the fortune of war; the army's eyes are on its successful leaders. The westward track of the pioneers was lined with the graves of the fallen; every new village contained its wounded spirits, but the spirit of the march was boundless hope. People saw before them more than the chance of winning a moderate livelihood in farm or shop. There was always a speculative thrill. The lucky ones located strategic townsites,

13

timber claims or mines, and acquired fortunes. Sometimes they were paper fortunes, blown away in the banking panics, but while they lasted they dazzled. These pioneers were hardy, kindly, steadfast; they were also wasteful, greedy and cruel. In other words, they were human. The only qualities they would have failed to recognize in themselves are those imputed to them by modern critics and historians with ideological axes to grind. But to understand a world different from ours it is more important to know how its inhabitants felt about it than it is to tag it with factory-made labels.

No American west of the Alleghanies in the first half of the last century would have known what was meant by the "pioneer mind." His village might be newly chopped out of the forest, but his dream of the place it was to take in national history was embodied in its name. It was not merely, or primarily, the high-pressure salesmen of the New Edens who sprinkled the map with Romes and Toledos and Palmyras. Anything could happen in the New World; Rome itself had been a village once; already American Boston and New York had outgrown their English forebears. But more significant than the grandiose evocations of ancient civilizations was the repetition in the Middle West of the names from the older communities of the East. Calling a raw new settlement Quincy or Mt. Vernon or Norwalk was a declaration of belief not in the "pioneer spirit" but in the continuity of American life from the Atlantic to the Mississippi.

The men who settled the Ohio and Mississippi valleys came from the East and South, and they purposed to create their new homes in the image of the older ones that bred them. They believed politically in the principles of the Declaration of Independence, and economically in the maxims of Poor Richard. But as their belief in the Rights of Man exempted Negroes and Indians, so their belief in industry and thrift did not debar speculation and gambling. No man reared in that era of expansion and optimism ever wholly freed himself from its basic dogmas even when changing times had invalidated them. And

Mark Twain, born near the high tide of the first simple, un-mechanized period of national growth, was a typical son of the westward migration. It formed his spirit and background; in his darkest moments his thoughts still expressed themselves in the patterns he had learned in Missouri and on the River before the Civil War.

But Mark Twain was also a son of the South. To think of him in terms of the Nevada mining camps where he made his first literary reputation, to think of his youthful homes as they look to a New Yorker of today—as too many of his critics have done—is to miss the strongest forces in his life. Hannibal, Missouri, cannot be interpreted in terms of that rebellion against village and farm which began with Ed Howe in the 1880's and Hamlin Garland in the 1890's. The society Mark Twain lived in was not ours; it must be thought of in terms of its own dreams, not ours.

The Clemenses came from Virginia. Their ideals were those of their class—the small planter or the professional man. They were gentlefolk but not magnates. Their class had furnished much of the brains and leadership of the old South in the days before the cotton aristocracy of the Gulf States took control and led their section to ruin. They clung to the graces of life. Lavish hospitality, and therefore sufficient means to indulge in it without worry, was part of their dream, and Mark Twain, keeping open house in Hartford in the 1880's, was expressing an essential part of his ancestral tradition. A gentleman of this stock was expected to be busy, but busy at a gentleman's affairs—directing slaves were he a landowner, practicing a pro-fession and not a trade were he landless.

The Clemenses of Virginia held a minor but honorable posi-tion in the community, but when the first Samuel Clemens was accidentally killed in 1805 he left a family none too well pro-vided for. John Marshall Clemens, first-born of Samuel's five children, was only seven years old. No doubt the responsibility of being the male head of the family intensified the natural austerity of his temperament. He was self-supporting from his early teens, and spent the evenings, when he was released from his clerkship in an iron foundry at Lynchburg, in reading and study. While he was still a minor, the family moved to Adair County, Kentucky, where his mother married again and where he studied law in Columbia, the county seat, fitting himself for a profession as the traditions of his class ordained. When he was twenty-one he wound up his father's estate, in which his own share was three slaves and a mahogany sideboard.

At twenty-five John Clemens met and immediately fell in love with Jane Lampton, five years his junior. Kentucky-born, the daughter of early settlers who had followed Daniel Boone across the mountains and who claimed kinship with the Earls of Durham, Jane Lampton was noted for her auburn-haired beauty and her wit—the latter expressed in the level, drawling tones which her son inherited along with her hair and her slender physique. She embodied a type hard to realize in the twentieth century—women who were ladies and belles though their setting might be only a score of log houses in a muddy clearing. When John Clemens met her, her pride had just shattered a romance. She had been deeply in love with a young medical student named Barrett, who loved her but was too bashful to say so. At last Barrett wrote to ask her uncle to drive her in his buggy to a party in a neighboring town and let Barrett drive her back, and thus have the opportunity to propose. Instead of doing as he was asked and saying nothing, the uncle read Jane the letter. Because of that unwanted knowledge, she refused to go to the party, and presently her disappointed lover left the country. So when John Clemens proposed, not long afterward, she married him out of pique, and to silence the neighbors' clacking tongues. Sixty-two years later she saw Barrett's name among those who were to attend an old settlers' convention in Iowa, and made a toilsome journey in the hope of meeting him again and asking his forgiveness. He had left three hours before she arrived.

But whatever the mood in which Jane Lampton entered upon her marriage, she was a loyal wife to John Clemens in continuously difficult circumstances. The young couple settled first in Gainsborough, Tennessee, on the Cumberland, and there in 1825 their first son, Orion, was born. Thence they migrated to Jamestown, county seat of the new county of Fentress, the Obedstown of *The Gilded Age*. Though his neighbors looked askance at his aristocratic ways—he wore "store clothes," and lived in a plastered house—John Clemens was quickly recognized as a leader and when, largely through his efforts, the new courthouse was built, he was elected circuit clerk. John Clemens was a thoughtful man, and planned for the future. Fentress County lay about midway between the upper reaches of the Cumberland and the Tennessee Rivers, the main arteries of commerce of two states. The region seemed certain of a swift development, and John Clemens saw how he could share that development and secure his family's future. When he got together about $500 capital, he invested it in 75,000 acres of land at a cost of a few cents an acre. The land contained coal and iron, and was richly timbered. It would yield, he was sure, a princely fortune to the man who merely paid the trifling taxes for a few years. Though he might not live to see the fortune, his heirs would be secure.

It was the reasoned optimism of the westward migration. John Clemens foresaw everything except the Middle West and the railroads, which were to divert the streams of traffic and development, and leave the hills of Tennessee in a backwater which had to wait for Sergeant York to give it national fame. Like his son with the Paige typesetting machine, John Clemens knew a good thing when he saw it. The trouble was, it was not the right thing. Half a century later his discouraged children at last let the great tract go for unpaid taxes, decades before its resources were finally tapped. But it supplied Mark Twain with a main theme for his first novel.

Meanwhile, though a fortune was just over the horizon, times were hard for its lawful owners. John Clemens' health was poor, and law practice in Jamestown, which had ceased to grow, was unremunerative. He opened a general store to help feed his

growing family, into which a daughter, Pamela, was born in
1827 and another daughter, Margaret, in 1830. For a short
time he tried storekeeping at the Three Forks of Wolf, and in
1832 was appointed postmaster of Pall Mall, where his second
son, Benjamin, was born. Finally, early in 1835, came a letter
from Jane Clemens' brother-in-law, John Quarles, who, following the main stream of the westward movement, had landed in
the new village of Florida, Missouri. Here he saw everything
which was lacking in the Knobs of Tennessee—ample fertile
acreage, and ready access to markets. The substance of his
letter was: Drop everything, sell out, come to Missouri and
make a fortune. John Clemens did not hesitate. Disposing of
everything salable, he loaded his family and movables and
started for St. Louis.

There is truth of atmosphere, if not of detail, in the arrival
of the Hawkins family at their new home in Missouri, as told
in *The Gilded Age*. "By the muddy roadside stood a new log
cabin, one story high—the store; clustered in the neighborhood
were ten or twelve more cabins, some new, some old." True to
fact is the Hawkinses' first meal—"hot corn bread, fried chickens, bacon, buttermilk, coffee, and all manner of country
luxuries," for the farms of which Florida was the center yielded
abundantly. Also true, probably, is the summing up of the inhabitants: "They were uncouth and not cultivated, and not
particularly industrious; but they were honest and straight-
forward, and their virtuous ways commanded respect. Their
patriotism was strong, their pride in the flag was of the old-
fashioned pattern, their love of country amounted to idolatry."

Because Florida is today a down-at-heel village it would be
easy to jump to the conclusion that John Quarles and John
Clemens were squalid people drifting naturally into squalid
surroundings. Actually, that straggling log village had reason
to be hopeful. At the nominal head of navigation on Salt River,
it was the center of a rich tract of agricultural land; it had a
good chance of becoming the county seat of Monroe County.
If this last hope were realized, it was a first-rate spot for a

lawyer to be established in; if the river could be made really
navigable for even part of the year, Florida would be the
natural center of a considerable trade. The country immediately fringing the Mississippi was already fairly well filled up.
The logical next step was the development of the interior sections and their connection with the commercial world by the improvement of the lesser waterways.

How much the neighborhood might yield to a homesteader
may be gleaned from Mark Twain's memories of his uncle's
farm as he knew it in the middle '40's. The family were still
living in the double log house of their early days—but how they
lived! "Fried chicken, roast pig; wild and tame turkeys, ducks,
and geese; venison just killed; squirrels, rabbits, pheasants,
partridges, prairie-chickens; biscuits, hot batter cakes, hot buck-
wheat cakes, hot 'wheat bread,' hot rolls, hot corn pone; fresh
corn boiled on the ear, succotash, butter-beans, stringbeans,
tomatoes, peas, Irish potatoes, sweet potatoes; buttermilk, sweet
milk, 'clabber'; watermelons, muskmelons, cantaloupes—all
fresh from the garden; apple pie, peach pie, pumpkin pie, apple
dumplings, peach cobbler."

But John Clemens was a professional man, not a farmer.
While his brother-in-law could stay on his farm and prosper
comfortably with his thirty slaves to work the soil, John
Clemens' only hope was a growing community where his talents
would have scope. He resumed storekeeping, with John Quarles
as his partner, but that was only a stopgap; he looked forward
to a day when he would be able to return to the full-time practice of law. He quickly made himself felt as a leading citizen
of the little community. When the plans for making Salt River
navigable reached the point of legislative incorporation, early
in 1837, John Clemens was one of the commissioners; at the
same time he was one of the incorporators of an academy in
Florida. The silent, austere Virginian had something in him
which people instinctively respected.

But it was eighteen months before the Salt River Navigation
Company was incorporated that John Clemens made his greatest

contribution to the life of America. On November 30, 1835, his third son and fifth child was born, two months earlier than he was expected. The boy was christened Samuel Langhorne, after his Clemens grandfather and an old Virginia friend of John Clemens, but nobody expected him to live long enough to make much use of the names. A premature baby's chances of living through a winter in the two-room shack which housed the family seemed slender enough. But, as Mark Twain once said about his daughter, who had escaped death in a series of accidents, "I don't believe God cares much about meeting her." Despite the old wives' forebodings the baby lived and, after a fashion, throve.

Which was as much as his father was doing, or more. By 1838, when Henry, his youngest child, was born, John Clemens had dissolved his partnership with Quarles, and it was clear that he had guessed wrong once more as to the course of national development. The Salt River Navigation was stillborn, blighted with countless other brave plans by the panic of 1837, and now everyone was talking railroads. In Missouri the canal era had ended before it began. Though no one could foresee a time when the Mississippi itself would not be the chief highway of commerce, it was obvious that the feeders of that commerce would be rail lines heading from ports on the main river. People talked of a railroad from Hannibal on the Mississippi, clear across the state to St. Joseph on the Missouri. Hannibal seemed to have a future; by 1839 it was plain that Florida had not even a past. And so to Hannibal, population 450, John Clemens moved in the fall of 1839.

By that time young Sam had become something of a problem child, though that blessed term was not yet invented. He was still frail and sickly, and as his faculties developed he showed himself moody, imaginative and highly nervous. He walked in his sleep; he ran away; his mother testified that he got into more scrapes than all her other children combined. Jane Clemens, under the burdens of her large family and straitened means, left the younger children largely to the haphazard ministrations of their older brothers and sisters and to the two slaves, Jenny and Ned. From these latter Sam learned the countless superstitions and bits of folklore which Tom and Huck repeat; he also heard weird and gruesome stories like the tale of the Golden Arm, which did nothing to abate his nervousness and sleepwalking. From them, too, he learned a lifelong fondness for the simplicity and kindliness of the Negro race. Shortly before the family left Florida he also had his first intimate contact with death, in the first break in the family circle. His nine-year-old sister Margaret died in August 1839.

The move to Hannibal promised momentarily to improve the family fortunes. John Clemens—"Judge Clemens" for the rest of his life, because he had been justice of the peace in Florida— soon had a leading but unremunerative part in all plans for community betterment. He was first secretary, and later president, of the Hannibal Library Institute; whenever meetings were held to discuss the establishment of colleges, roads, railroads, or a city government, John Clemens was certain to figure prominently. Though he gave little attention to his children he was concerned for their education, subscribing on their account for *Peter Parley's Magazine,* and buying books when he could afford to. To all seeming he was a typical father of the old school, fearful of spoiling his children and content to rule by fear rather than love. Yet he was no Theobald Pontifex; Samuel remembered being whipped by his father only twice, and then not severely. One of the whippings was for telling a lie, "which surprised me, and showed me how unsuspicious he was, for that was not my maiden effort." The other children were never whipped; apparently the father awed them not by punishment or threats but by his stern austerity.

Always the dream of the Tennessee land hovered in John Clemens' mind, but the beginnings of the Hannibal venture brought more prestige than money. After the move Pamela and Benjamin were sent to school, but Orion, now fourteen, was apprenticed to a printer. It was a blow to Orion and to his family. They were by tradition gentlefolk; printers were tradesmen, and the difference was just as keenly felt, though not so obviously displayed, in Hannibal as in Virginia or in Devonshire. In Hannibal "everybody was poor, but didn't know it; and everybody was comfortable, and did know it. And there were grades of society—people of good family, people of unclassified family, people of no family. Everybody knew everybody, and was affable to everybody, and nobody put on any visible airs; yet the class lines were quite clearly drawn and the familiar social life of each class was restricted to that class. It was a little democracy which was full of liberty, equality, and Fourth of July, and sincerely so, too; yet you perceived that the aristocratic taint was there. It was there, and nobody found fault with the fact." And Orion knew it, along with the rest, and knew that he had taken a step down in the world, and had to console himself with the reflection that Benjamin Franklin had begun life as a printer.

For young Sam, however, the move to Hannibal brought no repinings. For an adventurous, imaginative boy it was heaven and Utopia combined, with an occasional dash of hell to give it flavor. Upstream, downstream, and behind the village were bluffs and hills, tracts of unbroken prairie and miles of virgin woodland. Fragments of the original forest still stood even within the village limits. It was a tamed and expurgated wilderness, to be sure; the Indians were gone; the larger beasts of prey were gone, and the game was going as fast as guns could slaughter it, but there was still so much left—wild turkeys, partridges, prairie chickens, quail, passenger pigeons, coons, possums and squirrels—that nobody could visualize a time when these too would go. And the fourth wall of the village was the mile-wide Mississippi—no wall; rather, a magic casement. Up and down the river flowed the life of America, in everything from Minnesota lumber-rafts to the gaudy packets that carried the luxury trade in passengers and freight. And all this traffic was likely to pause, however briefly, at the Hannibal landing and offer intimations of glory to staring small boys.

Though Indians and beasts of prey were gone from the forests the savages had not been eliminated from the community. Young Sam in the course of his boyhood saw a Negro killed when his master flung a lump of slag at his head. He saw old man Smarr shot down in a drunken brawl, and watched the wounded man cough out his life under the weight of a Bible some pious fool had laid upon his chest. He saw the rowdy young Hyde brothers try to kill their uncle—one kneeling on his chest while the other repeatedly snapped an Allen revolver that would not go off. He saw coffles of chained slaves on their way down the river to hell. He saw a drunken tramp burn to death in the jail, because some of the boys had kindly given him matches and tobacco. One night he saw a drunken ruffian set off with the avowed purpose of raping a widow and her daughter at "the Welshman's," and saw the sequel when the elder woman, after warning the scoundrel to be gone before the count of ten, riddled him with slugs from a steadily aimed shotgun. And once he saw a brutal Corsican chase his grown daughter through the streets with the intention of flogging her. The terrified girl fled to the Clemens house, and Sam saw his mother face the Corsican in the doorway, and heard her, in her level, drawling, ladylike tones, verbally take the hide off the bully until he cringed and wilted and slunk away. Past question, a high-strung child found plenty of the raw material of nightmares in the life of a village where the police power scarcely existed, and the chief restraint upon conduct was the innate decency of most of the inhabitants. Growing up thus, a boy had little left to learn about the darker sides of human nature and "the facts of life."

Life, though, held fun as well as tragedy. As Sam grew older, there was the big cave in the bluffs a couple of miles below town to explore, and get lost in. There were hunting and fishing expeditions on which, half-consciously, a boy absorbed all the traditional woods lore of Indians and frontiersmen. In winter the boys skated, and once Sam Clemens and Tom Nash, out on the frozen river at midnight without permission, were caught when the ice began to break. Leaping from floe to floe, Sam reached shore safely, but his companion missed his last jump, and took a disastrous ducking. The procession of diseases which resulted from his icy plunge culminated in scarlet fever, from which he emerged stone-deaf. Fifty years later Tom's experience became part of Nikolaus Bauman's destiny in *The Mysterious Stranger*. In summer the boys swam, and in the process of learning Sam came close to death more than once, and was hauled out in a limp and unpromising condition. Two of his chums were drowned; it was a rare summer that passed without at least one fatality. But Sam kept at it; Tom Sawyer could not let the rest of the gang surpass him. The greater part of the education that would matter most when he became a writer he acquired outside of school.

There was school, too. The spring following the move to Hannibal, Sam, aged four and a half, was sent to a school kept by a stern New Englander, Mrs. Horr. By his own account, he distinguished himself on his first day. When he broke rules a second time, after a warning, Mrs. Horr sent him outdoors to cut a switch. He returned with a cooper's shaving, "two inches broad, a quarter of an inch thick, and rising in a shallow curve at one end. . . . I stood before her in an attitude of meekness and resignation which seemed to me calculated to win favor and sympathy, but it did not happen. She divided a long look of strong disapprobation equally between me and the shaving; then she called me by my entire name . . . and said she was ashamed of me. She said she would try and appoint a boy with better judgment in the matter of switches, and it saddens me yet to remember how many faces lighted up with the hope of getting the appointment."

The episode typified much of his school days, both at Mrs. Horr's and later at Mr. Sam Cross's where, there being no public school, the older children were taught. He learned to read, and proved to be one of those phenomena of the English-speaking world, an instinctively good speller. He never won the good-conduct medal, but he was usually the champion speller of his class. By his own account, also, Mrs. Horr's exposition of the scripture, "Ask and ye shall receive," sowed his first religious doubts. He tried it, when he wanted some of the gingerbread the baker's daughter used to bring to school. It didn't work. He told his mother he wasn't a Christian any more, but that shrewd woman found out why, and did not despair of his salvation.

He likewise, as Howells phrased it later, learned to fear God and dread the Sunday school. Jane Clemens was an ardent Presbyterian; all her children had to go to Sunday school, and the older ones had to stay for the sermon. The pioneer communities had more culture than some moderns think, but it is safe to say that the ablest clergy seldom reached the frontier or stayed there long. The preaching was apt to be dull and certain to be long-winded; in the Presbyterian fold its emphasis was strongly upon Calvinistic doctrines. Sam heard long expositions of predestination and hell-fire, which began by scaring and ended by boring him. His father was a freethinker and so was John Quarles, and from the latter, to whose farm Sam returned for long visits every summer, he no doubt heard guarded negations of Sunday-school doctrines. But the preaching and teaching bit deep; all his life he thought of theology and philosophy in terms of the Hannibal Presbyterian church, continued to flog dead horses, and based his own explanation of human life upon a mechanistic theory which was Calvinism minus God.

Boredom was a commoner emotion in church than terror or rebellion. Even though the minister's argument "dealt in limitless fire and brimstone and thinned the predestined elect down to a company so small as to be hardly worth the saving," its droning delivery blunted the effect. Occasionally a picture would catch the boy's attention: the world's hosts, perhaps, assembling at the millennium, when lion and lamb should lie down together and a little child should lead them. Then Sam would yearn to be that supernally conspicuous child—if it was a tame lion. At intervals, too, revivalists came to town, and for a few days or even weeks filled the boys with fear of hell and love of good works, until a circus or a showboat restored their natural selves. But mostly he spent his hours of incarceration in studying whatever details of life he could find to focus his bored attention on, from a fly preening its wings on the pew back before him to the Sunday-school teacher's thumbnail. The teacher, a stonemason, "at some time or other . . . had hit his thumb with his hammer and the result was a thumbnail which remained permanently twisted and distorted and curved and pointed like a parrot's beak. I should not consider it an ornament now, I suppose, but it had a fascination for me then, and a vast value, because it was the only one in town."

Constant pressure from his mother and Pamela gave Sam intimate acquaintance with the English Bible. He was dragged through it reluctantly, but enough stayed with him to color his writing. Though he never essayed a scriptural style the Bible furnished him with endless imagery, for objurgation and praise alike, and at times helped him to hide the point of a jest under an unexplained reference to chapter and verse, as in Uncle Mumford's comment on the engineers' efforts to control the Mississippi: "What does Ecclesiastes 7:13 say? Says enough to knock *their* little game galley-west, don't it?"* Or the allusion to Exodus 32:4 which closes his discussion of the finances of Christian Science. These, as much as *What Is Man?*, were fruits of the Hannibal Sunday school.

But the Bible was not Sam's only literature. He absorbed his father's copy of *Don Quixote* so thoroughly that Tom and Huck spontaneously play their parts as juvenile American reincarnations of the Don and Sancho Panza—just as recollections of Poe, read in Keokuk, recur in the echoes of "The Gold Bug" which fill Tom's treasure hunt. Though Tom's knowledge of the literature of adventure doubtless surpasses his author's at the same age, and though family testimony specifies Orion and Henry as the bookish children, young Sam Clemens unques-

---

* "Consider the work of God: for who can make that straight, which he hath made crooked?" (*Life on the Mississippi*)

tionably read more than old Mark Twain remembered. There were books in the better homes in Hannibal and a bookstore in the village; current publications reached the West quickly enough. He thought he remembered his father reading *Hiawatha* aloud "with the same inflectionless, judicial frigidity with which he always read his charge to the jury," but it must have been some other poem, for John Clemens died nearly eight years before *Hiawatha* was published. Like all his later reading, Sam's boyhood acquaintance with literature was spotty and unsystematic, but he read.

His reading included a deal of informal literature such as historians are usually too scholarly to know. The great tradition of American humor was going through the crude processes of birth, in newspaper sketches reprinted as cheap books. Some of these sketches were the work of genteel scribes, like Augustus Baldwin Longstreet of Georgia, essaying Addisonian or Irvingesque character studies of the oh-so-crude-and-amusing "originals" in their newly settled neighborhoods. But others, like the books ascribed to Davy Crockett, T. B. Thorpe's "Big Bear of Arkansas," and J. J. Hooper's *Adventures of Captain Simon Suggs*, were authentic transcriptions of the folk humor of America. In Davy Crockett, Sam found the story of the coonskin repeatedly pilfered and resold to the storekeeper, which later he thought he remembered as an exploit of his own gang, and Simon Suggs's pretending to repent at a camp meeting and making away with a generous collection was the germ of a famous episode in *Huckleberry Finn*.

For one specimen of this humor, moreover, which he read in print, Sam must have heard dozens by word of mouth. The American was anecdotal, and on the frontier the anecdote served all purposes from laughter to sermonizing. Across the river in Illinois a rawboned lawyer named Lincoln was developing the use of the anecdote, sometimes genuinely remembered, sometimes invented for the occasion, into an art which supplied him with pungent and memorable comments on any topic which came up. The fun of the story disarmed the victim's resentment; it also made the implied criticism stick as no direct statement could. That some Easterners later thought Lincoln a buffoon because he told homely stories instead of veiling his opinions in clouds of empty phrases merely showed the critics' isolation from the folk life of their country. The plain people loved the indirection of criticism which put up to the auditor the responsibility of drawing the conclusion and making the application. Above all, they loved the tall tale in the mouth of an expert narrator who, with straight face and level inflections, could begin with plausible and unsuspicious detail and gradually lead the guileless listener farther and farther along the path of absurdity until he realized, too late, that he was a sucker and had been hooked.

Even this most native of American folklore, however, had its roots deep in the popular traditions of the English, Scottish, and Irish forebears of the settlers, and in Sam Clemens' boyhood world it mingled with other elements of like origin. The boys played games of Robin Hood and his merry men, as well as games of fighting Indians. They heard quaintly distorted versions of "Barbara Allen" and other ballads, brought, like many of the tunes the fiddlers played at village dances, by oral tradition from a remote Scotland. The youngsters who danced to "Money Musk" did not know that it bore the name of a Scottish village and had they known they would not have cared, for it was as much at home in Missouri as they were. And meanwhile, down in the slave quarters, another American art was flourishing unregarded—the singing of jubilees and spirituals, which seemed to Sam Clemens, even as a boy, to make all other vocal music cheap. Hannibal had plenty of food for the imagination of a sensitive child, even though some of the arts were so wholly absent that Sam never learned to understand them.

Broadly speaking, architecture did not exist. The westward migration had long since outrun the well-proportioned simplicities of colonial New England, and the relatively small scale of Missouri agriculture prevented the erection of plantation houses in the stately Southern style. Orchestral music was as unknown as sculpture. The graphic arts were represented by rigid steel engravings of Washington and Andrew Jackson, or by the mawkish illustrations in the gift books and annuals which lay on the table in the best parlor. Unless, of course, the daughters of the family had "studied art," in which case their flower pictures and ruins-by-moonlight copied from some album joined Washington and Jackson on the walls.

But during the first seven years in Hannibal Sam Clemens was probably blissfully unconscious that he was getting any education at all. From a puny child he developed into a slender but wiry boy, his head crowned with a shock of sandy hair, which later turned auburn, that distressed him by its insistence on curling. He became the unquestioned leader of a gang that included John Briggs and Sam and Will Bowen; his riotous imagination, vocalized in his drawling speech, was always fertile in suggesting fresh escapades. They explored the cave; they rolled boulders down the steep slope of Holliday's Hill; they raided melon patches and orchards. They learned to smoke, under the usual penalties. When their parents weren't looking they would foregather with Tom Blankenship, son of the village drunkard, in their eyes the most enviable boy in town. Nobody made him wash or dress, or go to school and church; he picked up his own living, precariously, out of other people's gardens or with fish from the river and game from the woods. He was destined to immortality as Huck Finn. Such a boy, five or six years Sam's senior, might easily have been the evil influence the village parents thought him, yet Tom seems to have been just a natural, amoral young animal. It was true that he helped a runaway slave, despite the temptation of the reward offered for the man's capture—a thing which no properly reared white boy would have dared do.

Tom Sawyer is not autobiography in its details, but in its personalities, altered or heightened for dramatic purposes, it is essentially lifelike. Aunt Polly is Jane Clemens with no embellishments beyond a dialectal crudity of speech which was not Jane's. Sid is a debased copy of the gentle Henry Clemens; managing Cousin Mary is Pamela. And Tom, with his reckless escapades and abject penitences, is Sam Clemens—Sam Clemens in boyhood, manhood and old age. Time and wisdom modified the fondness for practical jokes, but the exuberant high spirits, the plunges into gloom and remorse over real or imaginary errors, above all the delight in being conspicuous, were his to the end. The boy who joined the Christian Sons of Temperance for the sake of their gaudy red sashes became the man who about 1870 astounded genteel Boston with a sealskin overcoat, and in his old age paraded Fifth Avenue in white clothes and wore his scarlet Oxford gown at his daughter's wedding.

One episode of his boyhood has been magnified into a symbol, though even its date is uncertain, for in different allusions to it Mark Twain gave his age at the time as anywhere from ten to twelve and a half. An epidemic of measles struck the village; several children died, and terrified parents tried to quarantine the ones who had not yet been exposed. Among these was Sam Clemens, who at last could bear the suspense no longer and, escaping from the house, crept into bed with Will Bowen, very sick with the disease. The results were all he hoped for and more, for Sam came near dying. The incident has been interpreted as the Death Wish, draped with dire Freudian symbolism which proves merely that some critics know more about literature and psychology than about children. Parents whose children have not been early victims of an epidemic can testify that perfectly normal youngsters have declared that it's sissy not to have had the measles, and have rejoiced when they caught the disease, until fever and headache put a quietus on the glee. All the episode really proves is that Sam Clemens was normal.

One version of the story, however, connects it with the event which closed the Tom Sawyer period of boyhood. John Marshall Clemens had not flourished in Hannibal; the Tennessee land had not enriched his family, and his folly in backing a friend's note had taken him through bankruptcy which had swept away most of his little property, including his two slaves. In November 1846 he announced his candidacy for the clerk-ship of the circuit court at an election to be held the following August. It was a post that would offer an assured, if small, income; the general respect in which his fellow citizens held him seemed to make his election certain. But at the end of February 1847 exposure to cold and wet on a trip to the county seat at Palmyra resulted in pneumonia. His death left the un-stable Orion as the only breadwinner in a family of five. Child-hood was finished for Sam Clemens.

ᴀᴘᴘʀᴇNᴛɪᴄᴇsʜɪᴘs

IT WAS the third time death had struck the Clemens family. When his sister Margaret died, Sam had been too young to retain much emotional impression. The death of his brother Benjamin in 1842 struck deeper; he always remembered kneeling by the dead boy's bedside with his mother. She was moaning inarticulately, while her tears flowed unchecked; Orion recalled that the only time he had seen his parents kiss each other was beside that deathbed. But this last death was the breaking of Sam's world. In his shock he remembered all his little sins of negligence and disobedience, and sounded the depths of hysterical remorse. As Orion described the scene, his mother comforted him, but begged him to be a better boy and strive to become as good a man as his father. Sam, ready to promise anything, begged in his turn that he might not be sent to school any more. Those who find profound psychological meanings in the episode know little about nervous children.

The last time Mark Twain himself told of the episode he described his mother's decision to take him out of school as the turning point of his life, the first step on his way to becoming a writer. But he remembered no hysterics, nor any promise to be a better boy. He connected her decision with the measles episode, which, he said, determined her to put him into more masterful hands than hers. But he would probably have had to leave school in any case. Even Mr. Cross's paltry fees were a drain on the budget. Orion, earning ten dollars a week as a printer in St. Louis, was sending three dollars of it to his mother. Pamela went fifty miles away, to the village of Paris, and supported herself for a time by teaching music, but her earnings were probably too meager to help her family much. Sam had to go to work; his brother's trade was the only one that offered much chance of continuing some sort of education.

In *Roughing It,* Mark Twain said that he had been a grocer's clerk for one day, had briefly assisted a blacksmith, had been a bookseller's clerk "for awhile," and had worked in a drugstore for "part of a summer." With the usual discounts for overstatements of his own incompetence, his claims were probably true. When he made them, he was much closer to the events than when he dictated his *Autobiography;* these were presumably his first efforts at wage earning during the spring and summer following his father's death.

In his old age he thought he had been apprenticed to Joseph P. Ament, editor and proprietor of the *Missouri Courier,* soon after John Clemens died. But Ament did not move to Hannibal until 1848, when he bought the *Gazette* and merged it with the *Courier,* which he had previously published in Palmyra. What really happened, apparently, was that Sam went to work in the summer of 1847 as delivery and office-boy for the *Gazette,* but was not apprenticed until after Ament bought the paper. Another of his memories supports this conjecture. He remembered being in charge of circulation and getting out extras during the closing months of the Mexican War. His always creative memory associated this work with the latter part of his apprenticeship, but Chapultepec, the last major battle of the war, was fought less than six months after John Clemens died. Hence Sam, instead of printing the extras, only delivered them, and such must have been his work for six months or more, until Ament took over the paper and the real apprenticeship began.

The terms of apprenticeship were the usual board and clothes—not too much of either—and no money. With two other apprentices and a journeyman printer named Pet MacMurray, the staff was large for a village paper. Records of Sam's two years as a learner are scanty. He remembered chiefly the pranks of his older fellow apprentice, Wales McCormick, a more daring practical joker than Sam himself. Wales was big for his age, and Sam was small; when they were both fitted out in Ament's castoff clothing they were figures of fun. Both boys raided Ament's cellar for potatoes and onions to supplement their inadequate meals, but it was Wales who, in printing a Campbellite preacher's sermon, turned the Savior's name into "Jesus H. Christ." It was Wales, too, who used to make extravagant love to Ament's mulatto maid, while Sam, young and careless as he was, realized that the girl had a refined nature and was taking the love-making in resentful earnest.

By the time his apprenticeship ended Sam had become a quick and accurate printer. Having mastered his trade, he apparently continued to work for Ament for wages for at least another year. Even with the Mexican War concluded, those were stirring days in Hannibal. Returned volunteers from the war told tales of their adventures, and the great overland trek to California and Oregon was on. In 1849 Sam enviously watched his schoolmate, John RoBards, ride off with his father on the way to California and the gold fields, and saw him return two years later covered with the ineffable glory of travel which had included a return voyage by way of Cape Horn. Sam wanted to travel, too, but his slender earnings were needed at home.

About three years after his father's death Orion came home from St. Louis. Apparently he worked for a time at wages, but in September 1850 he started a Whig weekly of his own, the *Western Union*. Early in 1851 another weekly paper, the *Journal*, came on the market, and Orion bought it with five hundred borrowed dollars. He merged his anemic *Western Union* with the *Journal*, and with boundless enthusiasm set out to make the paper succeed. Almost at once it became a family concern, for Sam joined the staff as printer and Henry as apprentice. Orion dreamed of founding a literary magazine, and in 1853 actually did add a daily to the weekly issue of the *Journal*. But by that time the whole enterprise was moribund. Probably there never lived a more earnest and conscientious man than

Orion Clemens, but the Curse of Reuben prevented his ever bringing any of his hopeful schemes to fruition.

Yet Orion's three years of struggle as a Hannibal journalist were crucial in his brother's life. Financially Sam soon found himself worse off than he had been as Ament's employee, for the *Journal* seldom earned enough to pay his wages. But in the course of those three years he experienced the thrill of getting into print, and took his first tottering steps as a humorist.

He himself dated his serious interest in history and literature from the day he picked up in the street a leaf from a book which contained part of the story of the imprisonment of Joan of Arc, whose name, even, he then learned for the first time. But in Ament's office, and later in Orion's, he had encountered a good many odds and ends of literature, especially in the form of quotations and anecdotes which the small-town press regularly used as fillers in the days before syndicated features. "One isn't a printer ten years without setting up acres of good and bad literature, and learning—unconsciously at first, consciously later—to discriminate between the two."

It must have been during the winter of 1850-1851, moreover, that Sam made his conscious debut as a humorous storyteller. In his *Autobiography* he placed it a year or more earlier, but 1849 was a favorite date of his, and the incident must have happened between Orion's establishment of the *Western Union* in September 1850 and Pamela's marriage to William Moffett on September 20, 1851. Orion had taken into his office a gawky, abnormally shy youth from Shelbyville, whose name was Jim Wolf. To Sam, Jim seemed a heaven-sent butt for practical jokes, though in time he learned that Jim was not so green as he looked and could retaliate in various painful ways.

One winter night Pamela and her friends had a candy pull. The boys were not included in the party, but late in the evening were awakened by a cat fight on the roof of the ell outside their window. Jim, under skillful goading from Sam, undertook to drive off the cats just as Pamela and her friends were bringing their saucers of candy out to cool in the snow. Jim's feet slipped on the icy roof, and he, simply clad in a brief nightshirt and a pair of socks, crashed the candy pull from above. Sam thought it the funniest thing that had ever happened, and told it next morning in full drawling detail to Jimmy McDaniel, son of the local confectioner. Though Sam knew the story was funny, he was not prepared to see Jimmy almost laugh his remaining teeth out. It was Sam's first realization of his own unique equipment for original humorous narrative; he had never been so proud and happy before. Perhaps it was this success which emboldened him a year or so later to try something similar in writing.

Among the exchanges which came to the *Journal* office were the popular humorous weeklies of the East. Chief of these was *The Spirit of the Times,* a New York sporting paper which specialized in reprinting the sketches mentioned in the previous chapter, which local humorists throughout the South and Southwest were contributing to their hometown papers, and in publishing original contributions of the same sort. This humor, as Mark Twain said in 1867 of George Harris' Sut Lovingood yarns, was popular in the West, but was tabooed as coarse by the more squeamish readers in the East. Another of these humorous journals, poorer and shorter-lived than *The Spirit of the Times,* was *The Carpet Bag.* It was published in Boston, and in 1852 a lanky towhead named Charles Farrar Brown, a year or so older than Sam Clemens, was setting type in its office. In *The Carpet Bag* for May 1, 1852, appeared a brief sketch entitled "The Dandy Frightening the Squatter." The scene of the sketch was Hannibal; the initials signed to it were S.L.C. It was merely a retelling of a yarn long popular along the river about an Easterner who undertook, for the amusement of his fellow passengers on a steamboat, to scare a Missouri squatter with a brace of pistols, and got knocked into the river for his pains. But it was Sam Clemens' first recorded appearance in print and crudely written though it was, it showed that even in his teens his ambition was to write humor, and not polite, bookish, Irvingesque humor but the rough, full-blooded comedy of his native region.

Soon he had a chance to try being funny at home. Late in the summer of 1852 Orion went to Tennessee on another effort to sell the land, and entrusted Sam with the duty of getting out at least one weekly issue of the *Journal* in his absence. It was a day when invective and personal ridicule were standard editorial equipment, even in the big cities, and Sam yearned to start something that would enliven his brother's paper. He began by continuing a controversy which had been started in July by a warning against mad dogs, published in a rival paper, the *Tri-Weekly Messenger*. Someone who signed himself "A Dog-be-deviled Citizen," and who may have been Sam Clemens, wrote a mock-serious letter to the *Journal* suggesting that the best way to avert the danger of rabies was to exterminate the dogs. Earnest citizens protested, and the editor of the *Messenger* kept the story going with some heavily facetious paragraphs which included a personal gibe at either Sam or Orion. As Sam recalled the affair nearly twenty years later, the *Messenger* editor, a newcomer in town, was a bachelor who had so taken to heart a rejection in love that he had resolved to drown himself in Bear Creek, but after getting wet had waded ashore. Quite possibly some such story was current in Hannibal, but when Sam brought out the *Journal* for September 16 he made no direct allusion to it.

What he did was to carve a crude woodcut with his jackknife, depicting the editor of the *Messenger*, with a dog's head, wading into the creek. In one hand he held a lantern; in the other a cane. On the bank stood a large bottle. An accompanying note explained the composition:

" 'Local,' disconsolate from receiving no further notice from 'A Dog-be-Deviled Citizen,' contemplates Suicide. His pocket-pistol (i.e. the *bottle*) failing in the patriotic work of ridding the country of a nuisance, he resolves to 'extinguish his chunk' by feeding his carcass to the fishes of Bear Creek, while friend and foe are wrapt in sleep. Fearing, however, that he may get out of his depth, he *sounds the stream with his walking-stick.*"

The same issue contained no less than three "feature articles" by the aspiring subeditor. At least one of them, entitled "A Historical Exhibition," must have been approved by Orion before his departure, for it was prefaced with Orion's note that "a young friend" had submitted it, and warning the readers that it might be a hoax. It described a fraud which bore a faint and far-off resemblance to "The Royal Nonesuch" of *Huckleberry Finn.* A traveling showman advertised a spectacle called "Bonaparte Crossing the Rhine"; the suckers discovered that the show consisted of passing the bony part of a pig across a piece of bacon rind. Another feature story described a drunken brawl on Holliday's Hill, and was signed W. Epaminondas Adrastus Perkins. The press of the day, from Thackeray in *Punch* to the humblest village paper in America, was full of contributors whose first and often only claim to being humorists was the devising of elaborate pseudonyms. Sam was conforming to fashion. He was also, in his first chance for free expression, trying wholeheartedly, but with the ill success to be expected of a village boy not yet seventeen, to be a humorist.

Whether or not the new features brought in the unparalleled number of thirty-three new subscriptions, they created a stir, especially in the *Messenger* office. The sorely tried editor of that paper described Sam as "a writer who has not the decency of a gentleman nor the honor of a blackguard"—words which suggest a basis of truth in the report of attempted suicide. Otherwise they were warmer than the occasion seemed to warrant even in that day of editorial free speech. But Sam had tasted blood and was out for more. For the next week's issue he made two more woodcuts, one depicting "Local's" astonishment at finding something interesting in the *Journal,* the other, "Local's" attempt to destroy the whole canine race with a cannon loaded, in default of lead, with copies of the *Messenger.* W. E. A. Perkins also appeared in another letter, in which he announced that by act of the legislature he had changed his surname from Perkins to Blab, "and if Congress takes the matter up and changes it back the way it was, the villainous President that signs the documents and makes it a law will never get *my support*—No, sir! not if he's NEVER elected again! As for Queen Victoria and Lord Derby, they may cut up as much as they like—it's none of their business." In the same issue Blab announced his retirement to the remote shades of Glascock's Island. In other words Orion had come home and was going to stop this foolishness before his reckless young brother got him and the paper into serious trouble.

These events of 1852 might seem to prelude a steady career of writing, but not for Sam Clemens. He may have been too busy to keep on writing or too poor to pay the postage on his efforts, but more likely he had for the moment used up his material. At seventeen creative thought seldom flows in quantity, and Sam valued having a good time with his friends more than the unprofitable glory of writing for such journals as would welcome his crude efforts.

But meantime the *Journal* was going downhill. In March 1853 Orion tried to arrest its decline by starting a daily issue. In May the elder brother was again out of town for a week or so, and again the irrepressible Sam was left in charge. The first contribution this time, in the issue of May 6, was a quite serious poem in the best gift-book style, entitled "Love Concealed." Telling the story, Mark Twain attributed the verses to a local poetaster, but they were probably his own. All human beings churn out such verses in their youth, he remarked long afterward of the "poems" of Mrs. Eddy. What distinguished it from its kind was its subtitle: "To Miss Katie of H——l." Again the author was following custom: it was still the fashion to disguise proper names with dashes or asterisks, "so that ingenuity may find them out," as Robert Burns had explained some sixty years before. But Hannibal thus disguised became an improper name. If Sam had not realized the fact when he set up the poem, it dawned on him soon after, and he forestalled comment by addressing a letter to himself to say that although poems had often been addressed to "Mary in Heaven," or "Lucy in Heaven," "Katie in Hell" was carrying the matter too far. To this caviler, Sam, as "Rambler" the poet, retorted by consigning "Grumbler" to a lunatic asylum, and presently imported another imaginary correspondent, "Peter Pencilcase's Son, John Snooks," to continue the argument. By May 13 Orion had evidently returned; an editorial note declared, "Rambler and his enemies must stop their 'stuff.' It is a great bore to us, and doubtless to the public generally."

That same issue of May 13, however, printed with Orion's editorial blessing a humorous essay in defense of redheads, obviously Sam's work. Evidently Orion was aware that Sam was restless and unhappy, and tried to offer him more scope for self-expression. Ten days after the end of the Rambler correspondence the *Journal* appeared with a new department headed "Our Assistant's Column." This was a miscellany of items ranging from local news to clippings from the St. Joseph *Gazette* about the number of California emigrants passing through the city. It excoriated "one Mr. Jaques" who had got drunk and beaten his wife and children, and wound up a controversy with the editor of the Bloomington, Illinois, *Republican* by interring him, in a heavy-handed parody of "The Burial of Sir John Moore." The column poked fun at the spiritualists, and joked about the Negroes sweating in the first warm weather. It displayed the Assistant's interest in steamboating by going into details to prove that the *Die Vernon,* not the *Jeannie Deans,* had made the fastest trip of the season from St. Louis to Hannibal. But only three of these columns appeared. At the beginning of June Sam Clemens left Hannibal, never again to return except on brief visits.

The eighteen-year-old youth was restless, and with reason. The *Journal* was sinking under his feet. Orion was seldom able to pay the meager $3.50 a week which was Sam's nominal wage, and besides its declining circulation the paper had suffered other disasters. To have a cow break into the office, upset the type case and eat two composition rollers was an accident that could have happened, one feels, only to Orion Clemens. Fire, on the other hand, can happen to anyone, but after the fire, to save rent Orion moved what was left of his establishment into the front room of the family home. He was desperately worried and depressed; the result was friction with his brothers. Pamela, meantime, had married William A. Moffett, a Hannibal boy who had established himself as a merchant in St. Louis, and it was to St. Louis that Sam announced his intention of going to seek a job.

Before he left, his mother asked him to swear on the Bible that he would not throw a card or drink a drop of liquor while he was gone. It seems a reasonable enough request for a mother to make of an eighteen-year-old son leaving home for the first time, though it has been interpreted as evidence that Jane Clemens began the work of blighting Sam's life which his wife is alleged to have finished. But it applied only to this first trip away. By the time she saw her son again Jane was obviously satisfied as to his ability to manage himself, and sought no renewal of the promise.

Sam had finished his first efforts at journalism, and had proved chiefly that as a precocious genius he was no Chatterton. Considered as literature his recovered juvenilia add somewhat less to his reputation than the poems of Victor and Cazire do to Shelley's. The country was full of village journalists who could do as well, or as ill. Yet they show him as part and parcel of the tradition of American humor. With similar squibs, somewhat better written, he would later make his journalistic reputation in Nevada; the genre, infinitely better written, survives in the pages of his *Autobiography*. Even in these first clumsy efforts his vocation was clear. Though almost a decade of varied activity intervened before he turned to writing for his livelihood, he had chosen his means of expression and never deviated from that choice. Degrading though it may seem to earnest-minded critics, his ambition was to make people laugh.

Though he told his mother that he was going to St. Louis, he had other intentions which he had not confided. The papers the country over were full of reports about the Crystal Palace exhibition in New York, started in emulation of Prince Albert's recent show in London. Sam's last "Assistant's Column" in the *Journal* had included a note that "from fifteen to twenty thousand persons are continually congregated around the new Crystal Palace in New York city, and drunkenness and debauching are carried on to their fullest extent." Sam wanted to see them carried on. As soon as he found a job, on the St. Louis *Evening News,* he began saving his money, and by mid-August had enough to pay his fare, with a few dollars over for emergencies. The trip, by steamboat and rail, via Chicago, Monroe, Buffalo and Albany, took five arduous days. On August 24 he broke the news to his mother in a long letter from New York which Orion published in the *Journal* with a prefatory apology for its "free and easy impudence":

"You will doubtless be a little surprised, and somewhat angry, when you receive this and find me so far from home; but you must bear a little with me, for you know I was always the best boy you had, and perhaps you remember how people used to say to their children—'Now don't you do like O[rion] and H[enry] C[lemens]—but take S[am] for your guide!' "

In this and subsequent letters he then went on to describe the sights of New York, including the Crystal Palace (with no mention of drunkenness and debauching), the Wild Man from Borneo and the crowds on Broadway. He was still thoroughly Southern in feeling: "I reckon I had better black my face, for in these Eastern States niggers are considerably better than white people," he remarked after an allusion to the activities of "the infernal abolitionists" in Syracuse. But he spent little time idling about. His confidence in his ability to fend for himself was justified; he soon found work, though at low wages, in a big printing house on Cliff Street, and proudly reported what clean proof he set and how easily he conformed to the exacting standards of metropolitan typography. As for his leisure, after he had exhausted the principal sights, "the printers have two libraries in town, entirely free to the craft; and in these I can spend my evenings most pleasantly."

But the thrill of the new experiences quickly wore off, and the noise, the crowds and the long hours of work began to fray his always irritable nerves. After less than two months in New York he sought the escape he would so often seek from irritations—he moved somewhere else. By mid-October he was in Philadelphia, where once more he quickly found work and once more wrote long descriptive letters home. But these were not published in Hannibal; Orion, giving up the *Journal* for the face of its $500 mortgage, had moved to Muscatine, Iowa, where he printed one of his brother's letters under the stately title, "Philadelphia Correspondence."

Increasing homesickness began to show in Sam's letters, but he would not yield to it yet. "There is only one thing that gets my 'dander' up," he wrote Orion from Philadelphia, "and that is the hands are always encouraging me: telling me—'it's no use to get discouraged—no use to be down-hearted, for there is more work here than you can do!' 'Down-hearted' the devil! I have not had a particle of such a feeling since I left Hannibal." But a month later, after learning that Orion was now publishing the *Journal* in Muscatine, he asked a series of searching questions about the pay and prospects of the new venture, and wound up by asking, "How do you like 'free-soil'? I would like amazingly to see a good old-fashioned negro." And to Pamela, early in December, he confessed that he would start for home right away if he hadn't spent all his money on clothes. So he stayed out the winter in Philadelphia, with one brief trip to Washington.

From the literary side, and apart from whatever reading he may have done in his leisure hours, the chief value of these months in the East was that they gave Sam his first opportunity to practice the kind of descriptive writing which later made his first national fame. His letters, however, showed little of his later style. They were almost devoid of humor: their writer was obviously an earnest sight-seer from the provinces, duly impressed by the mileage of the Croton Aqueduct and the acreage of Fairmount Park. Nevertheless, he had the root of the matter in him. He realized the value of clear and specific detail—"One has only to leave home to learn how to write an interesting letter to an absent friend when he gets back," he told Pamela. And though his style was for the most part stiff and colorless, it was far simpler and more direct than one would expect of an eighteen-year-old of a generation in which, even in humorous stories in the newspapers, judges were usually described as "dispensers of justice," and malefactors, instead of going to jail, "rusticated in the calaboose." Only rarely did Sam allow himself to be carried "in imagination, to the ruined piles of ancient Babylon," and the shambling, incomplete or incoherent sentences of so much youthful writing were wholly absent. He was still a long way from creating an individual style, but he had already learned how to put his observations clearly on paper.

Sometime in the spring of 1854 he returned from Philadelphia to New York, but no details of his second stay in the metropolis survive. Late in the summer his homesickness finally conquered. After a brief reunion with his mother, Orion and Henry in Muscatine, he resumed his former work on the *Evening News* in St. Louis. Orion urged him to stay with the Muscatine *Journal*, but he declared he would have to earn some money before he could afford that luxury. In St. Louis he roomed with Frank E. Burrough, a chairmaker with a taste for good reading, who more than twenty years later wrote to remind Mark Twain of their former association.

"As you describe me," Mark Twain replied, "I can picture myself as I was 22 years ago. . . . You have described a callow fool, a self-sufficient ass, a mere human tumble-bug, stern in air, heaving at his bit of dung, imagining that he is remodeling the world and is entirely capable of doing it right. Ignorance, intolerance, egotism, self-assertion, opaque perception, dense and pitiful chuckle-headedness—and an almost pathetic unconsciousness of it all."

Early in 1855, however, Sam rejoined his brothers in a last attempt to carry on a family business. Orion had married, in December 1854, Mary Ellen Stotts of Keokuk and, abandoning journalism, had taken over the Benjamin Franklin book and job-printing office in Keokuk, a town at the moment enjoying a feverish railroad and real-estate boom. Henry was still with him, and when Sam came up for a visit in the spring, Orion offered him five dollars a week and his board if he would join the firm. He stayed about a year and a half.

In one respect Keokuk offered what he had failed to find in New York and Philadelphia—congenial companions of his own age. Then, as always, he loved company. In after years some of these friends remembered that Sam used to read a good deal, and mentioned Dickens and Poe as two of the authors whose books they had seen him carry about. Though Mark Twain used to declare that he had never been able to read Dickens, it is hard to believe that any literate youth in the 1850's did *not* read him, and *Tom Sawyer* contains the proof that he read Poe. One friend, Ed Brownell, also recalled Sam's reading "a so-called funny book" and declaring that some day he would write a funnier book than that, himself—to which Ed retorted that Sam was too lazy ever to write a book.

But working under Orion's feckless management was a strain, and by the spring of 1856 Sam was fed up. In a letter to his mother, now living with Pamela in St. Louis, he complained of Orion's lack of system and the general slackness of the office. He was in the right mood for a new and dazzling dream of travel and adventure. He and some of his friends had been reading about recent explorations on the upper reaches of the Amazon, and began to plan an expedition thither. Among other things they had read of the wonderful properties of coca, and were sure they could return with an easily portable cargo of coca leaves which would pay all their expenses and leave a handsome profit in addition to the thrills of travel. But to reach the Amazon required cash in hand which Orion would not put up, even if he had it to put. The friends lost faith on sober second thought, but Sam continued to dream, and presently chance intervened.

On a windy November day a piece of paper blew past Sam on Main Street, Keokuk. When he picked it up he found it was a fifty-dollar bill. Though he honestly advertised his find, no claimant appeared. Here, by pure luck, was the bit of capital that would enable him to break away from Orion and Keokuk. He lost no time in starting, but for an adventurer supposedly bound for the Amazon his course was erratic. Instead of setting out directly for New Orleans or New York, he traveled by way of Quincy and Chicago to Cincinnati, as roundabout a journey as any since Chesterton's revelers went to Bannockburn by way of Beachy Head. Perhaps, like his whilom partners, he had begun to realize how impractical the enterprise was; perhaps he was merely waiting until he earned a little more money.

To this latter end he had arranged before leaving Keokuk to write a series of humorous letters to the most prosperous newspaper in the city, the _Post_. The editor agreed to pay him five dollars apiece for his contributions—his first literary earnings. One letter was written from St. Louis while Sam was there on a visit in October; two more were written from Cincinnati during the winter, and then the undertaking, like his earlier ones on the Hannibal _Journal_, died a natural death. It was just as well.

He still believed that the first requisite for a humorist was a comic pseudonym, so, with Dickens' help, he called himself Thomas Jefferson Snodgrass. The plague of illiterate dialect spelling, which had begun in the East a generation earlier in the Sam Slick and Jack Downing sketches, was already rife in the Middle West, and within a year and a half was to gain fresh impetus from the work of Artemus Ward. For the first and only time in his life Sam Clemens yielded to the contagion, and in the Snodgrass letters employed all the hackneyed devices of the genre. His purpose, he announced in the first letter from Cincinnati, was "to go a travelin, so as to see the world, and then write a book about it—a kind o' daily journal like—and have all in gold on the back of it, 'Snodgrass' Dierrea,' or somethin' of that kind, like other authors that visits forren parts." That passage fairly represents the labored humor of the three letters, which include such well-worn "comic" situations as the green countryman at the theater for the first time, who takes everything as real, and the guileless bachelor left with a foundling baby on his hands. The same dainty misspelling of "diary" was to reappear in March 1858 in one of Artemus Ward's early letters in the Cleveland *Plain Dealer*. All that can be said of Snodgrass is that he was no worse than most of the newspaper humor of the day—but to be worse than that would have been, for anyone with Sam Clemens' native intelligence, impossible. For all his twenty-one years he was still mentally adolescent, and had neither anything individual to say nor any individual medium to say it in.

But as he looked back upon his winter in Cincinnati it seemed to Mark Twain that he began to grow up mentally during those months. He lived in a boardinghouse populated by commonplace people of various ages and both sexes. "They were full of bustle, frivolity, chatter, and the joy of life, and were good-natured, clean-minded, and well-meaning; but they were oppressively uninteresting." The one exception was a Scotsman named Macfarlane, a humorless, self-taught man twice Sam's age.

All his life long a keen intellectual curiosity drew Sam Clemens naturally to anyone who had ideas to express, just as an innate fastidiousness appears to have kept him, even on river and frontier, away from the grosser forms of debauchery and self-indulgence. Behind his fierce intensity, his wild pleasure in shocking people with ribaldries and profanities, Clemens' central and final personality Howells discerned as something exquisite. "He was the most caressing of men in his pity, but he had the fine instinct of never putting his hands on you." In Philadelphia he had roomed with a quiet Englishman named Sumner; in St. Louis he and Frank Burrough had spent their evenings taking the world to pieces; now, in Cincinnati, he listened while Macfarlane with devastating Scots thoroughness expounded a version of the evolutionary theory. Though Darwin's *Origin of Species* was not yet published, Macfarlane was far from being as original a thinker as Sam then and later thought him. His ideas, indeed, were merely restatements of notions long familiar, though not in the Presbyterian Sunday schools of Hannibal except in their culmination, which Sam failed to recognize in its new environment. "Macfarlane considered that the animal life in the world was developed in the course of aeons of time from a few microscopic seed germs . . . and that this development was progressive upon an ascending scale toward ultimate perfection until *man* was reached; and that then the progressive scheme broke pitifully down and went to wreck and ruin!" The evidence of the ruin was that the heart of man was desperately wicked—a statement which Sam would have recognized and been bored by instantly had it come from the pulpit, but clothed in Macfarlane's half-scientific determinism it sounded like a new and depressing revelation.

At what time his revolt began against the strict theology of his mother's church cannot be determined, but Macfarlane apparently completed the work of emancipating him. He had read Tom Paine's *The Rights of Man* in Philadelphia; at some time before 1861 he also read, with fear and trembling, *The Age of Reason,* and upon these village-atheist foundations, aided by Macfarlane's version of Calvinism with God left out, he would in course of time, when the bitterness of living had entered into his soul, erect the philosophizings in which he took such great, though for the most part unjustified, pride.

The two Snodgrass letters and his memories of Macfarlane are the only surviving records of that winter in Cincinnati. When spring came and navigation reopened in the Ohio, Sam revived his dream of the Amazon—or later thought that he did. At any rate, he was ready to move on again, and during the winter had saved money enough to take him to New Orleans. In April he bought his ticket on the steamboat *Paul Jones.* Long before the boat reached its destination Sam's dream of the Amazon, if it existed at all, had joined his already extensive collection of discarded fantasies. One of the pilots of the *Paul Jones* was Horace Bixby, ten years Sam's senior; before the trip ended, Bixby had agreed to teach Sam the river.

CHAPTER III

THE RIVER

In *Life on the Mississippi* Mark Twain, as always, rearranged his facts for literary effect. He represented himself as considerably younger and vastly more ignorant than he really was in the spring of 1857. But there is no reason to doubt his statements about the lure of the river. For any spirited boy in a river village before the Civil War the steamboat symbolized adventure and romance: an exciting world in itself, and the means to other worlds still more enthralling. A number of Sam's contemporaries had gone on the river; all three of the Bowen boys had become pilots. Obviously Sam had a pretty clear realization that "learning the river" was hard work. But the glory of being a pilot was worth it.

Piloting was a highly skilled profession, and in those days of booming river trade it commanded pay commensurate with the skill it required. A pilot's wages ranged from one hundred and fifty to two hundred and fifty dollars a month, in a world where the purchasing power of the dollar was three or four times what it is today. For Sam Clemens, whose sole acquaintance with large currency had been the fifty-dollar bill which blew his way in Keokuk, such wealth was almost unimaginable. But other aspects of the profession were for him even more alluring than its wages. In that simple society the pilot was the only "unfettered and entirely independent human being that lived on the earth." His orders were obeyed on the run; from his decisions there was no appeal. In his high glass pilothouse, moreover, he was physically conspicuous as well as morally and legally absolute—all of which had boundless attraction for the eternal Tom Sawyer in Sam Clemens. But Sam Clemens had another side to which the life appealed—his sensitive shrinking from affronts and the crude practical joking that passed for humor—joking which he was still ready enough to indulge in himself, but which hurt and humiliated him when it was practiced at his expense. Even more than the freedom and prestige of the pilot's life, therefore, its security attracted him.

As the *Paul Jones* poked its way down the bankfull river, deeper and deeper into springtime, whatever dreams of the Amazon Sam may have taken with him from Cincinnati faded away. Two hundred miles below Cairo he mustered courage to ask Horace Bixby to take him on as apprentice. The pilot wasn't keen for the job; cubs were a great deal more trouble than profit. After some searching questions, however, he stated his terms: five hundred dollars cash, and the pupil to be responsible for all his own incidental expenses except his board while on the boat—board, by river custom, being free for learners as well as for their masters. Sam hadn't even one hundred dollars, let alone five, but after Bixby had firmly declined to take a few thousand acres of the Tennessee land in lieu of cash they agreed on a hundred down, the balance to be paid out of Sam's first earnings after he got his license. The final sealing of the bargain had to wait until they reached St. Louis on the return trip, when Sam borrowed the hundred dollars from Pamela's husband.

The one phase of Mark Twain's life which needs no retelling is the process of learning the river. To attempt to condense those matchless chapters of *Life on the Mississippi* is futile sacrilege; to quote them *in extenso,* an unwarranted affront to any literate American. From the time Sam embarked on the *Paul Jones* at Cincinnati to his last arrival in St. Louis as a passenger on the *Uncle Sam,* April 19, 1861, was four years, almost to a day. From the literary standpoint they were the four most important years of his life. His own oft-quoted words sum it up: "In that brief, sharp schooling, I got personally and familiarly acquainted with about all the different types of human nature that are to be found in fiction, biography, or history. . . .

When I find a well-drawn character in fiction or biography I generally take a warm personal interest in him, for the reason that I have known him before—met him on the river." When he entered on his apprenticeship he was, for all his twenty-one years, and for all that he had been self-supporting since his early teens, still a gawky small-town boy. Those four years made him into a poised and self-reliant man. But some of his experiences marked him for life.

Though in *Life on the Mississippi* he sets the duration of his apprenticeship as two and a half years, he was actually licensed as a pilot on April 9, 1859, a little less than two years after Horace Bixby took him on. He may have piloted freight boats during the last months of his training, for in those simple days fully licensed pilots were legally required only on boats carrying passengers. For Sam those years had included both adventure and tragedy.

A letter to Orion survives which gives a glimpse of the hardships of winter navigation—Sam and his chief out in the yawl for hours, sounding for the channel amid drifting ice that at one time held them trapped until the bow wave of another passing steamboat loosened the floes. When they got back on board they "looked like rock-candy statuary." The boat was the *Pennsylvania*, and Sam's chief at the time was not Bixby but another pilot named Brown (his given name is lacking, even in the casualty lists) to whom Bixby, temporarily engaging in the Missouri River traffic, had committed his cub. Of the mean, tyrannical Brown, and of his Shakespeare-reading copilot, George Ealer, Mark Twain left full-length portraits. But the acrid comedy of Brown's tyranny had a grim ending for Sam.

Henry Clemens had never become the skilled printer that his brother was, and in February 1858 Sam, finding him almost without employment in St. Louis, had helped him to get a berth as assistant "mud-clerk" on the *Pennsylvania*. About three months later came the fight with Brown. The captain had sent Henry to instruct Brown to make a certain landing; Brown, who was deaf but would not admit it, did not hear the order, and later denied that Henry had given it. When Henry next appeared in the pilothouse Brown struck him in the face, and Sam went into action with a fury that must have amazed himself. Brown was the bigger man, but Sam knocked him flat with a stool and then pounded him with his fists while the boat bowled on downriver with no one at the wheel. To interfere with a pilot on duty was the crime of crimes; Sam expected to be put ashore in disgrace at the next stop. But Captain Klinefelter was a just man whose personality shines in one of the innumerable thumbnail character sketches which fill Mark Twain's books. He told Sam, in substance, that Sam had been guilty of a great crime, and that his captain was damned glad of it. But Brown had a lawful grievance; either Sam left the boat, he proclaimed, or he would leave it himself. "Very well," said the captain, "let it be yourself." At New Orleans, however, Captain Klinefelter found no competent pilot available for the return trip and had to retain Brown. So it came about that in mid-June Sam was returning to St. Louis as a passenger on the *A. T. Lacey*, two days behind the *Pennsylvania*.

At Greenville the news was shouted that the *Pennsylvania* had blown up at Ship Island, below Memphis, with the loss of one hundred and fifty lives. From town to town that day the *A. T. Lacey* picked up more news, and before she landed at Memphis Sam knew that Henry was among the dying. He had been blown clear of the wreck, apparently uninjured, but after bravely swimming back to help in the rescue work had collapsed, for the scalding steam had penetrated his lungs. Sam found him with the other hopelessly injured in the improvised hospital at Memphis, and for four days and nights shared the watch by his bedside.

Every detail of the suffering around him burned itself into Sam's mind, and he remembered how, as the thoughtfully screened stretchers bore the dying from the room, a shudder went abreast of them like a wave. From his dying brother's bedside he wrote to his sister-in-law, telling the story of the disaster and hysterically reproaching himself as a hardened sinner who had really deserved all the suffering which was meted out to his innocent brother. And that nothing might be lacking to his morbid self-castigation, there was the torturing possibility that he himself had caused or hastened Henry's death by ignorantly giving him an overdose of morphine.

In one sense Henry's death was the end of his brother's youth. Though his humor and high spirits could not long be quenched, then or in later griefs, his face in repose took on the lined seriousness which for the next twenty years would make him look older than his years, and his mind commenced its endless beating of itself against the unanswerable problems of life and fate. Over and over in his dark moods he would review the Ifs—if he had not quarreled with Brown, if Captain Klinefelter had been able to get another pilot at New Orleans, if he and Henry had not in their last conversation resolved that in case of disaster they would stand by and do what they could, if he had not given that dose of morphine. . . . In this first of the many blows which life would deal him through his affections he first felt the mood of Captain Ahab, cursing the inscrutable malice of the universe which had wounded him.

But meantime life went on. About nine months after Henry's death Sam received his pilot's license and became full partner with his master, Horace Bixby. Much futile ink has been used to "prove" that Sam Clemens was never a good pilot; other ink, equally futile, has been applied to the thesis that his years on the river were the only period in his life when his artistic conscience was at peace, because he was doing the work that satisfied his inward cravings.

On the first point it would seem that no amount of irresponsible river gossip can outweigh the testimony of contemporary records. In 1859 Sam was able to boast to Orion that he was employed while most of the other young pilots were sucking their fingers—employed, moreover, on a good boat at top wages, so that he could bank a hundred dollars a month over and above his expenses—which included substantial contributions to his mother's support and equally substantial "loans" to Orion, who had lost his printing business in the panic of 1857 and was now unsuccessfully engaged in practicing law. (He had been admitted to the bar at Jamestown, Tennessee, in 1858, while living there in one of his many abortive efforts to sell the family land.) He had paid Bixby's tuition fee, and William Moffett's $100 loan. In the following year he gave his mother a spring excursion to New Orleans; the next fall he told of a ten-dollar dinner at a French restaurant. And since just after that dinner he still had twenty dollars to spare for Orion, he must have had steady employment. In that hard commercial and competitive world of steamboating neither Sam Clemens nor anyone else would have continued long at full employment had he not been competent. Nor is there record of any serious mishap to any boat which Sam piloted.

When Albert Bigelow Paine interviewed the aged but still wholly alert Horace Bixby about 1908, the pilot had nothing but good words for the abilities of his most famous pupil and partner. On a later occasion, however, and not for publication, Bixby is reported to have said that "Sam was never a good pilot. He knew the Mississippi River like a book, but he lacked confidence. This developed in him soon after he came on my boat. It never left him. . . . Sam Clemens knew the river, but being a coward, he was a failure as a pilot." It seems reasonable to infer that Bixby was remembering some of the episodes of Sam's apprenticeship. His pupil gave full details, in *Life on the Mississippi*, of the hard and humiliating public lessons by which Bixby taught him to have confidence in his knowledge of the river. Whatever Bixby may have said in 1912, he was not likely to have taken as his partner in 1858 and again in 1860 a man whom he considered a coward.

Yet in a different and subtler way Bixby's statement may well have been true. In 1906 Mark Twain told his biographer, "There is never a month passes that I do not dream of being in reduced circumstances, and obliged to go back to the river to earn a living. It is never a pleasant dream, either. I love to think about those days; but there's always something sickening about the thought that I have been obliged to go back to them; and usually in my dream I am just about to start into a black shadow without being able to tell whether it is Selma bluff, or Hat Island, or only a black wall of night."

One of the most obvious facts of dream psychology is the way in which the subconscious employs the memory, often forgotten by the waking mind, of a long-past strain or shock as the symbol of some current anxiety. It is an ironic commentary, both upon Mark Twain's own oft-repeated nostalgia for the river and upon the critics who assert that only on the river was his mind at peace, that piloting should have supplied one of his three recurrent nightmares. Later on, the lecture platform furnished the second; the third was the familiar and universal dream of appearing in public in a nightshirt. If a dream can be said to prove anything, this one proves that Sam Clemens had too much imagination for his own good as a pilot. The "lightning" pilot, like Bixby, was sure of himself and his knowledge at all times, and never allowed his mind to dwell on the possible consequences of an error. He didn't expect to make an error; if he did, then would be time enough to deal with the consequences. Nothing in all the voluminous records of Mark Twain's life and personality even remotely suggests that he could at any time or in any circumstances have achieved that sort of iron serenity. His courage and self-control were the nervously expensive sort which comes from thrusting back the over-vivid pictures furnished by the imagination. It is not without interest to speculate how long he would have lasted on the river without a nervous breakdown had he continued to be a pilot.

The toil of learning the river put a stop to Sam's literary ambitions, if any, for two years. Early in 1858 Orion had apparently suggested a renewal of the Snodgrass correspondence or something similar, for his brother replied, "I cannot correspond with a paper, because when one is learning the river, he is not allowed to do or think about anything else." By May

1859, however, Sam, now his own master, saw what he thought was a heaven-sent opportunity to be funny.

One of the most famous figures on the river was Captain Isaiah Sellers. Mark Twain describes him as a fine figure of a man, physically and morally, "and in his old age—as I remember him—his hair was as black as an Indian's, and his eye and hand were as strong and steady and his nerve and judgment as firm and clear as anybody's, young or old, among the fraternity of pilots. He was the patriarch of the craft; he had been a keelboat pilot before the day of steamboats; and a steamboat pilot before any other steamboat pilot, still surviving at the time I speak of, had ever turned a wheel." One gathers from the description that the Captain was a Methuselah; actually, in 1859 he was only fifty-six, so it is not surprising that his natural vigor was unabated. It was apparently true, however, that he had been in continuous service longer than any other man on the river. Because of his long experience and his prodigious pilot's memory, the Captain had got in the habit of contributing to the New Orleans papers reports and forecasts on the state of the river. It was long before the day when accurate measurements of the rainfall in the upper basin of the Mississippi made it possible to predict within an inch or two the stage which the lower river would reach at any given date; hence the Captain's guesses were better than no warning at all.

The Captain was almost illiterate: the man who could write, "In the winter of 1852 the Supervise inspectors enterduced the whisel as a Signal for metin and pasen Boats I wars a pose to it but after a time com over & am in favor of the whisal and hope it will prove yousfull," could have given points to Artemus Ward. His notes for the papers must have had heavy editing at the city desk. It was Mark Twain's firm belief in after years that these notes had been signed "Mark Twain"—in other words, two fathoms, which was safe water for any boat on the river. Yet no note thus signed has so far been unearthed in the files; their standard form appears to have been that of the item which was Sam Clemens' inspiration:

"VICKSBURG, MAY 4, 1859.
"My opinion for the benefit of the citizens of New Orleans:
The water is higher this far up than it has been since 1815. My
opinion is that the water will be four feet deep in Canal Street
before the first of next June. Mrs. Turner's plantation at the
head of Big Black Island is all under water, and it has not
been since 1815.

"I. SELLERS"

What graveled Sam Clemens and his fellow youngsters in the
craft was not the forecast but the calm certainty with which the
Captain declared that the present flood was higher than any
since 1815. With that statement as a starting point and the
applause of his fellows as stimulant, Sam dashed off a burlesque.

He prefaced his parody with a description of "our friend,
Sergeant Fathom, one of the oldest cub pilots on the river,"
whose reputation for safety—"he has made fourteen hundred
and fifty trips in the New Orleans and St. Louis trade without
causing serious damage to a steamboat"—was due to his caution
in seldom running his boat after dark. After laboring this point
with a series of illustrations intelligible only to his fellow pilots,
Sam referred to the Sergeant's "overflowing stream, without beginning, or middle, or end, of astonishing reminiscences of the
ancient Mississippi," and poked fun at the intense interest his
communications aroused in all classes of the population. Then
followed the "communication" itself. It began with the statement that the river was higher than at any time since 1813, and
then went on to recall some *really* high-water years, beginning
with the summer of 1763, when the Sergeant came down the
river on the old first *Jubilee*. "A singular sort of a single-engine
boat, with a Chinese captain and a Choctaw crew, forecastle on
her stern, wheels in the center, and the jackstaff 'nowhere,' for
I steered her with a window-shutter, and when we wanted to
land we sent a line ashore and 'rounded her to' with a yoke of
oxen." On that trip, the Sergeant continued, the water covered
all but the highest hills; in every flood year since, the river had

risen less, and the time was coming when it would cease to rise at all.

It was burlesque, crude and heavy-handed. Unlike its author's best mature work it was really the humor of exaggeration which bemused critics assert to have been always characteristic of him. It has none of the felicity of phrasing we associate with Mark Twain, though its prose, like that of his boyish letters from New York and Philadelphia, has the virtues of clarity and coherence. But its greatest demerit, apart from the unconscious cruelty of its ridicule of a man who had in no way offended the writer, is its tone. Sam Clemens had a long way still to go before he would learn the true tone of great humor, which is humility. As Irvin S. Cobb has summed up the matter, the tone of the satirist, whether he be Jonathan Swift or the neighborhood smart aleck, says, "What fools *you* mortals be"; never, "What fools *we* mortals be." The humorist, on the other hand, in whatever he writes says to his readers, between the lines, "My poor friend, you're an awful ass, addicted to all manner of nonsensical performances. But in your most asinine moment you never came anywhere near to being the ass that I am. So in all humility, as one ass to another, let's sit down here together and talk about ourselves and our failings. For the Lord knows we'll have plenty to talk about."

Sam's burlesque hurt Captain Sellers deeply, but it drew nothing but applause from the audience it was written for. Yet it does not seem to have stimulated its author to continue writing. He was too prosperous and having too good a time with his cronies when he was off watch to bother with his pen. His mind, nevertheless, was not lying fallow. He must have done a good deal of desultory reading, and he made the most of whatever "cultural" opportunities were available when he was in port. A letter to Orion in 1860 describes the sight which he and Pamela had had of the "most wonderfully beautiful painting" St. Louis had ever seen—Frederick E. Church's "Heart of the Andes." There is something pathetic about his rhapsodizing; as he later told Olivia Langdon, he loved beauty, but here on the river he saw few of the works of man that were not tawdry. Meantime the country was drifting steadily toward civil war, but so far as Sam's surviving letters show, he took no interest in politics and States' Rights. By January 1861, however, secession was no longer a theory: on the twenty-sixth Louisiana joined the Confederacy, and William Tecumseh Sherman's resignation from the superintendency of the State Military Academy became effective. Five days before, a letter entitled "The Expedition to Baton Rouge" was published in the New Orleans *Daily Crescent*. This letter, with five others which followed at irregular intervals until March 30, was signed Quintus Curtius Snodgrass. There is little reason to doubt that they were the work of Sam Clemens.

Snodgrass addresses himself to his friend, Charles Augustus Brown, whose surname was to reappear in 1865 in Mark Twain's California writings, and who was to serve as Mark's low-brow traveling companion from the beginning of the Sandwich Island tour to the end of the *Quaker City* excursion. The letter describes how Snodgrass, who had yearned for the military life ever since an uncle had given him a wooden sword to play with, decided to enlist in the Louisiana Guard. With other recruits he embarked for Baton Rouge "at the cheerful hour of 2 A.M. amid the cheers of about 34 individuals, all of whom exhibited unmistakable signs of intoxication. We were then ordered to go to bed, an order which, viewed theoretically, was a most desirable one; but as going to bed consisted in sitting upon a chair or lying down on the bare floor with a spittoon for a pillow, it was, practically speaking, not as luxurious as an unreflecting mind might deem it."

Snodgrass, in changing his name from the democratic Thomas Jefferson to the classical Quintus Curtius, discarded all the labored illiteracy of the letters of 1857. He quoted Daniel Webster and *Dombey and Son* and Jaques, mingling this highbrow material with such crude humor as the above allusion to using a spittoon for a pillow, and a mention of the first lieutenant's kindness in allowing him "two or three pulls at the bottle where he kept his toothwash . . . which he told me, in his impressive way, to 'use with discretion.' " Occasionally the style suggested the drawling rhythms of the mature Mark Twain:

"Brown, never make a bosom friend of an orderly sergeant! I am willing to concede the fact that in private life he may be all that is estimable—a loving husband, an affectionate father and an obedient son; but as a public character he has a duty to perform, and to that duty he will sacrifice his dearest friend should said dearest friend happen to turn his toes in or his chin out."

But if Sam Clemens was Quintus Curtius Snodgrass, he must at least have dallied with the idea of enlisting in the Confederate forces in Louisiana. The satire upon the ways of drill sergeants and the fatigue of standing at parade rest has a specific quality which suggests firsthand knowledge. It is on record that Horace Bixby believed his pupil had entered the Confederate service for a short time before his final return to St. Louis. The probability is that Sam did not enlist, but merely turned out with some of his friends for a few informal drills in the intervals between trips on the river. That he would heartily dislike the experience is obvious. He was always physically indolent except when he was doing things he enjoyed, and taking orders would be particularly distasteful to a pilot who had been in the habit of giving them. At any rate the only surviving personal letter of the period, written two weeks after the publication of the first Snodgrass letter, says nothing about enlisting. It is devoted wholly to telling Orion about a session Sam had had with Madame Caprell, a New Orleans fortuneteller. And Sam was still in funds: he had just sent his mother and Pamela $30 in quarters because they were always complaining about a shortage of small change, besides keeping his mother so well supplied that Orion was authorized to go to her for money if he needed it.

Apparently, then, Sam was still working as a pilot during the first three months of 1861, though the impending war was already dislocating trade on the river. On April 15 Lincoln issued his first call for troops; four days later Sam Clemens reached St. Louis on the last trip he would ever make as a licensed pilot. But he was not working on this trip; he was a passenger on the packet *Uncle Sam*. His biographer's statement that the *Uncle Sam* was the last boat to make the trip is, as Professor Lorch has pointed out, dramatic but incorrect. The river was not wholly closed to traffic until near the middle of May, and there is no contemporary confirmation of the story that the *Uncle Sam* was fired on as she passed Jefferson Barracks.

Sam found St. Louis seething with the divided allegiance of a border state. The governor, Claiborn Jackson, and the legislature were strongly pro-Southern, but outside of official circles Union sentiment in the city was strong. On May 10 Union troops seized Camp Jackson, and immediately thereafter the Confederate flag was hauled down for the last time in St. Louis. Four days later the governor, newly authorized by the legislature, began enlisting militia for Confederate service. During all these events Sam was apparently still in St. Louis. On May 22 he was initiated Entered Apprentice in the Polar Star Masonic Lodge, and on June 12 he passed to the Fellowcraft Degree. It must have been immediately after this latter date that he entered upon the adventure which he described, nearly a quarter-century later, in "The Private History of a Campaign that Failed."

On June 12, when Sam received his second Masonic degree, Governor Jackson called the militia into active service. Immediately thereafter Sam went to Hannibal. The town had been strongly pro-Southern at first, but when Sam reached there he found that sentiment had changed. Union Home Guards were in complete control, and the secession newspaper had been suppressed. But a dozen or so young men, including such graduates of Tom Sawyer's band as Sam Bowen and Ed Stevens, thought it would be fun to organize a Confederate battalion, and Sam joined them. He had been kicking his heels in St. Louis for nearly two months, and was ready for almost anything that promised activity. They could not organize openly in Hannibal, so they slipped out of town in the darkness and marched ten miles to the neighboring village of New London to complete their formation. Missouri was full of such groups at the moment—so thoroughly "volunteers" that they had gone through no formal enlistment and taken no oath of allegiance, electing their own officers and fully prepared to oust them if they got too uppity. Some of these groups degenerated into the bushwhackers who terrorized Missouri and Kansas all through the war—bandits and ruffians like the Quantrill gang, for whom war was merely an excuse for plunder and murder.

Nobody knew enough about drill to be able to inflict any of the military precision which the Snodgrass letters had ridiculed, but even so the adventure turned out to be less fun than they had anticipated. On June 17 Governor Jackson and his troops were defeated at Boonville, and the Governor proved less of a fire-eater in the field than he had been on paper. Hundreds of regularly enlisted militiamen straggled back home, with no one to call them deserters or take any action against them. Wellfounded reports began to circulate that Union regiments from Iowa and Illinois were moving into the state and taking control of the lines of communication. The little unit to which Sam belonged was kept constantly on the move. They found the farmers none too hospitable about handing out supplies, and they lacked both the authority and the nerve to levy what they could not beg.

To add to their troubles a long spell of dry weather broke in torrential rains which continued all through the latter part of June. The boys had no tents, and were shelterless except when they could induce a farmer to let them sleep in the barn or the corncrib. But the two most dramatic episodes of "The Campaign That Failed" never happened. The shooting of the strange horseman in the dark was admittedly introduced for its dramatic value in the narrative, and though Mark Twain liked to believe that he had come near being captured by Colonel U. S. Grant, in cold fact Grant did not arrive in the neighborhood of Salt River until three weeks after Sam Clemens and his friends had left. They had had enough. Two weeks of tramping and bivouacking had sated their martial ardor; they dissolved their battalion as informally as they had organized it and went home. It would take months and years of hard drilling, of lessons driven home by one rout after another of green troops, to convince the average Middle Westerner of the necessity of military discipline. Sam Clemens and his friends were doing only what thousands of others were doing in those opening months of a war that people were still unable to realize. And Sam, to an even greater degree than most of his fellow Missourians, had reasons to be divided in his allegiance. Though he had been reared in slave territory, he had lived in free-soil Iowa, and he must have realized that the prosperity and security of the river trade which had been his livelihood depended on the absence of tariff barriers and custom houses. But most of all he was disillusioned with the romance and adventure of campaigning in the mud.

Whether or not a sprained ankle kept him in hiding for some days in the house of Nuck Matson, a more or less friendly farmer, Sam Clemens was certainly back in St. Louis on July 10, for on that date he was made Master Mason. Six days before, Orion had reached the city, en route to a post which promised more congenial adventure than that of the campaign that failed.

CHAPTER IV

WEST AND AWAY

FOR the first and only time in his life Orion Clemens had backed the right horse. His years in Muscatine and Keokuk had converted him into an ardent Unionist and Abolitionist; during the campaign of 1860 he had supported Lincoln by an energetic stumping tour of northern Missouri, where he was practicing law in the village of Memphis. By the political code he was entitled to his reward, but the rewards were nicely proportioned to the power and prestige of the applicants. Back in Ohio, for instance, a young newspaperman named William Dean Howells had written a minor campaign biography of Lincoln, and was rewarded with the charming but unremunerative post of American consul at Venice. Orion's contribution, in terms of possible votes swayed, was smaller than Howells', but he had a friend in the Administration. In January had come the announcement that Lincoln had appointed Edward Bates of St. Louis as his Attorney General. Orion, in the '40's, had abortively studied law in Bates's office, and as soon as the cabinet appointment was announced Orion hastened to St. Louis to solicit the new Attorney General's patronage.

At the end of March Orion learned the results of his application. He was to be Secretary of the Territory of Nevada, at a salary of $1,800 a year—"an office of such majesty that it concentrated in itself the duties and dignities of Treasurer, Comptroller, Secretary of State, and Acting Governor in the Governor's absence." The new Governor was James W. Nye, later Senator from Nevada and a good friend of Sam's. But now that Orion had the appointment there remained the problem of reaching his post. The Overland stage fare from St. Joseph to

64

Carson City was $150; Orion, as always, was hard up. On July 4 Orion came to St. Louis to say good-by to his mother and sister, and probably also to try to borrow money for his trip. Sometime between the fourth and the tenth, Sam, as has been mentioned, also returned to St. Louis to take his final Masonic degree.

To the morbidly conscientious Orion, en route to an official position under the Union government, it must have been a severe shock to learn that his younger brother had just been playing round with a Rebel military unit. Mollie Clemens' journal records that her husband "prevailed upon" Sam to accompany him to Nevada. What form the persuasion took is uncertain. Past question, Orion wanted to stop his brother's dallying with the Southern cause, but the statement in *Roughing It* that Orion offered Sam the position of private secretary is surely literary embroidery. Both brothers must have known that the government appropriations carried no funds for such an appointment. Most likely the chief appeal was to Sam's spirit of adventure. The river was now completely closed to traffic unless Sam chose to enlist as a military pilot and act as a target at wages little more than half the peacetime maximum. But fabulous tales had been coming east of the gold and silver in the Nevada hills; a lucky man might make a fortune in a few months. By that time the unpleasantness between the states would be over, and he could come home and enjoy his wealth.

When Sam made up his mind he acted quickly. He had funds in the bank, the savings from his piloting, and with these he financed the expedition. On July 18, two weeks after Orion's arrival in St. Louis, the brothers boarded the Missouri River steamboat *Sioux City* for St. Joseph, through territory now firmly in Union hands. Sam Clemens had entered on the last lap of the long and roundabout journey which was to make him a man of letters.

Behind him lay nearly twenty-six years of experience. He had seen more of all varieties of raw and finished human nature than the average man of sheltered and sedentary pursuits encounters in a lifetime. Whatever Hannibal had failed to exhibit, the brief, sharp schooling of the river had supplied—all the types who furnished characters for his books, as well as the gamblers, pimps and prostitutes who infested the river boats but whom he omitted from the picture. So far as the creative part of his writing was concerned, the next five years in Nevada and California completed his equipment. Every character he ever wrote about, including Joan of Arc, was either drawn from the intensive experience of his first thirty years or conceived in its spirit.

That he had continued his literary self-education during the years on the river, his letters attest. Paine points out that such a locution as "between you and I" ceases to appear after 1859; other crudities of diction, however, survived much longer—not until after he settled in the East did he cease to write "it don't." He had written little, and that little not over well, but if the Q. C. Snodgrass letters are his he had obviously done some thinking about the art of humor, and had realized that it was possible to be funny without mangled spelling or labored puns.

Now, setting out for the Far West, Sam threw himself into the new role with the same enthusiasm that marked every new venture in his life. He began by dressing the part with the ardor of an Easterner newly arrived at a dude ranch. In his prosperous days as a pilot he had been something of a dandy, but as soon as he reached St. Joseph he took to cowhide boots and flannel shirts, and Orion followed his example with such disastrous completeness that when they finally reached Carson City the reception committee which had turned out to greet the new Territorial Secretary retreated in dismay at sight of the dusty and untidy brothers. Tom Sawyer could always be counted on to play a role to the limit.

For the exact facts of Mark Twain's Western years *Roughing It* is about as reliable a guide as Herman Melville's books are for his years at sea. The scenery is correct; most of the subsidiary characters have recognizable originals; but some of the adventures never happened, and others have for purposes of literary effect been colored and heightened out of all semblance to history. The Overland trip is the most accurate part, for in telling it Mark Twain was relying upon Orion's sober journal and not upon his own prodigal memory.

The brothers left St. Joseph on July 26, and reached Carson City on August 14. The coaches were faster than the covered wagons of the emigrant trains, but they concentrated about as much discomfort into their three weeks on the road as the wagons suffered in their five months. Sam Clemens was still young enough not to mind discomfort so long as he was having a good time and was going places. Once established in a board-inghouse with Governor Nye's other camp followers, he appears to have devoted himself for several weeks leisurely to taking stock of his surroundings. After having been the family leader for three years, as the result of his success on the river, he now found himself distinctly overshadowed by Orion. But he still had funds on hand, the mining fever had not yet infected him, and in response to an exhortation from his mother to "tell everything as it is—no better and no worse," he wrote long letters home.

The country, he reported, was fabulously rich in gold, silver, copper, lead, coal, iron, quicksilver, marble, granite, chalk, plaster of Paris, thieves, murderers, desperadoes, ladies, children, lawyers, Christians, Indians, Chinamen, Spaniards, gamblers, sharpers, coyotes, poets, preachers and jackass rabbits. "I overhead a gentleman say, the other day, that it was 'the d——dest country under the sun'—and that comprehensive description I fully subscribe to."

The unnamed gentleman was right for more reasons than Sam Clemens was likely to realize at the moment. The California and Nevada frontier was unique in history. Prior to 1849 the advance of white culture in America had been basically agricultural and had followed a simple and well-defined pattern. Behind a far-extended skirmish line of hunters, trappers and Indian traders had come the frontier farmers, more or less

equally divided between the shiftless, restless and defeated
fugitives from the older settlements and the adventurous but
impecunious homeseekers on whom the spotlight of history and
myth has been focused. After the farmers came the trades,
crafts and professions, as the new communities grew and prospered. Throughout the first half of the nineteenth century
capitalism in various manifestations had quickened the tempo
without changing the pattern except as it began large-scale exploitation of timber and minerals. Land companies had speeded
the influx of population, sometimes honestly, sometimes dishonestly. Canals, and the growing mechanized transport of
steamboats and railways had made possible the large-scale
marketing of the products of the newly opened districts. But
the odyssey of the Clemens family from Virginia to Tennessee
to Missouri remained typical of the whole country until gold
was discovered in California.

Upon the swift and ruthless exploitation of that discovery
every available resource was immediately concentrated. The
first highly individualistic stages of the exploitation were carried on by that huge and unorganized army of volunteers whose
epitaph Mark Twain wrote with pardonable overstatement, for
this was how the pioneers thought of themselves:

"It was a driving, vigorous, restless population in those days.
It was a *curious* population. It was the *only* population of the
kind that the world has ever seen gathered together, and it is
not likely that the world will ever see its like again. For, ob-
serve, it was an assemblage of two hundred thousand *young*
men—not simpering, dainty, kid-gloved weaklings, but stal-
wart, muscular, dauntless young braves, brimful of push and
energy, and royally endowed with every attribute that goes to
make up peerless and magnificent manhood—the very pick and
choice of the world's glorious ones. No women, no children, no
gray and stooping veterans—none but erect, bright-eyed, quick-
moving, strong-handed young giants—the strangest population,
the finest population, the most gallant host that ever trooped
down the startled solitudes of an unpeopled land. And where

WEST AND AWAY 69

are they now? Scattered to the ends of the earth—or prematurely aged and decrepit—or shot or stabbed in street affrays—or dead of disappointed hopes and broken hearts—all gone, or nearly all—victims devoted upon the altar of the golden calf. . . .

"It was a splendid population—for all the slow, sleepy, sluggish-brained sloths staid at home—you never find that sort of people among pioneers—you cannot build pioneers out of that sort of material. It was that population that gave to California a name for getting up astounding enterprises and rushing them through with a magnificent dash and daring and a recklessness of cost or consequences, which she bears unto this day—and when she projects a new surprise, the grave world smiles as usual, and says 'Well, that is California all over.'

"But they were rough in those times! They fairly reveled in gold, whisky, fights, and fandangoes, and were unspeakably happy. The honest miner raked from a hundred to a thousand dollars from his claim in a day, and what with the gambling dens and the other entertainments, he hadn't a cent the next morning, if he had any sort of luck. . . ."

A ribald rhyme, which the judicious do not quote in the presence of Californians, declares that "the miners came in '49, the whores they came in '50." Bret Harte in one of his moments of realism shocked Emerson with his declaration that it was vice that had brought the graces of civilization so quickly to the Far West: "It is the gamblers who bring the music to California. It is the prostitute who brings the New York fashions in dress there, and so throughout." First came the miners, next came vice and after them came capital to organize and consolidate.

When Sam Clemens arrived in Nevada only a dozen years had elapsed since the beginning of the gold rush, but the days of placer mining already belonged to a remote and legendary past. The San Francisco of the desperadoes and vigilantes had become a solid city, with banks and able newspapers and even a literary magazine. The hills of Sonoma and Tuolumne were full of ghost towns where a few castaways eked a scanty living from exhausted diggings. Other towns were not even ghosts: save for the ravaged stream beds and gutted hillsides, nothing remained to show that men had ever lived there. Mining had changed from surface work, where a couple of brawny men, if water was available, could do the work by themselves with pick and shovel and rocker, to hard-rock work which required tools and explosives and hoisting equipment to get out the ore, and then stamping mills to reduce it. On this sort of mining Nevada Territory was founded.

In the early 1850's prospectors had penetrated the valleys on the eastern side of the Sierras and had found small quantities of placer gold, but had failed to find or to recognize the silver ores. Not until the spring of 1859 were the surface croppings of the great Comstock Lode discovered—the richest vein of mingled gold and silver ever discovered in the world.

The news of the bonanza spread swiftly. San Francisco capital supplied the funds to erect stamping mills and develop the ledges, which their discoverers seldom held on to long enough to profit by their luck. But everyone was willing to believe the country was full of ledges as rich as the Comstock, and prospectors scattered in all directions to hunt for them.

On the heels of discovery came speculation. The prospectors were without capital, and without capital these hard-rock mines could not be worked. Hence, as soon as a man discovered a likely ledge he sold "feet" or shares in the discovery in order to raise funds to work it. Soon everybody in the Territory who had any ready cash was buying feet in the expectation that somewhere among his speculations would be a big bonanza that would make him a millionaire. The center of activity in the mining country had shifted from gambling with pick and shovel to gambling with stocks. It was Wall Street of the Coolidge era on a local scale. Almost every day the papers carried stories of new discoveries, and while some ardent souls rushed to the new diggings in hopes of locating claims, others, equally ardent, hurried to acquire feet.

During the first weeks of Sam Clemens' stay, however, the gambling fever did not impress him much. His first move was toward a secondary source of wealth. Timber for mine shafts and lumber for building was in enormous demand in the booming mining towns, and Sam, in company with a young Cincinnatian named John Kinney, set off on a camping trip to Lake Tahoe—Lake Bigler, they called it then—with the intention of locating a timber claim. They located their claim and held it four days. Then a carelessly managed campfire got out of control, and the resulting forest fire destroyed their own claim and a lot of other timber as well. They returned to Carson City undamaged, but Sam's distaste for active physical labor was intensified by the experience.

When he was going places no amount of toil deterred him. His delight in the hardships of the Overland trip is matched by his account of the joys of camping out—though we may question his statement to his mother that when they were lost for four hours in the rocky forests above Tahoe it was Kinney who did all the swearing. Later, he made long journeys on foot, carrying a pack, to Mono Lake and the Yosemite; his energy and endurance during his journeys in Hawaii and the Holy Land were to be phenomenal. But working hard in one spot was another matter. He tired of the labor of building a cabin and fencing their claim as quickly as he later tired of hard-rock mining. His restless spirit is summed up in a letter to Pamela not long after the Tahoe adventure:

"Tell Mrs. Benson I never intend to be a lawyer. I have been a slave several times in my life, but I'll never be one again. I always intend to be so situated (*unless* I marry), that I can 'pull up stakes' and clear out whenever I feel like it."

That same letter contains the first hint of the mining fever which would occupy Sam's whole time and attention for the next nine months. He had been on a trip to the Esmeralda district, had acquired feet in the unprospected Black Warrior claim, and now, receiving encouraging reports, planned to return there in the spring to help work it. With unconscious irony he repeatedly wished that his uncle, James Lampton—original of Colonel Sellers—could come to Nevada. He would make a fortune in a few months. Not even in the 1880's, the days of the Paige typesetting machine, would Sam Clemens show his kinship with Uncle James so clearly as he did during the winter and spring of 1861 and 1862.

His first manifestation of the fever was in setting out in December, across two hundred miles of desert, on a prospecting trip to the newly discovered Humboldt district, ecstatically reported in the papers to be the most fabulously endowed region on earth. His companions were Billy Clagget, whom he had known in Keokuk, A. W. Oliver and an elderly blacksmith named Tillou, whom he immortalized as Mr. Ballou in *Roughing It*. In his share in the wagon, the team of horses and eighteen hundred pounds of supplies Sam apparently invested most of the money he had left. The trip lasted two months—one month of actual prospecting, and one consumed in getting to the Humboldt and back again. Sam, Judge Oliver remembered, "was the life of the camp; but sometimes there would come a reaction and he could hardly speak for a day or two." His temperament had not changed since boyhood; it would never change as long as he lived.

The expedition was a failure. Gold and silver were not lying about loose, and the young men soon wearied of the drudgery of sinking shafts on doubtful claims. By the first week in February Sam was back in Carson City, en route to Esmeralda, where by this time he owned feet in other ledges besides the Black Warrior. His earlier letters home had been so enthusiastic that Pamela and her husband were thinking seriously of coming West, and Sam had to advise them to wait a bit until his claims really began to pay dividends. And meantime Orion was in trouble again. He had been demonstrating his complete unworldliness by trying, as a government employee, to save government money. The result was what might be expected. Orion had set up his office in a shack, because the high rents demanded for regular business quarters appalled him, but when he tried to apply the savings in rent on the costs of public printing, which were much higher than the official allowance based on Eastern prices, he was rebuked from Washington and the extra payments on the printing were deducted from his salary. Governor Nye was annoyed by his subordinate's refusal to practice the gentle political art of padding his accounts in one direction in order to take care of unauthorized expenses in another. Sam defended his brother in a fiery interview with the Governor, with the result that Orion remained in his post until ousted by political changes after Nevada became a state, and the Governor and Sam Clemens became warm friends.

But Orion by this time was as much infected as Sam with the speculative fever. He was buying every stock that was offered to him, and for the six months from February to August 1862 he financed Sam and Sam's speculations in the Esmeralda district. The surviving letters of those months are a monotonous reiteration of the theme of rich prospects ahead and no money in hand. To one of his temporary partners, Calvin Higbie, Mark Twain later dedicated *Roughing It*, "in memory of the curious time when we two were millionaires for ten days." But the story of the "blind lead" in that book is mostly fiction, compounded of two different episodes with a large infusion of dreams. It is true, apparently, that Clemens and Higbie did forfeit a claim because of failure to work it within the statutory ten days after location, but the riches existed only in their imaginations; the Wide West mine never paid dividends. More important for Mark Twain's literary development were the trips already mentioned, which he and Higbie took to Mono Lake and Yosemite.

In the height of his mining fever the literary bacillus began to stir again in Sam's blood, as it had stirred during the prosperous days as pilot. Some of his letters home had been printed in Keokuk newspapers, as Orion had printed the earlier ones from New York. During the spring in Esmeralda, while bad weather confined him to the cabin, he began to contribute to the chief newspaper of Nevada Territory, the *Territorial Enter-*

prise of Virginia City. It was not a move of desperation: the earliest allusion to it comes in a letter of May 11 to Orion at a time when Sam was asking, "What the devil does a man want with any more feet when he owns in the Flyaway and the invincible bomb-proof Monitor?" Of his writing he says merely, "I suppose you saw my letters in the *Enterprise.*"

None of these letters have survived, and there is no way of telling how many Sam wrote. They were signed "Josh," and some of them may have been humorous accounts of the Esmeralda diggings. But descriptions of two of the later ones have been preserved. Both were burlesques. The first parodied an egotistical lecturer whom "Josh" called "Professor Personal Pronoun," explaining that it was impossible to report his speech in full because the type case hadn't enough upper-case *I's.* The second, presumably written for Independence Day, was a burlesque of the spread-eagle school of oratory, and began, "I was sired by the Great American Eagle and foaled by a continental dam." It is unnecessary to believe that either represented much advance in subtlety over the Isaiah Sellers burlesque of 1859. But they made people laugh, and among the laughers was William H. Barstow, the business manager of the *Enterprise,* who suggested to Joseph T. Goodman, editor and part-owner of the paper, that here was a man they ought to have on their staff.

While these things were happening in Virginia City, Sam in Esmeralda was at the end of his rope. He had not yet abandoned hope in his mines, but he had been counting up his debts and his funds, and the tally was not encouraging. The debts exceeded the cash in hand, and "how in the h——l I am going to live on something over $100 until October or November, is singular. The fact is, I must have something to do, and that *shortly.*" His first thought was to get a contract as Esmeralda correspondent for a California newspaper. "California is full of people who have interests here, and it's d——d seldom they hear from this country." Accordingly he asked Orion to write in his behalf to the Sacramento *Union.* "Tell them I have corresponded with the N. Orleans *Crescent,* and other papers—and the *Enterprise."* The terms he was willing to accept were ten dollars a week and his board. He already knew at least one newspaper custom—that of not understating one's previous experience. That all his correspondence had been unsolicited and, with the doubtful exception of the first Snodgrass letters, unpaid, was not a detail to put into an application for work. But the position of depending on doles from Orion had become intolerable to his pride, and there was no work in Esmeralda that he could do. He had tried a week in a stamping mill, with no results except catching a violent cold and being almost salivated by the mercury used in reclaiming the gold and silver. "Now," he told Orion, "it has been a long time since I couldn't make my own living, and it shall be a long time before I loaf another year. . . . If I can't move the bowels of those hills this fall, I will come up and clerk for you until I get money enough to go over the mountains for the winter."

That was on July 23. A week later he announced, "Barstow has offered me the post as local reporter for the *Enterprise* at $25 a week, and I have written him that I will let him know next mail, if possible." But a week later he had not wholly made up his mind. He had written Barstow that he guessed he would take the job, and asked how long before he must come to Virginia City. Then came the passage which has been the basis of perhaps more unsubstantiated theorizing than anything else Mark Twain ever wrote:

"I shall leave at midnight tonight, alone and on foot for a walk of 60 or 70 miles through a totally uninhabited country, and it is barely possible that mail facilities may prove infernally 'slow' during the few weeks I expect to spend out there. But do you write Barstow that I have left here for a week or so, and in case he should want me he must write me here, or let me know through you."

"So," wrote Paine dramatically, "he had gone into the wilderness to fight out his battle alone," and Mr. Van Wyck Brooks found the passage symbolic of a sense of degradation in accepting a position as a mere writer and a humorous one at that. But why a man intent merely on thinking things over and coming to a possibly distasteful decision should find it necessary to slip out of town at midnight is far from clear. The likeliest conjecture is that Sam had heard one more rumor about the Whiteman Cement Mine, or some other legendary bonanza, and had determined to go and investigate before he finally quitted the Esmeralda district. Secrecy in such a quest was imperative if his heels were not to be dogged by a mob of other hopefuls.

The brevity of his stay in "the wilderness" supports this conjecture. Though on August 7 he had expected to be absent a "few weeks," on the fifteenth he was back in Esmeralda, and writing a letter to his sister. It had not taken long to discover that this last mining hope, like all the others, was illusory. He had just received a letter from Pamela, in which she must have suggested that he return to his old work on the river. In view of his alleged reluctance to join the *Enterprise,* and his much-advertised devotion to the fine art of piloting, his reply is significant.

"What in thunder are pilot's wages to me? . . . I never have *once* thought of returning home to go on the river again, and I never expect to do any more piloting at any price. My livelihood must be made in this country—and if I have to wait longer than I expected, let it be so—I have no fear of failure." These are not the words of a man who had sacrificed his ideal occupation. He need not have become a military pilot with the Federal forces, had he returned to the river; there was plenty of commercial traffic on the upper river and the Ohio and the Missouri. But even in this hour when he was bidding farewell to hopes of immediate wealth from the mines he regarded the river as a chapter of his life that was closed forever. He had a strong fiber of stubbornness in his nature, however; having abandoned one form of livelihood, he would not quit Nevada until he had proved his ability to support himself in Nevada in spite of disappointment and homesickness. When he found that old Californians had been promising themselves for a dozen years that

they would go home in the fall, "I stole a march on Disappointment, and said I would *not* go home this fall. . . . This country
suits me, and—it *shall* suit me, whether or no."

He had spent a year chasing the pot of gold at the rainbow's
foot. In a country mad with speculative fever he would have
been more, or less, than human if he had not caught the infec-
tion. Any survivor of the Florida land boom or the Coolidge
market has only to examine his own memories honestly to realize
what had happened to Sam Clemens. The dream died hard,
but Sam was no Micawber to linger on, sponging on Orion and
waiting for a barren shaft to strike the ledge. The basic realism
which underlay the enthusiasm of his nature told him that he
was through in Esmeralda. He had hoped for cake, and had
not got it. Very well, he would take bread, and a half loaf if
necessary. He accepted the *Enterprise* offer, and set out to cover
the hundred and seventy dusty miles between Esmeralda and
Virginia City. The long series of detours was ended. At last he
was on his way to fulfill his destiny as a man of letters.

CHAPTER V

E*N*TER*P*R*I*SE

IN THE mines four years brought more changes than a stable community might show in a lifetime. The *Territorial Enterprise* was the first newspaper established in Nevada. It began its career as a weekly on December 18, 1858, in Genoa, when that settlement contained two hundred people. Eleven months later it moved to Carson City, and after a year there migrated to Virginia City. By that time it had passed into the hands of Denis E. McCarthy and Joseph T. Goodman, who were to make it one of the best-known papers in the West. Published at first in a one-story shack with a lean-to annex which served as kitchen and bunkhouse for the entire staff, it had prospered with the booming mines, and when Sam Clemens shambled into its office on that hot August afternoon in 1862 it had recently been moved to larger and more substantial quarters on C Street.

In response to McCarthy's inquiry as to his business, the dusty and unkempt wayfarer dropped his blanket roll on the floor and himself into a chair, drawling:

"My starboard leg seems to be unshipped. I'd like about one hundred yards of line. I think I'm falling to pieces." A pause— one of those dramatic pauses which became part of Mark Twain's platform technique. "I want to see Mr. Barstow, or Mr. Goodman. My name is Clemens, and I've come to write for the paper."

It was a trick Sam Clemens never outgrew, to cover awkwardness or embarrassment with a whimsicality—the same impulse that made him, six years later, say to General Grant on their first meeting, "General, I seem to be embarrassed. Are you?"

It was an effective trick. Now he was caught coming among strangers, to undertake work of a sort he had never practiced except as an amateur. Naturally he was somewhat embarrassed, but it is needless to seek deeper symbolism in his remark.

Joe Goodman, the other proprietor of the *Enterprise,* and Dan De Quille (William Wright), its mining expert and chief reporter, promptly took charge of the new recruit. Goodman was slightly younger than his new employee; De Quille was six years older. Both were self-educated, but effectively so. Wright, Ohio-born of Philadelphia Quaker stock, had served his journalistic apprenticeship in Iowa before coming to California in 1857. Goodman, Mark Twain later told his bride, might have been a poet had he not married an unresponsive woman. A poetic impulse so easily smothered cannot have been robust. As it was, Goodman ultimately made himself something of a scholar, and in his later years was one of the first men to attempt to decipher the Mayan hieroglyphics. De Quille, who was about to return to the States for a visit, took Sam to his own lodgings; Goodman gave the few instructions he felt necessary. The gist of Goodman's advice was to go to headquarters, get the absolute facts and then report them in full. This policy, he added, might result in your becoming shot, but at least you would preserve the public's confidence in your paper.

Nominally, Sam Clemens was a reporter; actually he was a miscellaneous feature writer from the start. Virginia City was prone to violent self-expression; brawls which ended in pistol shots and homicide were commonplace—so commonplace that few citizens wanted to bother reading about them. Long before the *Enterprise* was off the press everybody in town knew all the details, anyway. What the *Enterprise's* public wanted was either something to read that they hadn't heard before, or something that had bearing on their fortunes. Business doings were news; the handouts and rumors regarding the output and prospects of the mines were news; homicides were not unless they were extra-special. If rival editors could work up a vitriolic feud, if self-important citizens or incompetent officials could be lampooned or if the public could be hoaxed by carefully contrived tall stories, the readers felt they were getting their money's worth.

So far as the feuds were concerned Sam Clemens was on familiar ground. It was the same sort of thing he had tried a dozen years before on the Hannibal *Journal*. So were the lampoons on public characters. But the elaborate hoaxes were a branch of journalism which had reached its finest flowering on the Pacific Coast, though Edgar Allan Poe and others of less note had tried their hands at them in New York in the '40's. The lampoon might be an elaborate practical joke, or it might be merely the retelling of some folktale as old as Joe Miller's, with local personalities inserted at the proper places. Dan De Quille's *The Big Bonanza* contains a dozen or more, ranging from the faked duel in which the hoaxer with the aid of some chicken blood feigns a fatal wound after receiving the fire from the hoaxee's pistol which the seconds had double-charged with powder without any bullets, to the yarn of the drunkard whom the jokers laid to sleep in an open grave. When he woke at daylight and saw his surroundings he exclaimed, "The day of resurrection, and I'm the first son of a bitch out of the ground!" (Every community probably had its version of that one: a popular Scottish variant gives the drunkard's remark as, "It's a puir turn-oot for Kirkintilloch!")

But in the dozen years between '49 and '62 the West Coast had developed a folklore of its own in such matters. The archetype of the large-scale public leg-pull was the work of Ferdinand Cartwright Ewer, editor of the *Pioneer*, San Francisco's first literary magazine. In 1854 Ewer had published in the *Pioneer* an elaborate burlesque of spiritualism, which at the time was attracting hosts of credulous people. Ewer mailed a copy of his magazine to Judge John Worth Edmonds of New York, a convert to spiritualism who was publishing a magazine to spread his discoveries. Ewer then sat back and awaited results. What he expected is unknown; he certainly could not have expected all he got. Edmonds not only reprinted the entire hoax in all good faith, but proceeded to have spirit communications on his own account from the wholly fictitious soul whom Ewer had invented. What had started as a joke became almost a tragedy as one spiritualistic publication after another took up the tale, and correspondence asking further details poured in on the astounded author. When he publicly confessed the hoax, through the columns of the New York *Herald*, the more earnest spiritualists refused to believe him, and Judge Edmonds demonstrated to his own satisfaction that the manifestations were genuine but the work of a malignant spirit—the ghost of a man who had shot himself while insane and who had not yet recovered his sanity in the other world.

That story was the progenitor of a whole cycle of legends. The Coast reveled in the yarn. But the name of its perpetrator was soon lost, because Ewer abandoned journalism for the ministry. At the same time, however, George Horatio Derby was writing the first of the series of sketches which made his pen names of "Squibob" and "John Phoenix" famous the country over. During the editor's absence in 1853, for instance, Derby took charge of the San Diego *Herald* and thought it a grand joke to reverse the paper's politics. All California guffawed, and when, a couple of years later, Derby contributed to the San Francisco *Herald* a scientific report by "Dr. Herman Ellenbogen" on zoological discoveries in the mountains of Washington Territory, California made the most of it. The report detailed the finding of living specimens of those remarkable beasts, the Gyascutus and the Prock. *The Spirit of the Times,* New York's sporting paper, promptly reprinted the skit, and the *Alta,* with the thin argument that the editor had not labeled the story as a joke, asserted that it had been taken seriously. The tradition that solemn Easterners could be gulled by Western humor was established now; the popular mind would take care of the rest of the legend, with some effectual help from Mark Twain.

Before Sam Clemens had been four months on the *Enterprise* he made his first contribution to the tradition. Darwin's work and the recent discovery in Europe of the first remains of the Neanderthal race had roused discussions of the antiquity of man in which California's nascent scientific societies joined. Two years later the Pliocene skull, allegedly discovered in a Calaveras mine, made the scientists so wary of hoaxes that it took them many years to admit the genuineness of the Folsom and other relics of ice-age man in America. Sam Clemens capitalized on the current discussions by describing the discovery in the Sierras of a petrified man, seated in a pensive attitude on a rock ledge, one hand propping his eyelid open in a then popular gesture, and the other hand raised with the thumb applied to the nose and the fingers extended. (Seven years before, John Phoenix had equipped a clipper-ship's figurehead with the same derisive gesture.) Every feature was perfectly preserved, even to a wooden leg. The Humboldt coroner was alleged to have hastened to hold an inquest on the remains; his jury of miners brought in the verdict that the deceased had come to his end as the result of protracted exposure. Because the limestone drippings had cemented the man firmly to the ledge on which he sat, burial proved impossible unless he were first blasted loose, which the coroner with characteristic delicacy forbade.

Everybody laughed, except perhaps Coroner Sewell. The San Francisco *Bulletin* reprinted the story with the caption, "Another Washoe Joke." No doubt other papers did, too, but if any editor was silly enough to take it seriously, the item has not been discovered. But ten years later Mark Twain, turning out "Memoranda" for the *Galaxy*, remembered this occasion and improved it. Suppressing the wooden leg, and vastly exaggerating the subtlety with which he had introduced the details of the thumbed nose, he asserted that the hoax had been seriously reprinted all over the country, had reached Europe, and had finally wound up in sublime and unimpeached legitimacy in the columns of the august London *Lancet*. Ten years' experience had taught Mark Twain a lot about the spoofing value of corroborative detail. In its revived and revised form the jest took in everybody, including Albert Bigelow Paine and Bernard De-

Voto; before he died, Mark Twain probably believed it himself.

But the Comstock had taken the jester to its heart, and Goodman and McCarthy were well pleased with their recruit. There was nothing of the backwoods in their ideas or in their standards of English. They appreciated a man who could pull the public leg, as Dan De Quille had done, or was to do, with the tale of the solar armor—a refrigerated suit in which the inventor froze to death in Death Valley in midsummer because a valve had stuck and he couldn't turn off the power. This tale likewise became part of the cycle of jokes which the outer world was believed to have swallowed, though again corroboration is entirely lacking. Perhaps De Quille himself helped this story to grow, though its companion tale of the traveling stones of the Pahranagat Mountains apparently owes its embellishments to other hands than his. As he told it in *The Big Bonanza,* it has no marks of a hoax. The traveling stones were merely small spherical lumps of magnetic iron ore which when placed on a smooth table would roll together—a plausible enough story.

But however rowdy the *Enterprise* humor might be, it was a sound training school for a writer. Sam Clemens took to heart Joe Goodman's insistence on specific detail; a few months after he joined the paper he lectured his sister on the importance of names in your news: "An item is of no use unless it speaks of some *person,* and not then, unless that person's *name* is distinctly mentioned." De Quille, who after his return from the States became Sam's roommate, was fastidious in the use of exact and picturesque English, a man who could sum up the sensation of dangling in a mine shaft at the end of fifteen hundred feet of springy steel cable by saying, "The less one has of this peculiar motion the more he enjoys it," or who could gravely assert that after a really severe Washoe zephyr, "it is said, drifts of hats fully fifteen feet in depth, are to be seen in the bed of [Six-mile] Cañon. All these hats are found and appropriated by the Piute Indians, who always go down to the

Cañon the morning after a rousing and fruitful gale, to gather in the hat crop."

When a State Mineralogist was appointed in Nevada, the *Enterprise's* summary of his duties included the following:

"He will be expected to foretell cloudbursts, and to cause them to burst by degrees.

"When Venus transits he is to go up to the top of Mount Davidson, the day before, provided with a shot-gun and other nautical instruments with which to stop her, if, in his opinion, what she does on that occasion is liable to have a bad effect on any of the leading industries of this State—particularly the anchovy-fields and the bologna marshes.

"In the spring, when the farmers have sown their cereals, he is to go down into the valleys and reduce the atmospheric pressure, in order that the grains may sprout without painfully straining themselves in swelling. . . .

"In the case of foreign invasion, by the Piute Indians, or any other intestine foe, he is to so alter the boundary lines to our State, as to throw the part containing the war into California— reserving, of course, our right to the free navigation of the waters of Lake Tahoe."

Mark Twain at any stage in his career might have written that. But he didn't. The author was Dan De Quille, Mark's first real instructor in his chosen art.

Six months of work on the *Enterprise* found Sam getting restless, in spite of a trip over the mountains to San Francisco. He had discarded the name of "Josh" under which his first contributions had been submitted, and in the anonymity of the *Enterprise* columns had nothing except his style to identify his work. He seemed, moreover, to have exhausted the jesting possibilities of Virginia City, and routine reporting, even of homicides, bored him. His chance for wider activity came when the paper's Carson City correspondent was chosen clerk of the territorial legislature, and resigned as reporter. Sam asked Goodman to give him the job. He admitted a comprehensive ignorance of legislative procedure, but Goodman decided, correctly, that whatever Sam's letters might lack in technical accuracy would be more than atoned for by their readability. The first letters from Carson were anonymous, and contained some boners which drew the ridicule of Clement T. Rice, reporter for the *Enterprise*'s Virginia City rival, the *Union*. Sam, retorting in kind, christened Rice "The Unreliable." The war continued, on paper, while Sam and Rice continued bosom friends when off duty, just as Sam and Dan De Quille made newspaper capital out of charging each other with drunkenness, wood-stealing, and other miscellaneous crimes and misdemeanors. The Carson letters, in short, justified Goodman's hunch: they were widely read and widely reprinted. But they didn't satisfy their author because they bore no name.

He told Goodman, finally, that he wanted a by-line, and when Goodman agreed he chose the inspired name Mark Twain. As he recalled the matter in after years, he had just heard of the death of his one-time victim, Captain Sellers, and appropriated the name which that worthy in heaven no longer needed. Actually, Captain Sellers did not die until 1864 and it is still to be proved that the old man had ever used the signature. But it makes no difference if the story should be merely another of the inventions which Mark Twain ultimately came to believe himself. The river had furnished its one-time pilot with a name which was to become a household word. It was the river's best gift to him, and in 1863 it was all he wanted of the river.

He had found his name and found his profession. The brief interlude of poverty was over, for besides his earnings from the newspaper he continued dabbling in mining stocks. It was the simple custom of the Comstock to give "feet" to reporters to encourage them to mention the donors' mines, and Mark Twain took his share of the loot. He sent money to his mother frequently, and still had enough for good living and for travel. The flannel shirts and rough clothes of his mining days he discarded, along with his beard; he dressed for journalism in broadcloth and clean linen.

In May 1863 he was in San Francisco again, having high

times with his friendly rival, Rice the Unreliable. "Rice says: 'Oh, no—*we* are not having any fun, Mark—Oh, no, I reckon not—it's somebody else—it's probably the "Gentleman in the Wagon"!' (popular slang phrase). When I invite Rice to the Lick House to dinner, the proprietors send us champagne and claret, and then we *do* put on the most disgusting airs. Rice says our calibre is too light—we can't stand it to be noticed!" He was having so good a time, in fact, that he hated to return to Nevada, but when his mother improved the occasion with some good advice about working hard and aiming for a job on one of the big San Francisco papers, he was wrathful.

"Why, blast it, I was under the impression that I could get such a situation as that any time I asked for it. But I don't want it. No paper in the United States can afford to pay me what my place on the *Enterprise* is worth. If I were not naturally a lazy, idle, good-for-nothing vagabond, I could make it pay me $20,000 a year. But I don't suppose I shall ever be any account. I lead an easy life, though, and I don't care a cent whether school keeps or not. Everybody knows me, and I fare like a prince wherever I go, be it on this side of the mountains or the other. And I am proud to say I am the most conceited ass in the Territory."

He wrote thus in August 1863, just a year after he had joined the *Enterprise*. In that year his name had become familiar all over the Pacific Coast. Grant had captured Vicksburg, and the river again flowed untroubled to the sea, but the ex-pilot revealed no hint of desire to resume his old work. He had tasted the power that lies in printer's ink, and the petty authority of a pilot over the handful of people on a steamboat had lost its allure.

On October 28, 1863, he made his most memorable contribution to Comstock legend—the "Bloody Massacre" hoax. This time he apparently took in his readers for the nonce. The narrative described in gory detail how a man named Hopkins had gone mad, slaughtered his wife and seven of his nine children, cut his own throat from ear to ear, and then, dangling his wife's head by its long red hair, had ridden wildly into town to fall dead in front of the Magnolia saloon. All this was a build-up for the conclusion, which explained that Hopkins had gone insane because he had been persuaded to take his money out of sound Nevada mines and invest it in the San Francisco waterworks, which had just "cooked" a dividend. Mark, relying on the geographical and other absurdities in the narrative to reveal the hoax long before the climax, had not realized that his sanguinary details were so appalling as to blind the average reader to everything else. The sensation which the article created was long remembered; when he left the territory in the following year the Gold Hill *News* singled out this story as its example of what Nevada would miss with Mark Twain no longer resident. But the day after the item appeared he had to publish a postscript: "I take it all back." As in the case of the petrified man, however, evidence that the story was anywhere reprinted in good faith is wholly lacking. Both legends owe their currency to Mark's own revival of them in 1871.

So far as his earliest work for the *Enterprise* can be judged by these fragments which survive, he had acquired the capacity for terse and picturesque expression, but his humor was still slapstick. His drawling utterance of narrative or invective was a joy to his friends, but he had not yet found the written equivalent of his spoken style. The boys in the *Enterprise* office made a regular practice of hiding his candle and playing other tricks that would rouse him to describe his wrongs, for they had never heard such richness of imagery from any other lips, even in uninhibited Nevada. Gently, slowly, with no profane inflections of voice—so Elizabeth Wallace described Mark's swearing in his old age—but irresistibly as though they had the headwaters of the Mississippi for their source, would come the stream of unholy adjectives and choice expletives. He had only to learn to write as he talked.

In December 1863 Artemus Ward appeared in Virginia City in the course of a casual lecture tour of the West Coast. The *Enterprise* staff promptly gathered him to their hearts. It has been denied that Artemus Ward exerted any influence on Mark Twain. So far as his written work is concerned, the denial is probably true, for in print the popular humorist still depended on the elaborate misspellings which Mark Twain had left behind in the letters of Thomas Jefferson Snodgrass. But Artemus Ward on the platform was not Artemus Ward in print. Now Mark Twain had a chance to see a first-class humorous artist at work. He was too acute not to see that much of Artemus Ward's stuff was commonplace. What put it across was his delivery. The lean, consumptive young man on the platform never smiled; he appeared earnest and ill at ease. He would begin to tell with great animation something which he seemed to think was wonderful; then lose confidence, and after an apparently absent-minded pause add an incongruous remark in a soliloquizing way. "I once knew a man in New Zealand," he would begin eagerly, "who hadn't a tooth in his head." Then his animation would die out; a silent reflective pause would follow, then he would say dreamily, and as if to himself, "And yet that man could beat a drum better than any man I ever saw." Or he would mention that his musician was a Count in his own country—"but not much account here," came the studied afterthought. It was all obvious and even heavy-handed when transferred to print. But Artemus Ward on the platform fitted Howells' description of the later Mark Twain there: he just straddled down to the footlights, took the audience up in his hands, and tickled it. Each perfectly slurred point brought howls of laughter, and at each salvo he would look up in innocent surprise, almost hurt that his utterances should be so received.

It was a liberal education in oral delivery. Artemus Ward was doing to a crowded house precisely what young Sam Clemens had done to Jimmy McDaniel when he told the tale of Jim Wolf and the cats. This was the fine art of humor, and Mark Twain would have been a chump if he had not recognized it and studied it. His path and Artemus Ward's never crossed again, but thirty years later every detail of that platform manner was still vivid in Mark's memory when he wrote his little essay on "How to Tell a Story."

And Artemus Ward off stage was as good as Artemus Ward on. He was not one of the humorists who painfully compound a lecture or a sketch for the public, and have nothing left in their lockers for private consumption. His jest and fantasy were innate. The man who, shivering on a winter night in a cheap hotel room, had searched for something to stuff a broken pane with, and finding nothing except the frame of a hoop skirt, solemnly propped that against the window, remarking through chattering teeth that "perhaps it w-would k-keep out the c-c-oarsest of the c-cold"—that man gave his best to the congenial spirits on the *Enterprise*. The week he had expected to spend in Virginia City stretched out to three, amid laughter and libations.

Over the cocktails before one epic dinner Artemus Ward solemnly rose, and with lifted glass said, "Gentlemen, I give you Upper Canada." The toast was drunk in fitting seriousness, and then Joe Goodman inquired *why* he had given them Upper Canada. "Because," responded Artemus Ward reasonably, "I don't want it myself." And either that dinner or another in those wet three weeks produced a precious memory which Mark Twain transmitted to Thomas Bailey Aldrich eight years later. At 2:30 A.M. Artemus Ward, Goodman, De Quille, and Mark Twain were still at table, the "remains of the feast thin and scattering, but *such* tautology and repetition of empty bottles everywhere visible as to be offensive to the sensitive eye." It was the right occasion for Artemus Ward to rise and recite a hundred-line poem, which he did amid applause that exploded in salvoes at the end. When he could be heard again he said, "Let every man 'at loves his fellow man and 'preciates a poet 'at loves *his* fellow man, stan' up! stan' up and drink health and long life to Thomas Bailey Aldrich!—and drink it stanning!" Everyone made fervent attempts to comply. Artemus Ward watched them for a few minutes, and then said, "Well—consider it stanning, and drink it just as you are!"

It is a delicious scene, however viewed, but for its light on the "frontier mind" of Nevada it is priceless. For Mark Twain was true to Joe Goodman's teaching, and named the poem which so stirred the enthusiasm of these journalists in the toughest mining town in the United States. It was "Baby Bell." The whole wide realm of Victorian poetry contains no more mawkish verses, with the possible exception of the Rev. George Macdonald's "Where Did You Come from, Baby Dear?" The closing stanza so vociferously applauded was this:

> "At last he came, the messenger,
> The messenger from unseen lands:
> And what did dainty Baby Bell?
> She only crossed her little hands,
> She only looked more meek and fair!
> We parted back her silken hair,
> We wove the roses round her brow—
> White buds, the summer's drifted snow—
> Wrapt her from head to foot in flowers . . .
> And thus went dainty Baby Bell
> Out of this world of ours."

Artemus Ward and Goodman, Dan De Quille and Mark Twain were not frontiersmen; they were Victorians, even when they were drunk, and they accepted Victorian literary tender at face value. For them the fact that they were working in Virginia City instead of Boston was the most trifling of accidents. The suggestion that the "frontier" had its own code of morals and esthetics they would have scorned.

Artemus Ward's influence on Mark Twain was not limited to wet nights, or to the sight of a humorous lecturer plying his trade. On New Year's Day, 1864, he wrote to Mark from the mining camp of Austin, recalling their good times, telling his own misadventures, and reiterating a promise he had made:

"Why did you not go with me and save me that night?—I mean the night I left you after that dinner party. I went and got drunker, beating, I may say, Alexander the Great, in his most drinkinist days, and I blackened my face at the Melodeon, and made a gibbering, idiotic speech. God-dam it! I suppose the *Union* will have it. But let it go. I shall always remember Virginia as a bright spot in my existence, as all others must or rather cannot be, as it were . . .

"I shall write soon, a powerfully convincing note to my friends of *The Mercury*. . . .

"Some of the finest intellects in the world have been blunted with liquor.

"Do not, sir—do not flatter yourself that you are the only chastely-humorous writer onto the Pacific slopes. . . ."

Artemus Ward had urged Mark to contribute to Eastern periodicals, with the result that "Those Blasted Children" soon appeared in the New York *Sunday Mercury*. The sketch was neither better nor worse than the regular work he was doing at the time. It described his sufferings at the hands of a parcel of lawless brats who infested the Lick House in San Francisco. After some paragraphs detailing the juvenile squabbles he heard outside his locked door—paragraphs dimly and heavy-handedly suggesting scenes to be written a decade later in *Tom Sawyer*—he continued:

"It is a living wonder to me that I haven't scalped some of those children before now. I expect I would have done, but then I hardly felt well enough acquainted with them. I scarcely ever show them any attention anyhow, unless it is to throw a bootjack at them or some little nonsense of that kind when I happen to feel playful. I am confident I would have destroyed several of them though, only it might appear as if I were making most too free."

There followed a section of medical hints for the care of children—hints which suggested administering arsenic to make a measles patient sleep, advised the removal of the brain in cases of brain fever, and offered amputation of the lower jaw as an infallible cure for stammering. For worms, "administer a catfish three times a week. Keep the room very quiet; the fish won't bite if there is the least noise."

The *Mercury* published it, and the *Golden Era* reprinted it.

New York and California both thought it funny. Another New York paper, *Yankee Notions,* about the same time reprinted from the *Enterprise* Mark's review of *Ingomar,* which summarized that pompous Victorian melodrama in terms of Nevada society and scenery, with Comanches and Piutes mingling indiscriminately in the minor parts. It was more intellectual fun than "Those Blasted Children," for it was literary analysis of a sort. Mark Twain had realized that for all its Greek costumes and inflated speeches the play, as to plot and motives, was no different from Beadle's dime novels, and his parody underscored the resemblances. John Phoenix before him, and Artemus Ward in his time, used burlesque as literary criticism.

But he was still content to be a Western newspaperman. This double success in the East did not inspire him to follow up his conquests. The incentive was insufficient. Neither as literature nor financially was the *Mercury* any better than the *Golden Era,* which was regularly reprinting his *Enterprise* sketches and paying for original ones. And *Yankee Notions* was a struggling journal of the rag-bag type then prevalent; if it paid at all, its rates were negligible. At the moment he was content to be the biggest frog in the small literary puddle of Nevada.

About two weeks after Artemus Ward wrote his letter to the *Mercury,* the Carson City newspapermen elected Mark Twain Governor of the Third House. They had decided to stage a burlesque of legislative procedure as a benefit for a local church, and Mark was the logical person for the star role. His outspoken comments upon legislative proceedings, good and bad, had given him fame and influence in the capital of the territory which was about to become a state for the sole but sufficient reason that two more Republican votes were needed in the United States Senate. Mark's acceptance came closer to his mature style than any of his previous writing had.

"Certainly. If the public can find anything in a grave state paper worth paying a dollar for, I am willing that they should pay that amount, or any other; and although I am not a very dusty Christian myself, I take an absorbing interest in religious affairs, and would willingly inflict my annual message upon the Church itself if it might derive benefit thereby. You can charge what you please; I promise the public no amusement, but I do promise a reasonable amount of instruction. I am responsible to the Third House only, and I hope to be permitted to make it exceedingly warm for that body, without caring whether the sympathies of the public and the Church be enlisted in their favor, and against myself, or not."

The speech—Mark's first prepared utterance on the platform—has perished, but that it was an overwhelming success was attested by the memories of all who heard or read it, and by the substantial gift of a suitably inscribed gold watch. Yet tragedy mingled with the comedy. A week after he wrote that letter of acceptance, Mark Twain sat with his sister-in-law, Orion's wife, by the deathbed of her only child, nine-year-old Jennie Clemens. But he had not yet reached the age when private tragedy was reflected in his public writings. He was riding high, this early spring of 1864, when a swift series of events exiled him from Nevada.

The territory was in the midst of a lively campaign to raise money for the Sanitary Fund, the Red Cross of the Civil War. The repeated auctioning of a sack of flour had developed a rivalry between communities which was highly remunerative for the Fund, but which inevitably strained the feelings of the rivals. The ladies of Carson City decided to do their bit by giving a benefit ball, and in a typically unwise moment Mark Twain declared in his *Enterprise* column that there was some question as to whether the proceeds would go to the Sanitary Fund or to a Miscegenation Society somewhere in the East. It was the jest of a Missouri Copperhead; it could not have been worse timed or in worse taste. The boundless wrath of the Carson ladies was not limited to the author; Mollie Clemens found herself suddenly ostracized because she was his sister-in-law. On May 23 Mark addressed a letter of abject apology to Mrs. W. K. Cutler of Carson City, the only one of the ladies concerned who had not included Mollie in her resentment. The situation, he admitted, called for public instead of private apology, but that was impossible for reasons which he tried to explain.

When the *Enterprise* published this ill-timed item, its old rival the *Union* seized the opportunity to excoriate the author. What terms were used the surviving records do not show, but they were such that Mark, in a characteristic fury, wrote to James Laird, editor and proprietor of the *Union*, to demand instant retraction or "the satisfaction of a gentleman." But all he got was a published statement in which one J. W. Wilmington avowed the authorship of one of the offending items and declared that he had nothing to retract. Mark declined to deal with Wilmington and in a peremptory letter, reminding Laird that he had always assumed full editorial responsibility for all items appearing in his paper, demanded "the satisfaction of a gentleman, without alternative." Laird was contemptuous. He told Mark, in substance, if he wanted to fight, to fight Wilmington, who was ready and willing to oblige; after Wilmington finished with him, Laird was prepared to take him on. "If you decline to meet him after challenging him," Laird concluded, "you will prove yourself to be what he had charged you with being, 'a liar, a poltroon, and a puppy,' and as such cannot, of course, be entitled to the satisfaction of a gentleman."

But Mark was not to be turned aside. Wilmington had avowed the authorship of only one of the offending articles; for the other, an editorial, Laird alone was responsible, and Mark would not deal with the subordinate until he had settled with the principal. When Laird still refused, he wound up the correspondence by calling Laird an unmitigated liar—"a liar on general principles, and from natural instinct"—an abject coward, and a fool. These were fighting words, but Laird would not fight, and in the full tide of his fury Mark had not noticed the predicament he was landing himself in.

Nevada, about to achieve statehood, was not proud of its sumptuous record of homicide. Though formal dueling had not been a major contributor to its graveyards, the legislators decided to make an example of duelists, and accordingly had enacted a law which made the sending of a challenge, whether or not it resulted in combat, a felony. In other words, Mark's extremely public demands upon Laird, instead of merely enabling him to make a fool of himself, had created a perfect test case for the new law. Though the authorities showed no speed in acting, it was obvious that they would have to act or else admit that the law was not to be enforced. Mark was warned of the unwisdom of standing upon the order of his going, and before the end of May he and Steve Gillis, the bantamweight fighter of the *Enterprise*'s composing room, who was to have been his second, hurriedly crossed the Divide on their way to San Francisco. The duel which was never fought became a part of the Mark Twain folklore of the West, told in various graphic but untruthful versions by Steve Gillis and by Mark himself in his *Autobiography*. But that when he had cooled off Mark realized how ridiculous he had made himself is proved by the fact that seven years later the subject was still too sore for him to mention it in *Roughing It*.

In 1873, however, he published in *Tom Hood's Comic Annual* a sketch called "How I Escaped Being Killed in a Duel." Presumably the yarn was part of his *Roughing It* lecture, and bore the same relation to fact as did the "Mexican Plug." When he was dictating the *Autobiography* in 1906, the needle of his subconscious memory slipped into the familiar groove of the old record, and reproduced as fact the old fiction of the platform.

It was an inglorious exit for the Governor of the Third House, but it merely hastened a remove he would have made before long in any case. He had grown weary of the dust and sagebrush of Nevada; its smalltime doings could not have contented him much longer. His twenty-two months on the *Enterprise* had made him as well known in San Francisco as in Virginia City, and those months, moreover, had settled his career. He was a professional writer at last, and in all the forty-six years he had still to live he was never again anything else.

CHAPTER VI

CALIFORNIA

MARK TWAIN was no friendless exile in San Francisco. A year earlier he had told his mother that he knew two thousand people in the city, and even the ninety percent discount which Jane Clemens said she applied to her son's stories still left a substantial group of acquaintances. Neither was he penniless. He had cash in pocket, and a miscellaneous collection of mining shares in his trunk, from which he expected great returns. But he was not inclined to loaf. He soon found a berth as reporter on the *Morning Call*, and Steve Gillis entered the paper's composing room.

Mark had arrived without difficulty at the place on a metropolitan paper which his mother had exhorted him to, but he soon found it less to his taste than the old job on the *Enterprise*. There he had been a columnist and feature writer; he had no beat to follow and no regular assignments to cover; all that Joe Goodman had expected was readable copy. On the *Call* he must make the daily rounds of the courts, getting the names and facts in an endless series of cases which all came to look and sound alike to him. As the only full-time reporter he had also to cover fires and the other excitements of a city of 130,000 people, and to wind up his day by acting as dramatic critic. Late in the evening came the task of spreading the day's collection out into words and phrases, and making it cover as much acreage as possible. "It was fearful drudgery—soulless drudgery—and almost destitute of interest. It was an awful slavery for a lazy man, and I was born lazy."

Added to the irksomeness of the work was the problem of finding lodgings where he and Steve could sleep late in the morn-

96

ing. Always some disturber of the peace appeared—children, pianos, dogs or traffic—and the roommates moved at least once a month. Even when they didn't move they had difficulties. Mark, high-strung and insomniac, wanted to read after he went to bed; Steve wanted to sleep. But to ask Mark to put out the light was too simple a device for a Comstock humorist to stoop to. Steve, with a nail tied to a string, imitated the sound of a deathwatch beetle, and when the ticking had driven his nervous companion to the verge of hysterics, Steve would suggest that perhaps it would stop when the light went out. When Mark finally caught the joker in the act there was a storm, yet it did not break their friendship.

Before he had been on the *Call* three months, Mark had offered to take less salary if he could be released from night work. So much is certain from his contemporary letter to his mother. Forty years later, in his *Autobiography*, he added picturesque details which may or may not be true. Probably not. According to this account, the editor assigned as Mark's assistant an earnest, hulking youth whom he remembered only by his nickname, taken from a popular song of the '60's, of Smiggy McGlural. Smiggy was willing to do the drudgery, and Mark was more than willing to let him. Within a month Smiggy was handling most of the work; it was obvious that he could handle all of it. So the editor kindly gave Mark Twain a chance to resign in order to avoid the humiliation of being fired.

Despite his insistence upon the drudgery and upon his own laziness, neither work nor long hours would have bothered him had his heart been in the work. The loss of his by-line, and the demand for routine fulfillment of routine assignments undoubtedly came hard, but what really discouraged Mark with the *Call* was the discovery that he couldn't express himself freely in its columns, coupled with the discovery that he could do so elsewhere.

Once, for instance, he saw a gang of hoodlums stoning a Chinaman while an Irish policeman watched and grinned. He wrote up the incident in hot indignation, and sent it in with the rest of his copy. But the story did not appear, and on inquiry he learned that the editor had killed it on the unimpeachable commercial ground that the Irish were the *Call's* chief supporters and the paper couldn't afford to offend them. Even though the editor later allowed him to excoriate to his heart's content a coroner who had refused information to the press, the zest was gone from the job, and without zest Mark Twain could never stay long at anything.

Almost immediately after his arrival in San Francisco he had sold two sketches to the *Golden Era*—one of them a burlesque of the sort of evidence that he had to listen to every day at the police court; the other a John Phoenix-like diatribe against early rising as illustrated by a sunrise visit to the Cliff House. In the very week in which Mark reached San Francisco Charles Henry Webb and Bret Harte had published the first number of a new literary magazine, *The Californian.* Though Harte soon resumed the editorship of the *Era,* its new rival gained reputation for a time, and seemed to the enthusiastic Mark the best literary paper in the United States. Abandoning the *Era,* he agreed, for the lavish pay of fifty dollars a month, to write an article a week for the *Californian.* During his last months on the *Call,* his real interest centered in the *Californian* office, which, together with the offices of the Mint that furnished Harte's bread and butter, was in the *Call* building.

In 1871 Mark told Thomas Bailey Aldrich that it was Harte "who trimmed and trained and schooled me patiently until he changed me from an awkward utterer of coarse grotesqueness to a writer of paragraphs and chapters that have found a certain favor in the eyes of some of the decentest people in the land." But that handsome acknowledgment was made when he was repudiating a charge of plagiarizing Harte, and when, moreover, he was smarting from Harte's first break with him. In these San Francisco days, before Harte's national reputation began with the launching of the *Overland Monthly* and the publication of "The Luck of Roaring Camp," Mark Twain openly and generously admired his clever junior. When they first met,

Harte had written nothing but some derivative verses and essays, the first of the brilliant *Condensed Novels,* and the two versions of *M'liss.* In 1866 Mark told his mother that Harte and not himself deserved to be called the best writer in California, but the contemporary evidence gives small support to Harte's reputed trimming and training.

Unfortunately for his claim that Harte had civilized him, the things Mark Twain wrote for the *Golden Era* and the *Californian* are extant. They are not markedly different from the things he had written for the *Enterprise.* His first *Californian* contribution was "A Notable Conundrum," published in October 1864—two months before Harte turned the editorship over to Webb. It included the combination of a love letter with a soap boiler's advertisement, described the process of getting drunk at the Cliff House bar, and made great play with the aroma of a stranded whale:

"The whale was not a long one, physically speaking—say thirty-five feet—but he smelt much longer; he smelt as much as a mile and a half longer, I should say, for we traveled about that distance beyond him before we ceased to detect his fragrance in the atmosphere. . . . A whale does not smell like magnolia, nor yet like heliotrope or 'Balm of a Thousand Flowers'; I do not know, but I should judge that it smells more like a thousand polecats."

During the next year he showed the refining influence of Bret Harte by continuing the burlesque fashion notes he had begun, in emulation of John Phoenix, as early as 1863. They included the information that "Miss C. L. B. had her fine nose elegantly enameled, and the easy grace with which she blew it from time to time marked her as a cultivated and accomplished woman of the world." They also included an attack on Miss X., "with a brass oyster-knife skewered through her waterfall, and smiling her sickly smile through her decayed teeth." Besides these gems, he had some fun with the vestry of Grace Cathedral. He invented a correspondence with Bishop Hawks, the Rev. Dr. Cummings of Chicago, and Phillips Brooks, in which each clergyman in turn explained why he could not accept the call to San Francisco. Their reasons included speculations in cotton, petroleum and wheat. He began his mockery of orthodox religion, in terms which would not vary much from 1865 to 1910:

"I was brought up a Presbyterian, and consider myself a brevet member of Dr. Wadsworth's church. I always was a brevet. I was sprinkled in infancy, and look upon that as conferring the rank of brevet Presbyterian. It affords none of the emoluments of the Regular Church—simply confers honorable rank upon the recipient and the right to be punished as a Presbyterian hereafter; that is, the substantial Presbyterian punishment of fire and brimstone instead of this heterodox hell of remorse of conscience of these blamed wildcat religions."

In May 1865 the *Californian* published the sketch, "How I Went to the Great Race Between Lodi and Norfolk." It once more worked in the old joke about drinks, though it developed a mildly amusing climax in the revelation that the man who had invited Mark to accompany him to the race had invited one hundred and fifty other men as well, and announced his intention of going on foot. But it was no funnier, nor much better written, than the skit "Concerning Notaries," written for the *Enterprise* early in 1864, and reprinted in the *Golden Era*. And in December 1865 the *Californian* contained a brief study entitled "Uncle Lige." It was, to be sure, intended as a parody of Dan De Quille, who had suffered a temporary lapse into sentimentality, but even so—— Uncle Lige had lost his left shoulder in a sawmill; he was blind drunk; he had a wine-bred cauliflower on his nose; he spat on his shirtbosom and slurred it off with his hand. Such was the refining result of a year and half of Bret Harte's alleged tutelage. The magazines and the literati of San Francisco had only a trifling share in creating Mark Twain's mature style.

In *Roughing It* Mark pictured himself as penniless after his dismissal from the *Call*. Though he may have felt comparatively so, because a speculation in Hale and Norcross stock had gone sour—in after years he thought because Orion had been too careful about forwarding the funds he needed to cover his margin—he was not really suffering. Besides continuing his contributions to the *Californian*, he had rejoined the *Enterprise* staff as their San Francisco correspondent, a job which paid him as much as he had been getting from the *Call*. It was, moreover, congenial work. In his letters to the *Enterprise* he was able to blow off all the steam about municipal corruption, venal policemen and other hot topics which editorial caution had kept out of the *Call*. Thanks to these *Enterprise* items, within six months from his arrival in San Francisco he had made the city too hot to hold him. But Steve Gillis helped.

The chief of police was so incensed by Mark's letters that he filed a libel suit against the *Enterprise*—an empty gesture, since the *Enterprise* was published in another state. But Steve's pugnacity—perhaps intensified by his having recently been jilted—supplied the chief with means for retaliation at the *Enterprise*'s annoying correspondent. Steve had waded into a barroom brawl and had thoroughly beaten up a man much larger than himself. Unfortunately, the victim was a friend of Chief Burke's, who immediately had Steve arrested on the charge of assault with intent to kill. Mark Twain furnished bail, but when friends warned Steve that the chief intended to press for a conviction Steve returned to Virginia City. Thereupon Burke brought action against his bondsman, and Mark Twain in turn found it advisable to decamp until things cooled off.

It happened that Steve's brother, Jim Gillis, was in San Francisco on one of his occasional visits. Of course Steve had introduced him to Mark; the two took to each other at once. When Mark realized that he had better leave town for a while, Jim invited him to his cabin on Jackass Hill in the Mother Lode country. They arrived there on December 4, 1865.

Jim Gillis was an unaggressive Thoreau. He had come to the Mother Lode country when the great placer diggings were already playing out, and the more acquisitive miners were deserting the region. But there were still pockets of nuggets to be found in the hillsides by those who understood the art, and Jim was a pocket miner. When he needed funds, he would prospect about till he located a pocket; if it panned out, he took a trip to the city, renewed his clothing and supplies, bought some books, and settled back to enjoy himself in his cabin until funds ran low again. "Contented wi' little, an' canty wi' mair," he bore about as much resemblance to the brutalized frontiersman of Mr. Waldo Frank as Thomas Mann does to Hitler.

Besides Jim and his books, Mark found the cabin on Jackass Hill inhabited by Dick Stoker, Jim's partner, Dick's cat—later to figure in literature under the name of Tom Quartz—and Jim's young brother, William. The rainy season was on, and on many days the little group spent their time before the cabin fire. Mark smoked and read Jim's books or listened to Jim's yarns, for Jim was a finished artist in the realm of extemporized tall stories in which Mark was still only an apprentice. It was a postgraduate course in the fine art of oral humor. Some of Jim's tales were masterpieces, and Mark knew it. The Bluejay yarn long afterwards found its way into *A Tramp Abroad,* and the story of "The Burning Shame" furnished one of the finest chapters in *Huck Finn.* Mark had heard plenty of storytellers before, but now he was a professional writer looking for literary pay dirt, and he listened and absorbed as he never had in his earlier years.

When the weather permitted, the partners went out prospecting and initiated Mark into the art of tracing a pocket to its hiding place on a hillside. Afterwards they thought they remembered that only his refusal to carry another bucket of water on a freezing day kept them from finding a pocket worth several thousand dollars, and Jim used to declare that "if Sam had got that pocket he would have remained a pocket-miner to the end of his days, like me." Not likely, unless Sam had somehow acquired also Jim's Thoreau temperament which sought no more of life than a snug cabin and plenty of books. Two and a half years of success as a journalist had thoroughly rubbed the ink into Mark's fingers, and he could never have got it out again even had he conquered his inherent distaste for hard physical labor.

Moreover, Mark always craved society, and found it even on Jackass Hill. In a near-by cabin lived the pretty Carrington girls, the "Chaparral Quails," and when he and his friends weren't visiting them, Mark was likely to drift over to down-at-heel Angels Camp and let the more industrious Gillis and Stoker go on prospecting without him. And it was at Angels that he struck his real pocket.

Among the derelicts who clung to the barrooms of the moribund camp was a dull, slow-witted veteran named Ben Coon, who had once been a pilot on the Illinois River. Ben had an endless fund of pointless stories, and craved an audience. A few years earlier the Sam Clemens who described himself to Frank Burrough as made up of "ignorance, intolerance, egotism, self-assertion, opaque perception, dense and pitiful chuckle-headed-ness," would doubtless have fled Ben Coon as an intolerable bore. But newspaper work had sharpened his perception; now it was fascinating to hear Ben drone through story after story, blissfully unaware whether they had point or not. Presently, out of the chaos, something emerged which he thought worth making a note of:

"Coleman with his jumping frog—bet a stranger $50.—Stranger had no frog and C. got him one:—In the meantime stranger filled C's frog full of shot and he couldn't jump. The stranger's frog won."

It was a folk tale as old and almost as widespread as Dan De Quille's yarn of the drunkard laid in the open grave, but Mark had never heard it before. It was about the end of January 1865 that Ben Coon told the tale, and for the next three weeks Mark and Jim Gillis chuckled over it at intervals. There were other tales, too, such as the one about the San Franciscan who jumped a lot and built a house on it. The hogs congregated under it, and the man's wife poured hot water on them through holes in the floor. The struggling hogs lifted the house off its pins and dragged it downhill, and the lawful owner of the lot reoccupied it next morning. But that story lacked the color and the drama of the frog.

Finally, on February 25, Mark left Angels Camp, walked back to Jackass Hill with Jim and Dick through a snowstorm, and thence returned to San Francisco and three months' accumulation of mail. Among the letters was one from Artemus Ward, asking him to contribute to a volume of sketches which he was preparing to publish. Mark wrote at once, explaining his absence from the city, and apparently regretting that it was too late to take advantage of the offer. On Artemus Ward's replying that it was not too late, Mark wrote out Ben Coon's story and sent it on. The tale no longer rouses the wild laughter that greeted it on its first publication, partly because Mark Twain himself later did the same thing again, and did it better. But it was a turning point in his literary career. He had told plenty of funny stories before this, but he had created no characters. What made the "Jumping Frog" a literary landmark was its double layer of personality: Jim Smiley, who owned the frog, and Simon Wheeler, who told the story, were both sharply defined. For the first time, Mark Twain had projected vividly realized characters upon paper; a commonplace folk tale had become literature because it was restated in terms of recognizable human personalities. He had found the first half of his art: the ability so to transfer speech to paper that the speaker came alive for the reader. But he had still to create the character of Mark Twain himself. That achievement was a slower growth; it was not even well started until more than a year after he wrote the "Jumping Frog."

Meantime he was not too well satisfied with what he had done. The story finally reached New York too late, after all. G. W. Carleton, Artemus Ward's publisher, had not yet brought out the book, but the forms were closed and Carleton did not think the belated contribution worth reopening them for. He turned the manuscript over to Henry Clapp, editor of the moribund *Saturday Press,* and Clapp published it on November 18,

1865. Papers all over the country reprinted it—without payment, of course—and within a month it was back in San Francisco in the columns of the *Californian*. Its fame reached Jane Clemens and Pamela in St. Louis, and they wrote to congratulate the author. But their letters found him in one of his black moods. He was sick of San Francisco, sick of journalism—piloting was the only thing worth while.

"To think that after writing many an article a man might be excused for thinking tolerably good, those New York people should single out a villainous backwoods sketch to compliment me on!"

Yet the mood faded even as he wrote. He pasted into his letter a paragraph, highly complimentary to that same villainous sketch, which the *Alta California*'s New York correspondent had written, and added, "I am generally placed at the head of my breed of scribblers in this part of the country," though he protested that first place really belonged to Bret Harte.

His weariness of San Francisco, however, was more than a mood. As soon as he had returned to the city from Jackass Hill, he had resumed his correspondence for the *Enterprise*, besides contributing to the *Californian*, the *Golden Era*, and various newspapers. But he was exhausting the available materials in San Francisco. In January 1866, when he wrote so morosely about the "Jumping Frog," he was having fun with the spiritualists. He began with the Kearney Street Ghost, who "stacked up a whole litter of nine little bloody kittens" on a girl's pillow. "What," he asked, "would you think of a ghost that came to your bedside at dead of night and had kittens?" And then he attended some seances, had a lot of fun with the ghost of his old friend John Smith, and described Mrs. Foye, the medium, as "a good-looking, earnest-faced, pale-red-haired, neatly dressed, young woman standing on a little stage behind a small deal table with slender legs and no drawers—the table, understand me." These are as good lines as any still extant in Mark's writing, after three and a half years' apprenticeship to the literary craft.

But the fates that had propelled him thus far upon his literary road were ready for the next move. A new steamer, the *Ajax*, was put into service between San Francisco and Honolulu, and Mark Twain was one of the notables invited to share the maiden voyage. He refused, because he felt that he could not give up his regular work as correspondent, but the refusal left him more dissatisfied than ever. California was keenly interested in Hawaii—still called the Sandwich Islands—because of its commercial possibilities, especially sugar. Mark had become well acquainted with the proprietors of the *Sacramento Union,* and now proposed that the *Union* send him to the Islands to furnish detailed reports of their prospects.

On March 7, 1866, he sailed, on the *Ajax's* second trip, upon the excursion which was to carry him a long step further on his career. For purposes of comic relief he took with him his fictitious friend, Brown, of the Q. C. Snodgrass letters, who had first appeared in a *Californian* sketch as early as March 18, 1865, but whose place in the local items of that year had been subordinate to that of John William Skae, the punster from Nevada. Since Brown was an inseparable part of Mark Twain's writing from now until the end of the *Innocents Abroad* trip, he merits notice, the more so as Albert Bigelow Paine seemingly went to his grave believing Brown to have been a real person.

If a "source" for Brown must be found, it is obviously the young fellow John in *The Autocrat of the Breakfast Table.* Like the rest of literate America in the '60's, Mark had read the *Autocrat:* in 1869 he and Olivia Langdon used it as a "courting book," a post of honor usually reserved for old literary favorites. John made crude and materialistic applications of the Autocrat's loftier philosophical generalizations; he was the mouthpiece for occasional low comedy which the Brahmin Autocrat could not fittingly utter in his own person. Brown served Mark Twain in precisely the same way. The more vulgar utterances about smells, seasickness and insects were, from the beginning of the Sandwich Islands letters, all attributed to Brown, instead of being spoken by Mark himself. In other words,

Brown became a projection and dramatization of the coarser side of Mark's nature. He was becoming aware of his crudities; he could not yet bear to give them up, but he expressed them under an alias. By this conscious segregation of one group of his impulses he took a long stride toward the creation of the mature Mark Twain.

Humor, like lyric poetry, is a form of self-dramatization. The humorist, like the poet, does not express his whole nature, or the whole of his attitude toward life. He takes one aspect of himself and his relation to the world, and by projecting and magnifying that aspect achieves an expression which, while still personal, is sufficiently detached and concentrated to be communicable to other people through the impersonal medium of print. The reason why many people who are humorous *talkers* cannot write acceptably is simply their inability to achieve this self-dramatization. In talk their total personalities supply the background and the color; in writing all this color is lost. But though all humor is thus dramatic in essence, its variety and success depend upon the variety and richness of the total personality of which one facet is thus projected. Mark Twain's full personality was not yet unfolded, but he had made a real start.

But the invention of Brown was not the only or the chief literary effect of the Sandwich Islands excursion. For the first time in his writing career Mark Twain was entering scenes unfamiliar to himself and to his readers. The necessity of complete communication, the realization that none of the background could be taken for granted, put the special correspondent on his mettle. It was not enough to see and feel things himself; he must make his readers see and feel them too. To this stimulus, more than to any other circumstance, must be ascribed the literary superiority of the Sandwich Islands letters over any of his previous work.

He took his assignment seriously. All through the nineteen days of the outward voyage—except when he came down with the mumps—he was jotting in his notebooks all the information about the Islands he could collect from returning residents. He was a good sailor. The *Ajax,* a small screw steamer with auxiliary sail, was wholly unfit for such an ocean run, but when most of the passengers were seasick Mark Twain was still up and about and, in the person of Brown, extracted from the vomitings of the sufferers some crude humor to garnish his first letters to the *Union.*

When at last he landed, the tropic charm and the easy-going life of the Islands captivated him at once. "No careworn or eager, anxious faces in the land of happy contentment," he noted in an early memorandum; "God, what a contrast with California and Washoe." But he did not sink into languor, however much he appreciated the Islanders' indifference to strict schedules. The stay that had been planned to last a month stretched out into nearly four, and was one of the many occasions in Mark Twain's life which disprove his own favorite assertion that he was a lazy man. Nothing dismayed him— neither saddle horses and saddle boils nor the verminous inter-island schooners. Friends in San Francisco had loaded him with letters of introduction, and the Island hospitality did its best. Among the residents he found his old friend of Virginia City days, the Rev. Franklin Rising, who had conducted Buck Fanshaw's funeral, which is described in *Roughing It.*

His trips from Oahu to Maui and Hawaii were conducted on the principle of going everywhere and seeing everything, even to the hair-raising exploit of descending into the crater of Kilauea and crossing its floor on the lava crust. But the quest for thrills and color did not make him forget the original terms of his assignment, and he collected and transmitted detailed statistics not only about the sugar industry but about whaling, and the importance of the Islands as a halfway house for the vast Oriental trade which Californians hopefully foresaw as soon as the Union Pacific should be completed. He realized that as the commercial position of the Islands increased it was only a matter of time before one of the great powers would take possession of them, but he thought the taker was more likely to be France than the United States. Like Herman Melville before him and Robert Louis Stevenson after him, he did not think too well of the missionaries—"more missionaries and more row made about saving these 60,000 people than would take to convert hell itself." And he noted two dominant characteristics of the natives—"Kanakas will have horses and saddles, and the women will fornicate." It has been remarked that the frankness of this note is not reproduced in Mark's letters to the *Union*. But in *Roughing It* he said that the uplifting influence of the missionaries "has at last built up in the native women a profound respect for chastity—in other people." This may stand as a fair illustration of what Victorian taboos actually achieved in the way of repressing Mark Twain.

Toward the end of June he was back in Honolulu, disabled with saddle boils and, as he thought, at the end of his adventures. But the most important happenings of the whole trip were yet to come. Anson Burlingame, American Minister to China, stopped at Honolulu on his way to his post, accompanied by his eighteen-year-old son Edward, later the great editor of *Scribner's Magazine*. Young Burlingame had read the "Jumping Frog," and on learning that the author was in Honolulu was eager to meet him. The Minister's party sent word that they would call on Mark at his hotel, but Mark crawled out of bed, dressed, and went to them instead. The Burlingames were delighted with their new acquaintance, and Mark's self-esteem rose several points on discovering that he was interesting to public men of international reputation. Burlingame recognized genius in the careless young journalist who kept him and his party laughing. "We just made Honolulu howl," Mark wrote to Will Bowen. "I only got tight once, though. I know better than to get tight oftener than once in 3 months. It sets a man back in the esteem of peopie whose opinions are worth having." But Burlingame also recognized crudity, and gave some fatherly advice which Mark probably would have resented hotly from anyone less distinguished and less affable.

"You have great ability; I believe you have genius. What

you need now is the refinement of association. Seek companionship among men of superior intellect and character. Refine yourself and your work. Never affiliate with inferiors; always climb."

Taken literally, it was about as snobbish advice as was ever given. But neither Burlingame nor Mark Twain was a snob, and the advice, however unfortunately worded, was precisely what Mark needed. His years as printer, pilot, miner and journalist had done little to give him any social grace beyond his natural ability to talk freely and unrestrainedly in any company that didn't too obviously disapprove of him. Before he could be accepted as a welcome equal anywhere, he had a lot to learn, beginning with the simple matters of dress and deportment. The tropic warmth of the Islands had, for example, seemingly brought on a severe relapse in personal tidiness. But his whole subsequent life shows that he never took Burlingame's advice too literally. What it really gave him was the first clear intimation that he might aspire to a place in the world higher than that of a California journalist.

But Burlingame also helped him to his greatest achievement as a California journalist. On June 21 the fifteen survivors of the clipper *Hornet* reached Oahu after forty-three starving days in an open boat. Within a few days most of them were transferred to a Honolulu hospital. By any standard it was a first-class opportunity for a newspaperman, and in those days before the Pacific railway the fate of any ship bound for the Coast had a very vital interest for Californians. But Mark's exertions in making his first call on the Burlingames had reawakened his boils, and he was helpless in bed. The scoop of a lifetime was available; a ship left for San Francisco the next morning; but Mark couldn't get to the hospital for his material. Burlingame took charge. He had Mark carried to the hospital on a stretcher, and then stayed with him and interviewed the survivors himself, so that all Mark had to do was to listen and take notes. He wrote all night, and got his story—which made three front-page columns in a sight-wrecking type that averaged nearly one hundred words to the inch—on board just as the ship was casting off.

After that there was nothing to do but recuperate and enjoy the company of the Burlingames and all his many new Honolulu friends. Finally, on July 19, after the Burlingames had departed westward, Mark Twain embarked for San Francisco on a sailing ship which took twenty-five leisurely days for the trip. Several of the *Hornet* survivors were among the passengers, and Mark had the chance to talk further with them, copy their diaries, and prepare an article which he determined to send to an Eastern magazine. Another passenger was the Rev. Franklin Rising, for whose Sunday services Mark acted as one-man— and one-hymn—choir. On August 13 he wrote in his notebook:

"San Francisco, Home again. No, not home again—in prison again and all the wide sense of freedom gone. The city seems so cramped and so dreary with toil and care and business anxiety. God help me, I wish I were at sea again."

To outward seeming there was no ground for despondency. The amusing and informative letters in the *Union* had vastly increased his fame, and the publishers had paid him a $300 bonus for the *Hornet* story. The fuller account of the *Hornet* disaster he sent to *Harper's Magazine,* which accepted it promptly; not until December did he learn that the printer had managed to spoil his serious Eastern debut by printing his name as "Mark Swain." And yet he was so depressed that he declared long afterward that he once put a pistol to his head, but lacked the courage to pull the trigger.

The reason was not, as he said in *Roughing It,* that he was without means and without employment. He could have resumed his correspondence for the *Enterprise* at any time; in fact, any newspaper on the Coast would probably have given him a job the moment he applied. But he hated the idea of resuming the drudgery of daily letters, after the footloose freedom of his months in the Islands. Though he did not know it the Hawaiian experience had in fact determined the pattern that most of his future writing would assume. It was the pattern of the Mississippi; motion was its inherent quality. You went on from place to place and wrote about each in its turn. An endless flow of new topics was brought to you; you didn't have to go round a familiar treadmill looking for something to write about. Essentially, it was newspaper reporting, but reporting sublimated and glorified, with no deadlines to meet and no restrictions on subject.

But meantime there was the question of immediate livelihood when the *Union*'s bonus was spent. He thought of preparing out of his Hawaiian experiences a series of magazine articles which might ultimately become a book, but he would have to live while the book was being written. However, the Island articles in the *Union* had roused public interest and curiosity; why not try a lecture?

His only appearance as a public speaker had been his Carson address as Governor of the Third House. That had been a success, but the conditions were special—a small auditorium, and an audience of friends. To face a crowd of strangers took a different sort of nerve. While he was hesitating he mentioned the idea to John McComb, editor of the *Alta California*. To his surprise, McComb enthusiastically urged him to take the largest theater in the city and go to it. Accordingly he hired Maguire's Academy of Music, prepared his lecture and wrote the famous handbill which closed with the line, "Doors open at 7 o'clock. The trouble to begin at 8 o'clock."

It was only seven weeks after his return to San Francisco that he stepped upon the stage, to be greeted by a hurricane of applause from a house that was packed, aisles and all. Stage fright engulfed him like a wave; he uttered his first sentences in a daze. Then his vision cleared. Suddenly he realized that these people, too, were his friends, just like the Third House audience in Carson. He recovered his self-possession, and with it embraced the crowd. From that moment till his death, so far as the records show, he was immune to stage fright. The claque of friends he had stationed at strategic points in the house was superfluous; the audience needed no fuglemen. And in that hour, on the stage of Maguire's Academy of Music, October 2, 1866, Mark Twain took the last step that was needed to make him one of the greatest writers of his century. He began the process of infusing into his writing the charm of his drawling speech. Where his writing was crude or stiff, the test of oral utterance exposed the weakness and taught him how to mend it. Though time was still needed to make his finished utterance second nature, his apprenticeship to the craft of letters was complete. Mark Twain the personality had come to birth out of Sam Clemens, and all that he was to say and write for the rest of his life was to be merely an expansion and consolidation of this San Francisco achievement.

CHAPTER VII

~AT ~LARGE

IN EVERY way the results of the lecture were heartening. It showed a net profit for the lecturer of $400, and the papers added their critical acclaim to the audience's applause. In the light of future developments it was scarcely unbridled praise to say that Mark Twain was the "most piquant and humorous writer and lecturer on the Coast since the days of the lamented John Phoenix," especially as Phoenix had never lectured. More to the point was the *Bulletin*'s judgment that the lecture much surpassed Artemus Ward in point of humor, had none of his straining after effect, "and possessed some solid qualities to which Ward can make no pretensions." At his first essay Mark Twain had outdone the man who less than three years before had given him his first glimpse of a humorous artist at work on the platform. The new confidence in his own powers which Anson Burlingame had instilled was mightily reinforced.

With his customary resilience he rebounded from the black mood of the preceding weeks. Denis McCarthy, who had left the *Enterprise,* turned up opportunely in San Francisco, and with that old and reliable friend as his business manager Mark set out on a comprehensive lecture tour of central California. Starting with Sacramento, they played every stand within reach, even to decaying mining camps like You Bet and Red Dog. The tour was a personal and pecuniary triumph which incidentally furnished the lecturer with a fund of anecdote and reminiscence which lasted the rest of his life—the rival manager of a tightrope act who proposed that they combine their shows; the old man who inquired after the lecture, "Be them your natural tones of eloquence?"; the chairman who introduced him as

114

"the celebrated Mark Twain from the celebrated city of San Francisco, with his celebrated lecture about the celebrated Sandwich Islands."

The tour ended in Nevada, amid tornadoes of affectionate applause from his old friends. It also included that last and most elaborate of Steve Gillis' practical jokes, a burlesque holdup on the lonely ridge between Gold Hill and Virginia City. As a holdup, the thing was a success; as a joke, from Mark's point of view, it was not. He was never fond of a joke which turned upon himself, and the memory of this one rankled at intervals until he died. However, if we may trust his own statement that it finally cured him of his own propensity for practical joking, it was not without value in his career.

Early in December he was back in San Francisco, where he lectured again, this time on his overland trip in 1861. He was solvent now, he had a profession which promised continued returns, and he was sick of the Coast. He wanted to see his family, and was at last sufficiently in funds to face them without qualms. Moreover, the lecturing success made journalistic correspondence seem less irksome than when it was his sole dependence, and he arranged with Colonel McComb of the *Alta California* to supply a weekly letter on the model of the Hawaiian correspondence in the Sacramento *Union*. By this arrangement his routine living expenses would be taken care of, and he would have a completely free hand in selecting subjects to write about. Thanks to these *Alta* letters, his movements and adventures during the ensuing months can be accurately followed.

No longer needing to stint expenses, and eager to see as much of the world as he could, he set out to return to St. Louis and Hannibal by way of the Isthmus of Nicaragua, Key West, and New York. Accompanied by his alter ego, Brown, who continued his blithe custom of making remarks about seasickness and lice and his sweetheart who picked her nose with a fork, he found more adventures than he had anticipated.

The adventures began with the discovery that the captain of

the steamer *America,* which bore him from San Francisco to the Isthmus, was Ned Wakeman. All Mark Twain's delight in full-flavored personalities was stirred by this competent, roaring, pious, hard-fisted seaman, who subsequently figured in his books under the various aliases of Hurricane Jones, Ned Blakeley and Captain Stormfield. Even without the presence of an eloping couple to whom the captain promptly furnished the nautical equivalent of a shotgun wedding, the trip would have been a revel for Mark Twain, whose immunity to seasickness gave him abundant opportunity to listen to the Captain's thundering yarns.

When they reached the Isthmus Mark Twain's journal gives an inkling of how much he had still to do in order to pass acceptably in polite society. A deck hand on the San Juan River steamer refused to admit him to the upper deck because the man took him for a steerage passenger. The broadcloth and good linen of Nevada, the fine clothes of piloting days, had not yet become instinctive with Mark; when he traveled he relapsed into a slovenliness which may have been comfortable, but was obviously not prepossessing. But worse troubles were ahead, for the ship took cholera with her out of Greytown and passenger after passenger sickened and died. Timid survivors left the ship at Key West, but it is indicative of courage, fatalism or an undiminished zest for adventure that Mark Twain had no thought of following them.

On January 12, 1867, he landed in a New York which had grown out of all recognition since he had worked there as printer thirteen years before. It was the city of Mayor Oakey Hall and the beginnings of the Tweed Ring. Prices had soared and politeness declined in the postwar inflation; he soon found that his weekly $20 from the *Alta* would not even pay his board. But he plunged into a round of sight-seeing that took in everything from Henry Ward Beecher to *The Black Crook,* and described with equal gusto the great man's preaching and the legs of the clipper-built girls on Niblo's stage.

He had two publishing projects in mind when he landed: a

book about the Sandwich Islands, and a collection of his miscellaneous humorous sketches. For the former he could find no
market at all, and laid the material aside until he later used it
in *Roughing It.* The volume of sketches he carried hopefully
to G. W. Carleton, who had published Artemus Ward's collection and had rejected "The Jumping Frog." As to what happened, there are two stories, Carleton's and Mark Twain's.
According to the latter, the publisher pointed to his shelves, saying scornfully, "Books? I don't *want* your book; my shelves
are *full* of books now." According to Carleton, the author
looked too disreputable to bother with. For once it is likely that
both versions are true: this was the Mark Twain whom the deck
hand in Nicaragua had recently mistaken for an intruder from
the steerage. When they met years later in Europe, Carleton
laughingly admitted that his one claim to immortality was his
refusal of Mark Twain's first book.

But New York was full of traveling Californians, and among
them was Charles Henry Webb, late editor of the *Californian.*
Webb offered to back the publication himself and to pay the
author a royalty of ten cents a copy. The agreement was made,
and Mark was launched upon the first of his numerous inharmonious relations with publishers. Though he told his mother
that he did not expect to make much out of the book and published it mainly to advertise himself, he thought enough of it
before he sailed for Europe to ask Frank Fuller to serve as his
business agent and collect the royalties for him. The book was
hastily put together, but Mark had so far recovered from his
momentary distaste for the Frog story that he made it the title
piece. On the face of the record he had more ground for his
subsequent dissatisfaction with Webb than was the case with his
later publishers. The book paid him nothing; indeed, several
years later, he had to pay Webb $800 to recover his copyright.
But it did advertise him to a wider Eastern audience than had
heard of him before.

Once the arrangements with Webb were made, Mark did not
even wait to read his proofs, but set out on March 3 to pay the

long-deferred visit to his mother and sister. When he reached St. Louis, after fifty-two hours in the train, he had his first glimpse of the real bitterness of the Civil War. Political animosities still ran so high that it was unwise to invite Republicans and Democrats to the same dinner, and even the churches were divided on sectional lines. But he had a noble good time visiting with old friends, lectured twice in St. Louis to appreciative audiences, and then went upriver to revisit Hannibal, Keokuk and Quincy. He lectured in those towns also, described their generally down-at-heel condition in the *Alta,* and was reminded of the story of Jimmy Finn, Hannibal's town drunkard. Though the railways were cutting into the steamboat trade there was still plenty of traffic on the river. But it didn't interest Mark Twain. He had other plans.

In his last letter to the *Alta* before starting for St. Louis he had described at great length a recently announced pleasure excursion to Europe, and had told of provisionally booking his passage, subject to a possible veto from the *Alta,* against which he fervently protested in advance. When the letter was published the editors added in brackets, "No veto. He has been telegraphed to 'go ahead'." The *Alta* had really done much more than that. The paper had promptly paid his entire passage —$1,250—and had contracted with him for a series of letters about the trip, to be paid for at the same rate as the series he was then sending from the East.

By the middle of April he was in New York once more, with nearly two months to wait before the *Quaker City* sailed. To keep up the flow of letters to the *Alta* he visited the Bible House; he visited the bootblacks' mission; he visited Harry Hill's dance hall. He also visited the Academy of Design, and was glad that he knew nothing about art, because his ignorance enabled him to enjoy the pictures he liked—"all the sea views, and the mountain views, and the quiet woodland scenes, with shadow-tinted lakes in the foreground, and I just reveled in the storms." But he failed to admire "that picture, by one of the old masters, where six bearded faces without any bodies to

them were glaring out of Egyptian darkness and glowering upon
a naked infant that was not built like any infant that ever I saw,
nor colored like it, either. I am glad the old masters are all
dead, and I only wish they had died sooner."

Meantime his friend Frank Fuller, formerly territorial governor of Utah, had been organizing the Californians in New
York to demand a lecture from Mark Twain. With a spacious
enthusiasm reminiscent of Comstock, Fuller undertook all the
arrangements and hired Cooper Union, the largest auditorium
in the city, for the occasion. Fuller's zeal was greater than his
judgment; advance sales were so slow that they had finally to
paper the house by sending free tickets to all the schoolteachers
in the city. The lecture was financially a failure but critically a
success. Mark repeated it twice, in New York and Brooklyn,
and could have had more engagements if time and his preparations for his trip had permitted.

As the sailing date drew near he was more and more depressed, in spite of his getting acquainted with his roommate
for the trip, Dan Slote of New York, "a splendid, immoral,
tobacco-smoking, wine-drinking, godless" youth. But the noise
and other discomforts of New York were wearing his nerves
thin, and on the eve of sailing he wrote his mother and sister
one of the morbidly self-reproachful letters he was given to in
his low moments. He was remorseful because he had not gone
to Washington to wangle a job for Orion, who had lost his Nevada post. "I am so worthless that it seems to me I never do
anything or accomplish anything that lingers in my mind as a
pleasant memory. My mind is stored full of unworthy conduct
toward Orion and towards you all, and an accusing conscience
gives me peace only in excitement and restless moving from
place to place."

But the mood did not last long after the *Quaker City* finally
got under way on June 8. Cruise ships were a novelty in 1867,
but no more of a novelty than the menagerie—as Mark soon
called it—gathered on board. The emphasis upon the Holy
Land in the publicity had resulted in a disproportionate num-

ber of clergymen in the company; the high price had tended to restrict the passengers to the well-to-do middle-aged. But besides his roommate, Mark found a few other young men on board, chief among them Jack Van Nostrand of Jersey City, Julius Moulton of St. Louis, and Charley Langdon of Elmira. And though the stricter brethren shuddered at his profanity and looked askance at his cigars, he found some congenial souls among his seniors. He gravitated toward the people with journalistic connections. Moses E. Beach of the New York *Sun* was on board with his daughter Emma. Mary Mason Fairbanks, some dozen years Mark's senior, wife of the proprietor of the Cleveland *Herald,* was traveling with her friends, Mr. and Mrs. Solon L. Severance. Mrs. Fairbanks loved laughter, and the place whence laughter came oftenest on the *Quaker City* was the table where Mark Twain sat. Before long she was "Mother Fairbanks" to him and to all the other young people on board.

At this stage of his career nothing about Mark Twain is more interesting than his capacity for making friends with people unlike himself. He was untidy, he was profane, he was socially crude with the crudity of a man who is completely unaware of his violation of conventions. By the standards of the stricter church members he was dissipated, for he smoked constantly and drank without subterfuge. Yet among his warmest friends was a whole procession of clergymen. It all depended on whether or not the clergyman had allowed his profession to stifle his sense of fun. And now the gentle and cultivated Mrs. Fairbanks came to occupy a place in his confidence which his own mother scarcely had.

It was a pleasure trip for Mark Twain, but it involved plenty of work. During the four months that it lasted he wrote for the *Alta* a total of fifty-three letters, each two to three thousand words in length. Before leaving New York, moreover, he had arranged with the New York *Tribune* to send them letters also, and wrote some half-dozen. To average twelve or fifteen hundred words of copy every day, amid the fatigues of a ceaseless round of sight-seeing, was not the achievement of the lazy

man Mark was fond of calling himself. It is no wonder that
his shipmate, Bloodgood H. Cutter, the Poet Lariat, remembered him as always writing when he was on shipboard, and
found him curt and ungracious to interrupters. But he enjoyed
every minute of it, and was as tireless as he had been in Hawaii.

Even more than in the Hawaiian letters, too, he was under the
stimulus of trying to convey the look and feel of strange places
to his readers. It is a commonplace of criticism that Mark
Twain's mature style is first established fully in *The Innocents
Abroad*. But what is really remarkable is that it appears almost
equally in the *Alta* letters from which the book was compiled.
Many of the much-quoted purple passages, such as the descriptions of Fayal and Tangier, stand in the letters almost word for
word as they do in the book. Moreover, the passages newly
written for the book display no advance in taste and judgment.
Some are good; some are bad. Thus, the travesty of the legend
of the Seven Sleepers of Ephesus was written for the *Alta,* and
taken over unchanged into the book, but the travesty of Abelard and Heloise was composed later, in cold blood. In short,
the letters, like the book, show Mark Twain writing as he was
always thenceforward to write: sometimes producing eloquent
and genuinely humorous prose, sometimes producing buffoon-
ery, and never completely certain which was which.

Not but what the letters had blemishes which were later deleted. Mark was still accompanied by Brown, who asked asinine
questions of the guides, compared Leonardo's "Last Supper" to
an old fireboard, and said that he knew a painter in San Francisco who could dash off a picture forty feet long in two weeks
that would far surpass the Titian he was being shown. At the
Grotto del Cane Mark with vast effort procured a dog to see if
the gases in the cave would suffocate the animal as advertised,
"and then, after all my trouble and vexation, the dog went up
and smelt Brown's breath and laid down and died." In the
book, of course, Brown vanishes. One example of his quizzing
a guide is transferred to the Doctor; a few other experiences
are attributed to Blucher, who made his first appearance in

the Azores letter to the *Tribune;* the rest of Brown is scrapped. But Mark was capable of plenty of bad taste without Brown's help. The devout who are upset by his vehemently Protestant mockery of relics, and his skepticism regarding miracles, had better avoid the *Alta* letters. It was Mark Twain, not Brown, for example, who said of the Duomo in Florence:

"It takes three hundred flabby, greasy vagabonds in holy orders to run this awful ecclesiastical swindle. And they don't stand a watch worth twenty dollars a month. They begin dinner at noon, and gorge till 3; then they smoke, and swill, and sleep till 5, and then they come on watch for just two hours.

"I saw one of their performances. Sixty of them singing and talking Latin at once. And I say in all seriousness that the majority of them looked stupid, and brainless, and sensual beyond anything I have ever seen for many a day. Those fat-cheeked, sleepy-eyed, bull-necked fellows, may have been good men— of course I cannot say they were not—but their general build was better suited to a butcher shop than a cathedral. Whenever you see a Catholic priest in America, you can pretty safely set him down as a man of brains—a man of ability and intelligence, away above the average of men—but when you see one in Italy you can as safely set him down as altogether the reverse. It seems so to me at any rate, and I certainly could not conveniently jump out of a third-story window without mashing a priest or a soldier, one or the other. Both are plenty enough."

Similarly, when Mark got to the Holy Land, he let himself go in mockery of Biblical stories at far greater length than the book would indicate—Joseph, Gideon and the Prodigal Son were all so recklessly travestied that one can begin to understand why a clergyman in San Francisco denounced him from the pulpit as "that son of the devil, Mark Twain."

That the Holy Land letters were written under peculiarly trying conditions—even archeologists today avoid Palestine in midsummer—was doubtless one reason why they were cruder than the ones written on shipboard. But another reason was that Mrs. Fairbanks was not with Mark's detachment in the

Holy Land. She had taken the young genius in hand. "She sewed my buttons on, kept my clothing in presentable trim, fed me on Egyptian jam (when I behaved), lectured me awfully on the quarter-deck on moonlit promenading evenings, and cured me of several bad habits." To her, and the little group that surrounded her, he soon formed the habit of reading his letters for the papers, and got frank criticism. Once at least Mr. Severance saw him tear up and throw away what he had just written: "Mrs. Fairbanks thinks it oughtn't to be printed, and, like as not, she is right." It was the first time he had had a critic on the hearth, and the value of her criticism is proved by the superior quality of the letters he wrote under her eye.

Of other matters on which Mark Twain changed his mind between the writing of the letters and the book, Napoleon III is conspicuous. All his life long the humorist was impressed by material things. The scale on which Napoleon was rebuilding Paris took his imagination at once. When he saw the Emperor pass in procession with the Sultan, he went off the deep end:

"That he is the greatest man in the world today, I suppose there is no question. Bismarck may be shrewder in some things, but there his greatness stops, while there is no element of true greatness which Napoleon does not possess."

He was lyric in his descriptions of the Emperor's improvements, and later, comparing what he thought was the shakiness of Victor Emmanuel's Italy with what he thought was the stability of Napoleon's France, he called the Emperor "that giant." But when he prepared the *Innocents* he modified "giant" to "statesman," and though he retained most of the praise of the French regime he added qualifying touches—the Emperor "watching everything and everybody with his cat-eyes from under his depressed hat-brim, as if to discover any sign that those cheers were not heartfelt and cordial," and the passage about "his credulous victim, Maximilian, lying stark and stiff in Mexico, and his maniac widow watching eagerly from her French asylum for the form that will never come." Here, as so often elsewhere, Mark's second thoughts were better.

But the quality most evident in the letters is Mark's zest for experience, and his inexhaustible sense of fun. He was looking at Europe and Asia with eyes which, except for New Orleans and his few weeks in New York and Philadelphia, had never seen a city more than fifty years old. His knowledge of architecture had been nurtured by nothing older or more impressive than Southern plantation houses and Trinity Church, New York. His knowledge of painting went no further than Church's "Heart of the Andes," Bierstadt's "Domes of the Yosemite," and the chromos and steel engravings in people's parlors at home. He hated sham, and refused to pretend to admire what he could not understand. Besides, mocking at sacred cows was a sure means of getting a laugh, provided they were not the sacred cows of the majority of his readers. So he had a prolonged field day in the churches and galleries of France and Italy. But no man was ever more genuinely and profoundly impressed by the continuity of human experience when it was so expressed that he could visualize it. To him the hollows worn by generations of hurrying wayfarers in the streets of Pompeii meant more than sculpture and architecture. Here was evidence that people in all respects like himself had once thronged those empty streets. Whatever he could translate into terms of his own life came alive for him.

Sometimes, for all his mockery, this tendency brought him closer to the truth than the starry-eyed reverence of more conventional pilgrims did. He constantly visualized the stories of Scripture in terms of the ragged and verminous vagabonds whom he found inhabiting the holy places in 1867. It was not reverent, but it was probably nearer reality than the odorless reports of the pious. And his readers ate it up.

The personal results of the trip, moreover, were even more important than the literary ones. By the time the ship reached the Black Sea, Mark Twain, for all the disapproval of some of the clerical pilgrims, was recognized as one of the most distinguished men on board. He was chosen to draft the address to the Tsar of Russia when the pilgrims visited Yalta, and proudly proclaimed the fact in letters to both the *Alta* and the *Tribune,* though before he told the story in the *Innocents* he was heartily ashamed of the effort, and suppressed his authorship. These tourists were supposed to be a picked lot, socially and culturally; he found them accepting him as their equal, and probably began to feel himself superior to most of them.

He had courage and to spare—and impudence and irreverence as well. He was one of the little group who risked jail in Athens by slipping ashore, in defiance of the quarantine, to see the Acropolis by moonlight. He protested, vehemently but in vain, against the godly members of his party who insisted on forcing their miserable horses through a double march on the road to Damascus in order to avoid the sin of traveling on Sunday. On the return trip from Damascus to Galilee he spoke his mind still more freely. Dan Slote fell ill with cholera, of which Mark himself had had a light attack in Damascus. The other members of the party held a meeting, and resolved that after making Dan as comfortable as they could, they would push on without him. Said Mark: "Gentlemen, I understand that you are going to leave Dan Slote here alone. I'll be God-damned if I do." And he remained behind until the sick man was able to ride again. It may have been this incident that made Deacon Church, one of the deserters, say in after years that Mark Twain "was the worst man I ever knew. And the best."

Unquestionably Mark's ribald comments on the holy places influenced the Deacon's judgment. Though the remark, "No wonder Jesus walked!" when the pilgrims learned the price of boat hire on the Sea of Galilee, is ascribed to Jack Van Nostrand, it has a strong Mark Twain ring, and it was unquestionably Mark who summed up his whole impression of the Holy Land in the phrase, "No Second Advent—Christ been here once, will never come again." He was studying his Bible with the best of them, but to different effect. When the devout rhapsodized over the fulfillment of prophecy in the destruction of Gilgal and Bethel, Mark would drawl that with the same propriety you might point to the site of *any* city of that day and say the very same. Only Damascus and Jerusalem had survived, and even there the places of biblical times were buried thirty feet under ground. "It seems to me that the prophets fooled away their time when they prophesied the destruction of the cities—old Time would have fixed that, easy enough." He added, "I can go as far as the next man in genuine reverence of holy things, but this thing of stretching the narrow garment of belief to fit the broad shoulders of a wish, 'tis too much for me."

As inept a comment as was ever made on Mark Twain is the attribution of his notable advance in style in the *Quaker City* letters to his increased study of the Bible during the trip. To begin with, the vivid style is evident from the start, whereas he began intensive Bible reading only when the party reached the Levant. Next, he read the Bible mainly to get the history and tradition associated with the various spots he visited, and frequently as the material for heavy-handed burlesque. And finally, Mark's mature style is anything but biblical. Not from the Bible did he learn the art of building up a phrase with meticulously chosen adjectives, his vivid images, his skilfully contrived anticlimaxes. These were the result of learning to write as he talked.

By the time the pilgrims rejoined the ship at Jaffa even Mark Twain had had enough of sight-seeing. He wrote a letter to the *Tribune* about the fate of a colony of American Second Adventists who had migrated to Palestine to secure preferred places for the Second Coming, and who were now trying to get away because their leader's prophecies had failed to fit the almanac. He made a couple of pages of notes in Egypt, which later became a chapter in the *Innocents*, but the letters to the *Alta* carried the trip no further than Jerusalem and the Dead Sea. He wound up with a week's travel in Granada and Andalusia, but took no notes and wrote no letters. He had had enough of authorship for the moment.

On November 19 the *Quaker City* reached New York. The next day Mark Twain published in the *Herald* his summary of the trip. It would have been better, he concluded, to call it

"The Grand Holy Land Funeral Procession," instead of the "Grand Holy Land Pleasure Excursion," and he trod upon numerous toes with his descriptions of the pious seniors who made up the majority of the party. The letter was uproariously funny, but the galled jades winced. Nevertheless, Mark was not the only dissatisfied pilgrim. The next day the *Herald* had another letter, signed "A Passenger," which excoriated everything from the advance publicity to the ship's library, which latter, said "A Passenger," consisted of "a score and a half of the *Plymouth Collection* and two volumes of *Harper's Weekly.*" The writer criticized the discipline of the crew, charged the passengers with cliquishness, backbiting and gossip, and summed up the whole expedition as a failure. "It is true that we have visited a number of interesting places, but we have done so in the most hurried and unsatisfactory manner, while the expense has been much greater than if the travel had been made upon the regular lines." The likeliest ascription of authorship is to Mark Twain's friend, Moses S. Beach of the New York *Sun.* The letter shows that Mark was not the sole critic; other passengers shared his feelings; he got the abuse because he had expressed his feelings wittily.

But no summary of the trip as it affected Mark Twain is complete without the incident in Smyrna harbor on the fifth or sixth of September. Young Charley Langdon of Elmira had not been one of Mark's intimates on the trip. The lad was only eighteen, and Mark had probably felt more at home with Dan and Jack and Julius Moulton, who were nearer his age. But at Smyrna Mark dropped into Charley's cabin, and the boy showed him pictures of his family. The chief treasure was a miniature on ivory of his invalid sister Olivia, a girl with delicate, finely-chiseled features, her dark hair drawn back smoothly from her forehead with no concession to the fashionable "waterfalls" which had been furnishing Mark with material for humor ever since his Nevada days. Ever afterward he remembered that occasion as one of the main links in the chain of circumstances which made up his life.

He had arrived in New York to find himself far more famous than when he left, and the *Herald* letter did nothing to obscure his identity. His immediate program, however, he thought was all settled. While he was abroad a letter had come from Senator William Stewart of Nevada, offering him the post of private secretary. The job would give him the chance to maintain his newspaper connections in the guise of Washington correspondent; indeed, that was probably why Stewart made the offer. A popular correspondent, with free entry into the leading newspapers of the West, could be very useful in support of some of the Senator's political schemes. Mark left for Washington after only one day in New York, and entered upon his new duties.

They lasted about a week. No American who ever lived was less fitted than Mark Twain for the work of contact man and private secretary. The brief association left Senator Stewart one of the few people who disliked Mark Twain with a thoroughgoing, rancorous dislike. When he says in his reminiscences that his secretary was amazingly slovenly in his dress, he probably tells the truth. When he says that Mark's untidiness and his habit of smoking in bed were the despair of his landladies, he certainly tells the truth. But when he accuses Mark of carelessness about debts, and suggests that he had to threaten him with a thrashing, he makes charges which have no duplicate elsewhere in the records. It was a clear case of incompatibility. Mark's humor could not companion long with senatorial pomposity. His resignation gave him the material for a couple of comic articles, but for publication he named Senator Nye as his employer. Jim Nye could take a joke; Bill Stewart couldn't.

But he had already established himself as a Washington correspondent. He had begun with a regular contract with the New York *Tribune,* and quickly added another with the *Herald;* papers all over the country were asking him for regular or occasional letters from the capital. He was elected to the Correspondents' Club, and at their dinner on January 12 responded to the toast, "Woman," in the first of his public speeches to be reported verbatim. In its adroit use of anticlimax and, above all, of the pause, it showed him already a master of his art. "Human intelligence cannot estimate what we owe to woman, sir. She sews on our buttons; she mends our clothes. She ropes us in at the church fairs; she confides in us; she tells us whatever she can find out about the little private affairs of the neighbors. She gives us advice, and plenty of it. . . . She bears our children— ours as a general thing." He brought in a tribute to the mother of Washington, who raised a boy that couldn't lie. "It might have been otherwise with him if he had belonged to a newspaper correspondents' club." And he wound up his drolling with a serious and conventional tribute to Mother. He had learned a pattern for after-dinner speeches which he employed fruitfully for the rest of his career.

Within a month from his return to America he was an accepted member of an influential and nationally known group of journalists. At the end of January he told Mrs. Fairbanks that his contracts—presumably if he exploited them to the full —were worth six or eight hundred dollars a month. Numbers of his uncollected Washington letters are still buried in newspaper files. He might easily have settled permanently into the work of humorous commentary on national affairs, had not something bigger come along.

CHAPTER VIII

ESTABLISHED

AT THE head of the new notebook he began in Washington Mark Twain wrote: "Fame is a vapor; popularity an accident; the only earthly certainty is oblivion." As he was writing, a letter must have been waiting in the New York office of the *Tribune*, which for him was to give the lie, once and for all, to that particular piece of his pessimism.

Two days after the *Quaker City* reached New York, Elisha Bliss of the American Publishing Company of Hartford had written to propose a book based on the European travel letters. Bliss's was a subscription house which issued only two books a year, but got them up with elaborate and tasteless illustrations and bindings and sold them through a corps of house-to-house canvassers. Total sales by this method far exceeded what the ordinary trade houses of the day were able to accomplish—when the Company could secure volumes which appealed to their clientele. Until Bliss had become manager, the Company had dealt mainly in works of a heavily evangelical cast, which may have laid up treasure in Heaven, but had paid few dividends. Bliss had undertaken to liven up the list, with results that helped the directors' pockets but sometimes hurt their minds. At the moment his best seller was A. D. Richardson's *Field, Dungeon, and Escape*, a narrative of adventures in the Civil War.

It was ten days before Bliss's letter was forwarded to Washington, and when it reached Mark Twain at last it found him none too eager. He was just getting launched on his work as newspaper correspondent; preparation of a book would cut

130

heavily into his time. He wanted to be sure that the venture would be financially worth while. This detail, he said, "has a degree of importance for me which is almost beyond my own comprehension." But he was willing to discuss terms.

At this critical moment Bliss fell ill, and the correspondence lapsed for several weeks. In the meantime Mark had met the woman he wanted to marry.

Early in December "Mother" Fairbanks had told him that what he needed was a good wife. He took up her words in a letter written on the twelfth:

" 'A good wife would be a perpetual incentive to progress'— and so she would—I never thought of that before—progress from house to house because I couldn't pay the rent. The idea is good. I wish I had a chance to try it. But seriously, Madam, you are only proposing luxuries to Lazarus. That is all. I want a good wife—I want a couple of them if they are particularly good—but where is the wherewithal? It costs nearly two letters a week to keep *me*. If I doubled it, the firm would come to grief the first time anything happened to the senior partner. Manifestly you haven't looked into this thing. I am as good an economist as anybody, but I can't turn an inkstand into Aladdin's lamp. . . .

"But seriously again, if I were settled I would quit all nonsense and swindle some girl into marrying me. But I wouldn't expect to be '*worthy*' of her. I wouldn't *have* a girl that *I* was worthy of. *She* wouldn't do. She wouldn't be respectable enough. . . ."

Less than two weeks later Mark went to New York to spend the Christmas holidays with Dan Slote. A reunion of the *Quaker City* nighthawks was arranged. Julius Moulton was far away in Missouri, but Dan had invited Jack Van Nostrand, and Charley Langdon turned up from Elmira—he was in the city for the holidays with his parents and sister. The four laughed till their sides ached as they relived their Holy Land experiences, and before young Langdon left he had invited Mark to dine with the family a couple of evenings later.

Jervis Langdon was a businessman of a more conservative sort than Mark had known in San Francisco—an operator, not a speculator. He had a prosperous coal business in Elmira, and owned the mines that produced the coal. But Mark's attention was not focused on Mr. Langdon. He had eyes only for the original of Charley's miniature. After dinner the Langdons took him with them to hear Dickens give his *David Copperfield* reading at Steinway Hall. The only man of letters after Dickens whose ultimate place in the hearts and minds of the vast public was commensurate with the Englishman's was attentive enough to note and remember details of platform technique. But most of his thoughts were elsewhere.

Olivia Langdon fulfilled all the promise of her picture. She was twenty-two years old, and her features had a *spirituelle* quality which ill-health had intensified. When she was sixteen she had injured her spine in a fall on the ice, and adolescent hysteria had probably had its part, along with the excessive solicitude of her family, in keeping her helplessly bedridden for two years. At any rate, the dire Victorian technique of keeping an invalid in a darkened room had been given full play, and she did not recover the use of her legs until a "faith healer" had applied the salutary remedies of fresh air and sunshine to supplement his treatment by suggestion. Now a young woman, she was poised and self-controlled; for all her invalidism and her position as the petted darling of her family, firmness of character was evident in word and gesture. "Her habitual demeanor," says her daughter, "was full of gentleness and sweetness, so much so that to me she always lived the meaning of the word, 'lady'." Her sweetness, however, was not softness. After thirty-two years of married life her husband described hers as a "turbulent spirit," but the turbulence never got out of hand. Here was the girl Mark had jested about to Mrs. Fairbanks a fortnight before.

He lost little time in improving the acquaintance. Olivia was to assist a New York friend in receiving New Year's callers, and at eleven o'clock on New Year's morning Mark and Charley made Mrs. Berry's their first place of call. What followed, he told his mother and sister a week later:

"I anchored for the day at the first house I came to—Charley Langdon's sister was there (beautiful girl), and Miss Alice Hooker, another beautiful girl, a niece of Henry Ward Beecher's. We sent the old folks home early, with instructions not to send the carriage till midnight, and then I just staid there and worried the life out of those girls. . . ."

The first fruits of the day were invitations to visit the Langdons in Elmira, and the Hookers in Hartford.

The New York visit had other results also. There was a dinner at Henry Ward Beecher's in company with Harriet Beecher Stowe, the Hookers and Moses Beach and his daughter of the *Quaker City* party. "We had a gay time, if it was Sunday. I expect I told more lies than I have told before in a month," Mark informed his family. He had come a long way from Jackass Hill in three years. Preliminary arrangements were likewise made for improved newspaper contracts—two impersonal letters a week for the *Herald* instead of "wishy-washy squibs" for the *Tribune*. In the long run these did not matter much. More important was the advice which Beecher, an old hand at book publishing, had for the neophyte.

"With his usual whole-souled way of dropping his own work to give other people a lift when he gets a chance, [Beecher] said, 'Now here, you are one of the talented men of the age—nobody is going to deny that—but in matters of business I don't suppose you know more than enough to come in when it rains. I'll tell you what to do, and how to do it.' And he did."

But the visit to Hartford to talk business with Bliss had to be postponed until Mark had filled a lecture engagement at Washington and had caught up with the arrears of his newspaper work. Not until the last week of January did he finally come to terms with the American Publishing Company. He was the guest of the Hookers (Mr. Hooker was Beecher's brother-in-law) while in Hartford, and humorously told his family and Mrs. Fairbanks of his efforts to do the right thing. He wanted the respect of the sterling old Puritan community, and so he didn't dare smoke in the parlor, or after he went to bed—"in fact I don't dare to do *anything* that's comfortable or natural. It comes a little hard to lead such a sinless life. . . ." But in spite of restrictions he had a good time, and thanks to Beecher's advice came away with a contract which was the best stroke of business he had ever done.

Bliss had offered the choice between a cash payment of $10,000 and a royalty contract. The cash looked big, and the royalty was only five percent, but for once Colonel Sellers did the right thing and bet upon the credit instead of taking the cash. The manuscript was to be delivered on August 1, but because of the time required for preparing two or three hundred illustrations and getting canvassers in the field for advance orders, the book would not appear until the following year.

Back in Washington he went energetically to work upon the book. His visit to Paris had been very briefly treated in the *Alta* letters, and presumably his first task was expanding the account of this part of the trip to a more adequate scale. The interest in the new project quickened his disillusionment with Washington. It was only ten weeks since he had eagerly undertaken the task of making himself a general Washington correspondent, but he was already sick of the job. "This is the place," he wrote to Orion on February 21, "to get a poor opinion of everybody in. There isn't one man in Washington, in civil office, who has the brains of Anson Burlingame. . . . There are more pitiful intellects in this Congress! . . . I am most infernally tired of Washington and its 'attractions.' " He reduced his correspondence to the minimum necessary to live on, and labored at his book, declining offers of political patronage which included the San Francisco postmastership. The chief editor of the *Alta* wanted that job, and Mark felt that he would be taking money out of a friend's pocket if he accepted.

But just after this renunciation Joe Goodman sent him bad news from the Coast. The *Alta* proprietors, it appeared, had known a good thing when they saw it, and had copyrighted the

Quaker City letters. Now they were preparing to bring them out in a book. Nothing in their contract with the author prevented their doing so, but if they did they would wreck his arrangements with Bliss. An exchange of letters bringing no satisfaction, he determined to go at once to San Francisco and have it out with "those *Alta* thieves." Bliss gave him an advance on royalties, and in the second week of March he was on his way to California by the Panama route, where on the Pacific side he fell in again with Captain Ned Wakeman.

In 1901 Mark thought he remembered once buying a revolver and traveling twelve hundred miles with the fixed purpose of killing a man. That is the distance from St. Louis to New Orleans, and he may have been recalling some wholly lost episode of his pilot days. But more probably this was the occasion, and John McComb or someone else on the *Alta* was the man. On his arrival in San Francisco, however, he shed no blood. His return to the Coast was a triumphal reunion with old friends. McComb staunchly backed his claim, and the proprietors of the *Alta* presently conceded that they had already had the full worth of their investment and yielded the letters, though not without requiring from the author a public acknowledgment that they had "waived their rights," which still rankled forty years later.

He was short of money, but a lecture on the Holy Land excursion, followed by a repetition of the tour he had made in the fall of 1866, left him with comfortably lined pockets and the glow of a fresh triumph in his heart. He finished his book in San Francisco, at high speed. In his *Autobiography* he thought that he had made little use of the *Alta* letters, after all:

"I found that they were newspaper matter, not book matter. . . . They were loosely constructed and needed to have some of the wind and water squeezed out of them. I used several of them—ten or twelve, perhaps. I wrote the rest of *The Innocents Abroad* in sixty days, and I could have added a fortnight's labor with the pen and gotten along without the letters altogether."

Like so many of the memories of his old age this was highly

inaccurate. Before leaving Washington, he told Orion at the time, he had done ten chapters. Of these, the descriptions of the Azores and Tangier were taken over almost as they stood in the newspaper, and so was part of the Gibraltar chapter. The rest was new matter. As already mentioned, he greatly expanded his account of France; about half of the Italian chapters were also new. But the entire second half of the *Innocents*, beginning with the ascent of Vesuvius, followed the *Alta* letters throughout. The chief additions to the Palestine section were the scathing comments on J. C. Prime's *Tent Life in the Holy Land*, which incidentally was an instance of what became Mark Twain's habitual practice in writing travel and description: reading every book on the current subject which he could lay hands on. Only the concluding chapters, from Alexandria onward, were wholly new. The *Alta* letters, in fact, made up considerably more than half the book.

True, they were more or less revised. Besides suppressing Brown, Mark struck out most of the slang with which the letters were peppered, and dropped such bits of small-town humor as substituting Williamsburg and Baldwinsville for the Arabic place names of Palestine. The broader burlesques of Scripture were toned down, and a few passages, like a detailed description of the Russian custom of naked bathing, were deleted entirely in the interests of decorum. Stylistically the revisions were usually improvements. Superfluous words were omitted; exact and picturesque ones substituted for the commonplace. When they reached the Azores, for instance, he had originally said that "a swarm of chattering, gesticulating, dark-skinned, piratical-looking Portuguese boatmen climbed the ship's sides." On revision this became, "A swarm of swarthy, noisy, lying, shoulder-shrugging, gesticulating Portuguese boatmen, with brass rings in their ears, and fraud in their hearts." Comparisons aimed at Pacific Coast readers naturally went by the board—comparisons sufficiently illustrated by the remark that Abana and Pharphar "do not amount to quite as much as the Carson and the Humboldt." But there remained whole chapters, such as the descriptions of the Parthenon and the ruins of Baalbec, in which scarcely a word was altered.

In this first book, in short, Mark Twain did what he did in almost every subsequent book. He began with a burst of enthusiasm which carried him about halfway. Then the task became irksome; the enthusiasm of expression waned, and he snatched at any material which could be levied on to fill up the contracted number of pages. The most significant additions to the *Innocents*, perhaps, are those which have nothing to do with the subject. The memory of the night when he sneaked into his father's office in Hannibal and found a dead man there, interpolated after the description of the Milanese effigy of a flayed man, was an afterthought. It was also his first realization, apart from a casual reference to Jimmy Finn a year earlier, of the literary possibilities of his boyhood experiences. He similarly lugged in the story of the undermined boulder that wrecked the cooper's shop at the foot of Holliday's Hill to illuminate his account of the Great Pyramid. But the passages comparing Shepheard's Hotel to the Benton House, and citing stories from the apocryphal New Testament, are pure padding. He said he took the former from his notebook; actually, both sections were drawn bodily from his letters to the *Alta* in the spring of 1867.

The continuity of the *Innocents* is the continuity of the tour it records, nothing more. The architectonics of literature, the planning of a book as an organic whole, meant no more to Mark Twain in 1868 than they meant to him when he dictated his autobiography in his old age. What G. K. Chesterton said of Dickens applies even more forcibly to Mark Twain: all his books "are simply lengths cut from the flowing and mixed substance called Dickens—a substance of which any given length will be certain to contain a given proportion of brilliant and of bad stuff. . . . You cannot artistically divide the output into books. The best of his work can be found in the worst of his works."

But he finished the book, after his fashion, in June, and wrote to reassure Mrs. Fairbanks, who had been admonishing him. He had left out the week in Spain, he said, because he would be sure to caricature Miss Newell—Julia Newell of Janesville, Wisconsin, a fellow passenger—if he wrote much about it. He continued:

"According to the contract I have to put in that N. Y. *Herald* valedictory squib which worried you so much—but that is all right. I read it over yesterday and found that it gave a perfectly accurate idea of the excursion. I have marked out some sentences. That article is so mild, so gentle, that I can hardly understand how I ever wrote such literary gruel. . . . Let it stand as testimony that I *am* moved by gentle impulses sometimes. You know what they said about me at Gibraltar, when I was absent—and O, I could have said *such* savage things about *them*—and would have done it, too, if they had had full swing in the metropolitan newspapers to reply." The chief omissions were a long paragraph which poked fun at the pilgrims' nightly prayer-meetings, and a shorter one which repeated some of the irony about Jehu's missionary zeal which he had already used in his *Alta* letter from Jezreel.

On July 2 he lectured again in San Francisco, with hilarious success. He had outdone himself in preparing the publicity, which was an elaborate advertisement for his forthcoming book as well as for the lecture. It took the form of alleged protests from prominent citizens, "and 1500 in the steerage," against the infliction of the lecture, to which he retorted that nothing would move him from his fell purpose. "It only costs the public a dollar apiece, and if they can't stand it what do they stay here for?" He represented the Pacific Board of Brokers as offering to pay his passage if he would leave at once, and the Chief of Police as saying, "You had better go." So of course it was the lecture that went, with a bang.

Four days later he set out again by way of Panama, reached New York on the twenty-eighth, and had his manuscript in Bliss's hands by the contract date. Then a new hitch arose. Some of the directors thought the book irreverent if not downright blasphemous, and wanted Bliss to cancel the contract. So completely has John Bunyan fallen from his once high estate as the author of virtually another Testament, that it is difficult for the modern reader to understand why much of the protest should have been due to the proposed title, *The New Pilgrim's Progress*. In view of the blistering things Mark said about Bliss in his *Autobiography*, it is worth recording that in this crisis Bliss upheld him wholeheartedly, even to the length of threatening, if the directors persisted in their stand, to resign and publish the book himself. Thus forced to choose between battling for the Lord and losing the dividends Bliss had brought them, the directors executed a strategic retreat, and the manuscript was placed in the hands of the illustrators.

His business thus satisfactorily adjusted, Mark secured a renewal of the Langdons' invitation to spend a week with them in Elmira. His arrival was not auspicious. Instead of taking the Lackawanna express he was supposed to arrive on, he managed to get on a local which did not reach Elmira until late at night. He enlivened things for his prospective hosts by dispatching telegrams from various stations along the way, reporting his progress. Charley decided to go a few miles down the line to meet him. Mark, travel-stained and disheveled, was in the smoker, arrayed in a disgraceful linen duster and the wreck of what had once been a straw hat. No doubt the Nicaraguan deck hand would have recognized him instantly.

"You've got some other clothes, haven't you?" asked the dubious Charley. Mark assured him that he had a brand-new outfit in his bag, and would be presentable when he met the family in the morning.

It was the beginning of a week of shocks for Charley. Mark told his family that his only trouble was that the Langdons gave too much thought and time and invention to making his visit pass delightfully. Long before the week was over he knew that he was in love with Livy. Doubtless Livy knew it, too, but this was the Victorian age and she gave no sign. At first, indeed, she was probably more disturbed than gratified by his attentions. The elders apparently suspected nothing, but Livy's married sister, Sue Crane, had eyes in her head, and warned Charley that Mr. Clemens was after Livy. This was upsetting. Charley liked and admired Mark Twain, but he couldn't see him in the role of Livy's husband. When the morning of the last day of the visit came, Mark told Charley that he *ought* to go by the first train, because he was in love—in love with Olivia. With his sister's warning thus dramatically confirmed, Charley leaped into action.

"There's a train in half an hour. I'll help you catch it. Don't wait till tonight. Go now."

"No, Charley. I want to enjoy your hospitality a little longer. I promise to be circumspect, and I'll go tonight."

But when night came, he didn't go. Fate, or someone, had removed the bolts from the back seat of the station wagon that was to take him to the train, and when the horse started, the seat, with Mark and Charley on it, went over on to the cobblestones. Mark did some quick thinking as he lay in the gutter. He allowed himself to be carried into the house, was treated for shock and contusions, and made no unseemly haste about recovering. That fall gave him a good three days' extension of his visit, and he didn't waste his time. But he also was Victorian, and though his mind was made up he left Elmira without declaring himself to Olivia.

He declared himself elsewhere, however. From Elmira he went to Cleveland, where he told the whole story to "Mother" Fairbanks, and so won her approval that she became the confidante of far more details of his courtship than he told to his own mother. Next he returned to Hartford for conferences about his book, and while there made the acquaintance of one of the men whose friendship was a lifelong joy. The Rev. Joseph Hopkins Twichell has been sneered at by critics because he was a Republican and the pastor of a wealthy and fashionable Congregational church. But it is possible to be a good man even in such environment, and Twichell was both good and very much of a man. He had served as chaplain with General Daniel Sickles in the Civil War; he was athletic and fond of fun; his private charities ultimately bankrupted him.

It was only narrow-minded clergymen who were shocked by Mark Twain. Like Franklin Rising and Henry Ward Beecher before him, Twichell warmed to his new friend at once and so did Mrs. Twichell. Their house became a home to him whenever he was in Hartford, and it was the sort of peaceful, harmonious, well-ordered home that Mark was dreaming of for himself. One evening Mrs. Twichell repeated the advice Mrs. Fairbanks had given a year earlier, and asked him why he did not marry and settle down, now that his affairs were prosperous. He replied with boyish frankness:

"I am taking thought of it. I am in love beyond all telling with the dearest and best girl in the whole world. I don't suppose she will marry me. I can't think it possible. She ought not to. But if she doesn't I shall be sure that the best thing I ever did was to fall in love with her, and proud to have it known that I tried to win her."

At this point James Redpath, the leading lecture agent of the day, took a hand. He signed up Mark Twain for a heavy schedule of lectures during the late fall and winter, and Mark so handled his itinerary in New York State, Pennsylvania, and Ohio, as to manage at intervals to stop over in Elmira.

Financially and critically the tour was a huge success. He had prepared a lecture based on the *Innocents,* and everywhere delivered it to capacity houses. In Pittsburgh he played against Fanny Kemble, and had two thousand auditors to her two hundred. The papers made much of his "long, monotonous drawl, with the fun invariably coming in at the end of a sentence— after a pause," and noted the informal platform demeanor which seemed to contradict his formal evening dress. The public took him to its heart. The Langdons didn't.

When it became obvious that he was courting Olivia her parents were perturbed, and Olivia herself was not prepared to say Yes. Though Elmira, as Max Eastman has made clear, was intellectually no Gopher Prairie, it was socially conservative, like all the older American communities of the day. Mark Twain, for all his charm and humor, was a disturbing person, above all in his ignorance or disregard of the lesser social conventions. His unorthodox utterances on religion, for example, were no great shock to people used to the preaching of Thomas K. Beecher, but his careless attire, his cigars, his loose-jointed Western demeanor in a drawing room, were hard to get used to. His first proposal met refusal, polite but firm. That must have been late in October.

He continued his lecture tour. On Saturday, November 21, two days after his Pittsburgh triumph, while the Langdons were at breakfast, Mark appeared at the door with a characteristic greeting:

"The calf has returned; may the prodigal have some breakfast?" The following Saturday he wrote from New York to tell Twichell the events of the week:

". . . I have fought the good fight, and lo! I have won! Refused three times—warned to quit once—accepted at last! . . . She felt the first symptoms last Sunday—my lecture, Monday night, brought the disease to the surface—Tuesday night she avoided me and would not do more than be simply polite to me because her parents said NO absolutely (almost)—Wednesday they capitulated and marched out with their side-arms— Wednesday night she said over and over again that she loved me but was sorry she did and hoped it would pass away—Thursday I was telling her what splendid magnificent fellows you and your wife were, and when my enthusiasm got the best of me and the tears sprang to my eyes she just jumped up and said she was _glad_ and _proud_ she loved me!—and Friday night I left (to save her sacred name from the tongues of the gossips)—and the last thing she said was: 'Write immediately and just as often as you can!' Hurra! . . ."

But he also explained that the parental surrender was still conditional. Livy must have a chance to make up her mind thoroughly, and he must prove that he had done "nothing criminal or particularly shameful in the past, and establish a good character in the future, and settle down." But a letter to Mrs. Fairbanks at the same time gives a revealing glimpse of Jervis Langdon. "For all the old gentleman is so concerned, he knows he has not been so jolly himself for months, or had such noble opportunities for poking fun at helpless people. He makes her face crimson, and enjoys it. But he don't embarrass *me* any to speak of...."

One of the things Mr. Langdon wanted was character references as to the suitor's conduct and reputation in his Western days. Mark named half a dozen clergymen and other prominent San Franciscans, omitting Joe Goodman because, as he afterward explained, he knew Joe would lie unreservedly in his favor. Meanwhile he continued his lecturing, sitting up nights in small-town hotels to write long, tender, and sometimes broadly comic letters to Livy.

It was the first of February before he got back to Elmira to learn the results of Mr. Langdon's correspondence. All his references, it appeared, had spoken warmly of his talents, but all had agreed that as a husband he would be about the worst on record. For once in his loquacious life Mark was silent.

"I couldn't think of anything to say. Mr. Langdon was apparently in the same condition. Finally he raised his handsome head, fixed his clear and candid eye upon me, and said: 'What kind of people are these? Haven't you a friend in the world?'

"I said, 'Apparently not.'

"Then he said: 'I'll be your friend, myself. Take the girl. I know you better than they do.' "

On February 4, 1869, the engagement was formally ratified, and presently Mark once more resumed his lecturing. His happiness sent him into meditations on the chain of fate which had at last brought him to win Olivia's love. From Lockport, New York, on February 27, he imparted the results of his meditations to Mrs. Fairbanks—meditations which link backward with the Presbyterian Sunday school in Hannibal, and forward with *What Is Man?*

"I never yet had what seemed at the time to be a particularly aggravating streak of bad luck but what it revealed itself to me later as a piece of royal good fortune. Who am I, Mother, that I should take it upon myself to determine what is good fortune and what is evil? For about a week, Providence headed me off at every turn. The real object of it, and the real result, may not transpire till you and I are old and these days forgotten—and therefore is it not premature, now, to call it bad luck? We *can't tell*, yet. You ought to have heard me rave and storm at a piece of 'bad luck' which befel me a year ago—and yet it was the very individual means of introducing me to Livy!—and behold, now am I become a philosopher who, when sober reflection comes, hesitateth to rail at what seemeth to feeble finite vision ill luck, conscious that 'the end is not yet.' "

But amid all his happiness he was under the pressure of finding a settled means of livelihood. The lecture platform was profitable, but irksome. He loved his hour on the stage, when he could practice and refine his art of playing upon an audience as upon an instrument, but the other twenty-three hours of travel, of hurry, of strange and usually bad hotels, wore upon his always irritable nerves. Lecturing, in fact, soon provided him with the second of the anxiety symbols which appeared in his dreams for the rest of his life. To the dream of being lost in a fog on the Mississippi was now added the dream of getting up before an audience, finding that he had nothing to say, and seeing the audience walk out on him. The platform would do as an occasional money-maker in emergency, but he shrank from making it his lifework, as Oliver Wendell Holmes and John B. Gough and Anna Dickinson did.

He still thought of himself as primarily and professionally a journalist, but to support a wife as Livy deserved to be supported called for something better than a salaried job as reporter or editor, and more stable than free-lance correspondence. The best thing, he concluded, would be to buy a share in an established newspaper in which he could write as he had once written for the *Enterprise*, but with the greater freedom allowable to one of the proprietors. Thus he would have a settled position in the community, and thus also share the profits of whatever new prosperity his work might bring the paper.

Through the Fairbankses, he tried to buy an interest in the Cleveland *Herald*. To become the partner of one of his best friends seemed an ideal arrangement. But the negotiations fell through. Mr. Fairbanks' partner was unwilling to sell except at a price which Mark felt he could not afford. The Fairbankses were almost as disappointed as he was, and Mr. Fairbanks offered him a well-paid post as political editor. For the moment he was tempted. But he hated politics, and remembered how quickly Washington had got on his nerves. It would mean another apprenticeship, "to be tacked on to the tail-end of a foolish life *made up* of apprenticeships . . . *No* sir, I said, I'll prostitute my talents to something else. I am capable of slaving over an editorial desk without rest from noon till midnight, and keep it up without losing a day for three years on a stretch, as I am abundantly able to prove, but I am sure it has to be agreeable work." And then, while he was still hesitating, he learned that a third interest in the Buffalo *Express* was on the market.

The price was $25,000, and in order to raise it Mark began to think of a nationwide lecture tour, which might even take him back to California. But Jervis Langdon, now that he had accepted Mark Twain, was not doing things by halves. After an examination of the *Express* books had satisfied him that the investment was sound, he advanced the money himself. Early in August the deal was consummated, and on the fourteenth the new associate editor took his place on the staff. Four days later, in a "Salutatory," he assured the paper's readers that he was not going to hurt the paper deliberately and intentionally at any time, would avoid slang and vulgarity, would try not to use profanity even in discussing house rent and taxes, though he did not see how they could be discussed worth a cent without it, and promised to write no poetry unless he conceived a spite against the subscribers.

But before that date the *Innocents* had been published. With Livy to help him, he had read the final proofs in Elmira during the spring. The first copy was delivered on July 20, and by the time he joined the *Express* it was already on the full tide of success which brought sales of more than 30,000 copies in the first six months after publication. In January he was able to tell Mrs. Fairbanks that he would soon have paid off $15,000 indebtedness, besides sending his mother and sister a thousand dollars and taking out $10,000 in life insurance for his mother's benefit. And most of these funds had come from the book; he had not drawn a cent from the *Express*.

The book, moreover, was something more than a financial success. It was even reviewed favorably in the *Atlantic Monthly*, by that august journal's assistant editor, William Dean Howells. The praise, to be sure, was not describable as intemperate, but Howells was shrewd enough to recognize the brilliance of Mark's thumbnail character sketches, the pervasive irony of his style, and—and this was discerning, in view of what other critics said, then and later—the fact that the destructive humor was directed against "the standard shams of travel. . . . We do not remember where it is indulged at the cost of the weak or helpless side, or where it is insolent, with all its sauciness and irreverence. . . . There is an amount of pure human nature in the book that rarely gets into literature; the depths of our poor unregeneracy—dubious even of the blissfulness of bliss—are sounded by such a simple confession as Mr. Clemens makes in telling of his visit to the Emperor of Russia: 'I would as soon have thought of being cheerful in Abraham's bosom as in the palace of an emperor.' " After all, it was little wonder that when Mark first met Howells, soon after the publication of the review, he said, "When I read that review of yours, I felt like the woman who was so glad her baby had come white."

Mark was lecturing in New England when that meeting occurred—lecturing before audiences of four thousand Boston critics with the same success as before the intellectually unregenerate denizens of the Middle West and the Coast. He and Livy had planned to be married at Christmas or New Year's, but they decided to wait until he was through with his lecturing, and accordingly set the date for February 2, almost the anniversary of their formal engagement.

That year had done much for Mark Twain, and so had Livy. Deliriously happy and deliriously in love, he kept Mrs. Fairbanks acquainted with his progress. One of his letters was signed "Your Knighted and Ennobled Cub, Your Crowned and Sceptred Scrub"; another was dated, "Livy, Feb. 32, 1946," and substituted her name for half the nouns in the letter. Still another, a few weeks before his marriage, detailed both his own happiness and Livy's essays at reform:

"With my vile temper and variable moods, it seems an incomprehensible miracle that we two have been right together in the same house half the time for a year and a half, and yet have never had a cross word, or a lover's 'tiff,' or a pouting spell, or a misunderstanding, or the faintest shadow of a jealous suspicion. . . . *Could* I have had such an experience with any other girl on earth? . . . And yet she had attacked my tenderest peculiarities and routed them. She has stopped my drinking, entirely. She has cut down my smoking considerably. She has reduced my slang and boisterousness a good deal. She has exterminated my habit of carrying my hands in my pantaloons pockets, and has otherwise civilized me and well nigh taught me to behave in company. These reforms were calculated to make a man fractious and irritable, but bless you she has a way of instituting them that swindles one into the belief that she is doing him a *favor* instead of curtailing his freedom and doing him a fatal damage. She is the best girl that ever lived."

And so on for four pages. Past question, Mark loved to be reformed, when he loved the reformer.

The full nature, extent and durability of Livy's reforms will recur. What is abundantly evident is that his year and a half of courtship had quickened and refined the latent sensitivity of Mark Twain's nature. The Clemenses had been an undemonstrative family, Scottish or Puritan in their chariness of expressing the love they felt for each other. The Langdons were demonstrative, lavish with caresses and words of endearment. In their home, moreover, were the peace and beauty that love begets. Livy, at the age of twenty-three or twenty-four, had already the quality that was hers till death: the ability by virtue of which she was to create about her an atmosphere of serenity. Mark revealed to her that other soul side a man shows a woman when he loves her; she brought the peace his restless spirit craved.

"Livy," he wrote once, "you are just as kind and good and sweet and unselfish and just, and truthful, and sensible and intellectual as the homeliest woman I ever saw (for you know that these qualities belong peculiarly to homely women.) I have so longed for these qualities in my wife, and have so grieved because she would have to be necessarily a marvel of ugliness—I who do so worship beauty."

Humor was Mark's natural form of expression even in love. Livy, on the other hand, was naturally grave; she had a keen perception of humor but her first approach to things was serious. This gave her lover endless opportunities for tender teasing. He never tired of contriving elaborate traps for her, for the joy of seeing concern give way to shock, followed swiftly by helpless laughter and the despairing cry of, "Oh, Youth!"—the inspired name she always gave her ebullient husband.

In Howells' later opinion, Mark Twain showed himself at his best in the company of women. "He loved the minds of women, their wit, their agile cleverness, their sensitive perception, their humorous appreciation, the saucy things they would say, and their pretty, temerarious defiances." And he did not patronize them. The women he had known in his youth were capable and self-reliant, as women in new communities had to be. As a result, he had a respect for them far different from the sheltered-life "chivalry" of his fellow Victorians. But he never learned the technique of Victorian parlor manners. Long after his death old ladies in Hartford still remembered resentfully how he put his feet on their sofas or draped his legs over their chair arms as he talked.

Joe Twichell came on from Hartford to assist T. K. Beecher in the wedding ceremony at Elmira on February 2, 1870, and the next day the whole wedding party went on to Buffalo on a special train which Jervis Langdon had chartered. Mark Twain was married, and he thought he was settling down.

CHAPTER IX

BUFFALO TO HARTFORD

As SOON as they were settled in the fine house on Delaware Avenue which Jervis Langdon had bought and furnished as a wedding present, Mark Twain buckled down to work on his paper. Despite the success of the *Innocents* he still did not think of himself as a professional author. He seems to have regarded his book, like his success on the platform, as a lucky fluke. When the novelty wore off, the public would tire of him. Meantime he hoped to be established in what he considered his real profession, journalism. With wider scope and vastly improved powers of expression he would go back to the sort of work he had done on the *Enterprise*, writing humorous editorials, satiric parables and comic or bitter comments on items he found in the exchanges.

In a sense he was right; in a sense he never ceased to be a journalist, as anyone will realize who goes through his collected works and notes how many pages, even in the *Autobiography*, are essentially reporting, satirizing or fulminating against experiences of his own or events in the current news. Some of this writing, all through his life, was potboiling, done because he needed extra funds, but much of it was the instinctive expression of a man who had learned at the editorial desk to speak his mind fully and promptly on whatever came up in the day's news.

Before long, however, he was putting his best efforts into other columns than those of the *Express*. Not long after his marriage the *Galaxy*, a magazine which began with high hopes and high quality, but failed to weather the panic of 1873, had offered him a year's contract, at $200 a month, to conduct a humorous department which he called "Memoranda." Though long before the contract expired his domestic and other worries made the task irksome, Mark put good work into the series. It included those contributions to the growth of his own legend, "My Petrified Man" and "My Bloody Massacre," and a tall story, which might just as well have gone into the *Innocents*, about the Arab tobacco pipe which Dan Slote bought in Palestine. With the inconsistency which was always one of his most engaging traits, Mark denounced the "noble red man," and almost in the same breath championed the Chinese against their California oppressors. When the Rev. Mr. Sabine of New York, by refusing to read the burial service over George Holland, the actor, gave the neighboring Church of the Transfiguration its title of the Little Church Around the Corner, Mark erupted. After an eloquent, if rhetorical, defense of the moral values of the theater, he concluded with a blast that would have merited attention even among the *Enterprise's* staff:

"Was it not pitiable—that spectacle? Honored and honorable old George Holland, whose theatrical ministry had for fifty years softened hard hearts, bred generosity in cold ones, kindled emotion in dead ones, uplifted base ones, broadened bigoted ones, and made many and many a stricken one glad and filled it brimful of gratitude, figuratively spit upon in his unoffending coffin by this crawling, slimy, sanctimonious, self-righteous reptile!" No doubt this illustrates how his wife's censorship was beginning to emasculate Mark's natural vigor of expression.

Certainly his wife was working hard on him during these first months of their marriage. They were ebulliently happy, and wrote joint letters and separate ones to tell all their friends and relatives about it. And Mark, having taken a wife and established a home, was determined to make a good job of it. Livy brought with her the traditions of her own home, which included family worship. The worst shock of Joe Goodman's life was the sight of Mark Twain saying grace and reading the Bible when Joe visited Buffalo a few months after the marriage. Mark curbed his smoking because Livy thought he should—"not that

I believed there was the faintest *reason* in the matter, but just as I would deprive myself of sugar in my coffee if she wished it, or quit wearing socks if she thought them immoral," he explained to Joe Twichell. He couldn't stop swearing, but for the present he managed to avoid doing it in Livy's hearing. It looked like a thorough reconstruction of the wild humorist of the Pacific Slope according to the best parlor models of Queen Victoria, and as such some of his critics have treated it.

But the critics who find so much significance in the above passage would have done well to follow its themes a trifle further. Before long these reforms ceased, and ceased on Mark's terms, not on Livy's. The Bible readings were the first to go. After a few months all the skepticisms which dated from his reading of Tom Paine and his conversations with Macfarlane, and which had merely been intensified by his study of the Scriptures in Palestine, rose in revolt, even at the risk of hurting Livy's feelings.

"You may keep this up," he told her, "if you want to, but I must ask you to excuse me from it. It is making me a hypocrite. I don't believe in this Bible. It contradicts my reason. I can't sit here and listen to it, letting you believe that I regard it, as you do, in the light of gospel, the word of God."

Whereupon the Bible readings ceased in the Clemens home. Within a year after her marriage, moreover, Livy's crusade against tobacco was as if it had never been. Her husband resumed his stogies and his full-flavored corncob pipes throughout most of his waking hours at home and abroad. In the Victorian age gentlemen were not supposed to smoke in the presence of ladies, but Livy had made up her mind that her husband should be comfortable in his own home though the conventions suffered. According to Katie Leary, whose quarter-century of service ought to make her a reliable witness on this point, Livy determined from the start that her husband must be free to *say* whatever he wished to say, whether she approved or not. But she also let him *do* what he wished. All witnesses who were guests in the Clemens home agree in their accounts of Mark's wholly unconventional conduct—wearing his lounging slippers on all occasions, lying down on the floor before the fire when the spirit moved him, strolling about the dining room between courses, talking and flapping his napkin as he gesticulated. Before particularly formal dinners Livy would exhort him to remember his manners, but oftener than not her exhortations would be forgotten before the meal was half over, and after the guests were gone would come the scene which his children later described as "dusting off papa." Livy would enumerate his varied lapses; he would contritely admit his guilt—and do the same things next time. It relieved Livy's mind and it didn't bother him.

According to his own version, he held out longest on the matter of profanity. For ten years he claimed that he did his swearing in private, and dreaded the day when Livy should discover that he was "but a whited sepulcher partly freighted with suppressed language." But one Sunday morning in Hartford when he thought he was safely shut in the bathroom, he let his feelings over his buttonless shirts have full vocal expression. Too late, he discovered that the door had been ajar all the time, and when he finally mustered strength to return to their bedroom Livy's eyes were snapping and flashing with indignation.

"I stood silent under that desolating fire for as much as a minute, I should say—it seemed a very, very long time. Then my wife's lips parted, and from them issued—*my latest bathroom remark*. The language perfect, but the expression velvety, unpractical, apprentice-like, ignorant, inexperienced, comically inadequate, absurdly weak and unsuited to the great language. In my lifetime I had never heard anything so out of tune, so inharmonious, so incongruous, so ill-suited to each other as were those mighty words set to that feeble music. I tried to keep from laughing, for I was a guilty person in deep need of charity and mercy. I tried to keep from bursting, and I succeeded—until she gravely said, 'There, now you know how it sounds.'

"Then I exploded; the air was filled with my fragments, and

you could hear them whiz. I said, 'Oh Livy, if it sounds like *that,* God forgive me, I will never do it again.'

"Then she had to laugh herself. Both of us broke into convulsions, and went on laughing until we were physically exhausted and spiritually reconciled."

No marriage is wholly without storms. But it was Mark's gift of laughter, and Livy's quick appreciation of it, that cleared the air and left no charges of latent static behind.

Into the first happy months in Buffalo, however, crept shadows which were not of the young couple's making. Everything began smoothly, and Mark confidently told James Redpath that he had his finances ciphered down to a fraction; he had enough to live on comfortably, and never expected to lecture again. But in the spring Jervis Langdon was stricken with cancer and Livy, with her husband, went to Elmira to help Sue Crane and her mother with the nursing. The long agony dragged out until August, and they returned to Buffalo only to have death with them again in another prolonged siege, for a friend of Olivia's fell ill with typhoid and died in their home. Olivia was pregnant; her always frail health had suffered under the double strain; the result was that her baby, a boy whom they christened Langdon, was born prematurely on November 7.

It was the beginning of long months of anxiety. Livy was desperately ill and weak; the feeble life of the four-and-a-half-pound baby seemed likely to flicker out at any moment. The bleak, sunless Buffalo winter dragged on, and all the high hopes with which Mark had embarked on his undertaking in the *Expresss* faded out in the universal grayness. Nothing had gone right. Besides the constant worry at home, the paper itself had become a burden. Mark's connection with it had greatly increased its value as a source of clippings among its exchanges. A few items, such as the burlesque map of the fortifications of Paris—in which he reverted to the trick of his days on the Hannibal *Journal,* and carved his own illustration—had been laughed at all over the country. But this celebrity had not beer reflected in the subscription lists; his hope of making the *Express* into a paper with a national circulation, like the Springfield *Republican* or the Toledo *Blade*, was as far as ever from fulfillment. Nor had Buffalo furnished much in the way of congenial society, and illness and death had made it impossible for the Clemenses to cultivate what society there was. Convention prescribed a year of seclusion after a parent's death, and thus set up another barrier even had Livy's health permitted them to go out much.

Within thirteen months from the day of their marriage, Mark Twain had made up his mind that so far as Buffalo was concerned he was through. He would dispose of his share in the *Express*, sell his house and depend thenceforth on writing and occasional lecturing for his livelihood. Probably he would make his home in Hartford, where his publishing interests were centered and where he had already discovered congenial society, but at least he would get out of Buffalo. The first stop would be Elmira, and thither they went in the middle of March, with Livy carried on a mattress to a specially chartered invalid car on the railway. Their temporary home was Quarry Farm, the property of Theodore Crane, Livy's brother-in-law. On a breezy hilltop three miles from town, the farm commanded wide vistas of some of the loveliest countryside in the world and, like any home, seemingly, which the Langdon sisters had anything to do with, it was a center of peace and good will. Here Livy recuperated; the baby showed some signs, at last, of gaining; and Mark was able to return to his writing with something of the old zest.

The past months had wrought havoc with his plans. In July 1870 Elisha Bliss had proposed another book to follow up the huge success of the *Innocents*, and it was Bliss's suggestion that the book should deal with Mark's Western experience. So hopeful and well satisfied was Bliss that he offered the then unprecedented royalty of seven and a half percent on the new contract, and Mark eagerly went to work. But the series of domestic disasters soon wrecked his working schedule, and long before the deadline date of January 1, 1871, it was obvious that the book could not be finished on time. As a stopgap Mark first proposed a collection of his miscellaneous sketches. When Bliss was, justifiably, lukewarm to this, Mark had one of his sweeping, Colonel Sellers ideas. The papers were full of the recent discovery of the South African diamond fields. Let Bliss underwrite the expenses of a trained newspaperman to visit the fields, take copious notes and pick up any unstaked claims that might be lying about handy, and then Mark would ghostwrite a book that would knock the public eye out. Bliss agreed; Mark chose J. H. Riley, a newspaper friend of his Washington days, as the agent. The end was a grotesque anticlimax. Riley duly made the trip and collected his notes, but on the trip home managed to stab himself with a fork, and died of blood poisoning with the book unwritten.

Even Mark's incidental writing had suffered during the long period of strain. When his year's contract with the *Galaxy* was fulfilled he mentioned in his farewell item that doctors and watchers of the sick had been his daily and nightly companions for eight months. "I think that some of the 'humor' I have written during this period could have been injected into a funeral sermon without disturbing the solemnity of the occasion." But he had done worse than write dully or forcedly. He had on one occasion lost his sense of humor completely in allowing an item, which had been intended to pull the public leg, to be turned into a pull on his own. The *Saturday Review* of London had reviewed the *Innocents* in a rather heavy and condescending British style, which led an American paper to remark that the *Saturday Review* hadn't known that the book was meant to be funny. Without looking up the review to verify the charge, which was false, Mark had proceeded to concoct a burlesque of what he thought an utterly humorless Englishman might have written, which he offered to his readers as the genuine article. But the hoax backfired when some of the newspapers asserted that the review was really humorous, and that Mark had been too dull to realize the fact. When he made the fatal mistake of trying to explain his own joke he naturally laid himself open to further jesting, at which he lost his temper. The experience, however, cured him—almost—of practical joking in print, though he signalized the cure by launching the most successful of all his hoaxes, the expanded and glorified versions of his *Enterprise* yarns.

When at last he was free of the *Express,* where he took a $10,-000 loss in selling out, had closed out the "Memoranda," and had seen Livy and Langdon reviving in the sunshine at Quarry Farm, he returned to his work on the Western book, as yet untitled. Even at the start, in the previous July, he had found that his always erratic memory had failed him. He could remember scarcely any details of the Overland trip; not until Orion sent his own journal did his brother begin to recall the incidents which he worked up into some of the most striking chapters of the book. When he resumed work at Elmira he found it hard to get the right tone again. He told Orion, who for the moment was editing the *Publisher* magazine for Bliss, that "right in the first chapter I have got to alter the whole style of one of my characters and rewrite him clear through to where I am now. It is no fool of a job, I can tell you, but the book will be greatly bettered by it." The only two characters who appear in the first chapter, and continue to appear, are the author himself and Orion. Obviously, then, Orion was the character who was rewritten; Mark Twain had probably begun by ridiculing his brother, and had thought better of it. He should have. His lifelong tendency to make cutting fun of his gentle, honorable but ineffective brother was one of his least admirable traits. Nevertheless, he was profoundly discouraged with the whole book when Joe Goodman, early in the spring, came to Elmira on a visit. Goodman read, and applauded, and his praise bounced Mark back to the heights again, even to the point of offering Goodman a salary to stay until the book was finished.

By the middle of May he was able to report to Bliss that he was two-thirds done, and so engrossed in his work that he couldn't bear to stop even for a trip to Hartford to consult on the canvassers' prospectus. "When I get it done I want to see the man who will begin to read it and not finish it. If it falls short of the *Innocents* in any respect I shall lose my guess. Nothing grieves me now, nothing troubles me, nothing bothers me or gets my attention. I don't think of anything but the book, and I don't have an hour's unhappiness about anything and don't care two cents whether school keeps or not. It will be a bully book." And he was turning out two hundred or more manuscript pages a week—the equivalent of about 15,000 words.

But the finances he had ciphered down to a fraction when he settled in Buffalo were badly tangled again. Besides the enormous expenses of Livy's illness and the loss he had taken in selling out of the *Express,* he needed money for moving and setting up a new home. Once more he turned to James Redpath and the lecturing he had forsworn. During July he worked on a new lecture, and kept Redpath aquiver with constantly changing instructions about places and dates. "I am different from other women," he told the agent; "my mind changes oftener. People who have no mind can easily be steadfast and firm, but when a man is loaded down to the guards with it, as I am, every heavy sea of foreboding or inclination, maybe of indolence, shifts the cargo. . . . You must try to keep the run of my mind, Redpath, it is your business being the agent, and it always was too many for me." Among the places where he refused to lecture was Buffalo; he had few happy memories of that place.

He had now definitely decided upon Hartford as his home, and early in August was there looking for a house. He rented one on Forest Street from his friends the Hookers. It was pleasantly situated, with the promise of congenial society at hand, for among the near neighbors were Harriet Beecher Stowe and Charles Dudley Warner, six years Mark's senior, who looked "like a Western Reserve Yank," but was editor and part owner of the Hartford *Courant* and the author of some mildly humorous essays. Thanks to a substantial advance from Redpath, the Clemens family were able to move to the new home the first of

October, but for the next four months Mark Twain was there only for brief visits in the intervals of his lecturing.

All his former dislike of the huggermugger of travel quickly revived, and was only momentarily tempered by the fun he had with Nasby, Josh Billings, and other lecturers when the New England portions of their itineraries made it possible for the "talent" to forgather in Redpath's offices in Boston. Dissatisfied with his first lecture, "Reminiscences of Some Pleasant Characters I Have Met," he scrapped it in favor of one on Artemus Ward, and dropped that in turn to fill out the rest of his engagements with episodes from *Roughing It*. When the tour finally closed in February he told Redpath, "If I had another engagement I would rot before I would fill it." He had paid off all his debts, the advance sales of his new book had outdone those of the *Innocents*, and he confidently expected to be thenceforward a writer, and nothing but a writer.

Roughing It was published in February, and its sales were gratifying, though in the long run they failed to equal those of the *Innocents*, which, as its author told Howells, "sold right along just like the Bible." From the literary side, however, the new book marked an advance over its predecessor. Though large sections of it—the Overland journey, the factual descriptions of the mines, the Hawaiian tour—were more or less straight reporting, humorously colored, the book as a whole is nearer to picaresque fiction than to history. In it Mark Twain took his first tentative steps toward really creative writing, heightening and dramatizing episodes out of all resemblance to what really happened, and inventing freely when the needs of the story required it. In this book, too, the dramatic personality of Mark Twain, as distinct from Samuel Clemens, was for the first time fully defined in print—the guileless easy mark who got his surest laughs by Irvin S. Cobb's formula of showing himself as one of the prize asses of the asinine human race. The full possibilities of his own experiences as material for fiction had not yet dawned upon him, but he had ceased to be just a journalistic observer comically reporting the passing show.

But the shadow which had darkened them in Buffalo was not long in falling upon the new home in Hartford. In March 1872 the Clemenses returned to Elmira for a visit, and there, on March 19, Olivia Susan Clemens was born. She was a healthy, full-term baby, and Livy made a better recovery than she had after Langdon's birth. A few weeks later, however, little Langdon, whose hold on life was still feeble, caught cold, the cold proved to be diphtheria, and in the early summer the child died. "I killed him," said Clemens to Howells, with his usual bitter self-blame, for he had taken the child for a drive before the illness developed and, falling into one of his blank day-dreams, had not noticed that the carriage robe had slipped aside and exposed the baby to the chilly air. It added one more burden to the load of self-reproach he never ceased to gather until he found peace in the grave, but there is no hint that his wife reproached him, though the loss cut her to the heart, and she wrote, "I feel so often as if my path is to be lined with graves."

Yet his resilient spirit soon rallied, or else plunged into new activity to drown thought. The doctors having prescribed sea air for Olivia and the baby, they spent the summer at Saybrook, on Long Island Sound, instead of at Elmira. He invented and patented the Mark Twain Scrapbook, its pages coated with strips of dry adhesive to obviate the need of mussing about with a paste pot. Dan Slote of the *Quaker City* was a commercial stationer in New York, and Mark put the scrapbook in his hands to market. For a number of years it paid its inventor as large an income as he ever received from a newspaper, but in the end it brought estrangement between him and Dan. Sooner or later, Mark Twain's business relationships usually led to hostilities.

It may possibly have been at Saybrook that he resumed work on an idea that had been in his mind since the honeymoon days in Buffalo. In 1867 he had confessed to Will Bowen that almost all recollections of their Hannibal school days had faded from his treacherous memory. A couple of years later Bowen wrote a letter which, Mark said, stirred him to the bottom. "The fountains of my great deep are broken up and I have rained reminiscences for four and twenty hours. The old life has swept before me like a panorama; the old days have trooped by in their old glory again; the old faces have looked out of the mists of the past"—and he went on to detail boyhood adventures which are now known to millions of readers. The first assay of the new literary lode was in the form of a boy's diary, clumsily done but containing the germs of some immortal scenes. According to Paine—Mr. DeVoto questions the assertion—a dramatic version preceded the *Tom Sawyer* we know. Certainly the opening pages of the book seem to preserve vestiges of the dramatic form, with Aunt Polly's soliloquy as sufficient proof of Mark's inability to contrive good theater. But if he worked on Tom at Saybrook, it was not for long. On August 21 he sailed for England.

His determination to depend upon his books for his livelihood had awakened him to the value and importance of international copyright. It was an age of rugged individualism in which no author had any rights which a foreign publisher was bound to respect. American publishers were bigger pirates than English publishers, but only because they found more books that were worth stealing. To balance matters, however, English authors, especially Charles Dickens, were the more vocal in their protests. The English law, to be sure, contained one helpful provision not duplicated in this country; it granted British copyright to any book first published in the British dominions, regardless of the author's nationality. When *The Innocents Abroad* was published it was promptly reprinted, without royalties to the author, by John Camden Hotten, one of the most active of the London pirates. Its success encouraged Hotten also to issue Mark Twain's *Sketches,* which he expanded by including fugitive pieces from the Buffalo *Express* and elsewhere, of which Mark denied the authorship.

When *Roughing It* was ready Bliss and Mark Twain decided to attempt to copyright it overseas, and accordingly arranged to send advance sheets to the house of Routledge. There was a slight irony in their choice, for Routledge in the past had not been too scrupulous about getting permission from American authors before reprinting their works. It was, however, a strong and well-established firm, and though there was a technical flaw in the copyright, because Mark Twain had not been resident in the British dominions at the time the book appeared, Hotten did not venture to challenge them to a showdown. Mark Twain's avowed purpose in going to England was to see the Routledges and arrange for the protection of his future work. Another purpose, not avowed, was to gather material for a travel book about England.

London in 1872 was in a cordial mood toward American writers, especially the wilder and woolier ones. Artemus Ward's lectures in 1867 were still affectionately remembered; a couple of years before Mark Twain's visit Joaquin Miller, riding the wave of Bret Harte's popularity, had charmed the city by parading in the high boots, flannel shirt, and slouch hat of a California miner, though his actual connection with the mines was as tenuous as Buffalo Bill's with the Indian wars. By much the same process of reasoning which still leads the English to believe that only the possessor of a raucous voice is a typical American, they concluded that these wild men were typical American authors, and took them to their hearts. When they learned that Mark Twain was in London they confidently expected more of the same—perhaps something like the self-styled Byron of the Pacific Slope, who rimed "Goethe" with "teeth"— but were swept off their feet by what they really got.

From the day when a luncheon with the Routledges stretched on into a dinner, and then into an evening at the Savage Club, Mark Twain was the belle of London, as twenty years later he was called the belle of New York. Celebrities jostled each other in attempts to call on him; the roster of the friends and acquaintances he made during this London visit and the next reads like the index to the Dictionary of National Biography; Henry M. Stanley, Charles Kingsley, Charles Reade, Henry Irving, Herbert Spencer, Tom Hughes, William Black, Anthony Trollope, Robert Browning were among the literary visitors. He was a guest at the House of Commons; he was a guest at a Lord Mayor's dinner at the Guildhall. George Dolby, the manager of Dickens' last reading tours, looked him up and urged him to lecture. He received the final British accolade by being quoted and punned upon in *Punch.*

His onslaught in the columns of the *Spectator* upon John Camden Hotten did nothing to abate English interest in him. He began by disavowing any intent to protest against Hotten's piracy: "publishers are not accountable to the laws of heaven or earth in any country, as I understand it." What he really objected to, he insisted, was Hotten's expansion of the *Sketches* with spurious items which he pretended to believe were written by the publisher himself. "And, further, suppose that in the kindness of his heart and the exuberance of his untaught fancy, this thoroughly well-meaning innocent should expunge the modest title which you had given your book, and replace it with so foul an invention as this, 'Screamers and Eye-Openers,' and went and got *that* copyrighted, too. And suppose that on top of all this, he continually and persistently forgot to offer you a single penny or even send you a copy of your mutilated book to burn. Let one suppose all this. Let him suppose it with strength enough and then he will know something about woe. Sometimes when I read one of those additional chapters constructed by John Camden Hotten, I feel as if I wanted to take a broomstraw and go and knock that man's brains out. Not in anger, for I feel none. Oh! not in anger, but only to see, that is all. Mere idle curiosity." Hotten had asserted that "Carl Byng," the name of a contributor to the Buffalo *Express,* was one of Mark's pen names. "How would this sinful aborigine feel if I were to call him John Camden Hottentot, and come right out in the papers and say he was entitled to it by divine right? I do honestly believe it would throw him into a brain fever, if there were not an insuperable obstacle in the way." And Mark closed his letter by stating that Routledge was the only English publisher who paid him any copyright, "and therefore, if my books are to disseminate either suffering or crime among readers of our language, I would ever so much rather they did it through that house, and then I could contemplate the spectacle calmly as the dividends came in."

The sinful aborigine attempted to reply, but inasmuch as he could not deny the real point at issue his protest came off lamely. He asserted that the "Carl Byng" sketches had been generally circulated in America as Mark Twain's "without a single denial appearing." Actually, Mark's correspondence with Thomas Bailey Aldrich had been opened, a year and a half before, with a heated denial, in Aldrich's *Every Saturday*, of the authorship of one of "Carl Byng's" contributions to the *Express*. The *Spectator* letter doubtless helped establish the future security of Mark's English copyrights. Few publishers, however bold or greedy, would care to expose themselves to a repetition of the attack on John Camden Hottentot.

For the moment Mark resisted Dolby's offers, though he made tentative arrangements to return and lecture the following year. He spoke several times, however, at dinners in his honor, and always with applause and laughter. To find himself taken seriously as a man of letters, the friend and equal of distinguished writers, was a heady experience which he did not minimize in his letters home. But the social life played havoc with his plans for a book, though his hosts were assiduous in showing him the sights, even to the point of arranging such unusual privileges as a midnight visit to Westminster Abbey. The book about England was never written, but probably only in part for the reason commonly alleged, that "he could not write entertainingly of England without introducing too many personalities and running the risk of offending those who had taken him to their hearts and homes." His after-dinner speeches and his conversations had shown him that the English were well able to take, and enjoy, good-natured raillery at their own expense. Plenty of episodes, like the Shah's visit to England in the following summer, were ready material for burlesque which hurt no one's feelings. A deeper trouble was probably that his experience in England was too static. It centered in London. The peripatetic framework of his other travel books, past and future, was lacking; without it, he could not unravel the tangled skein of his impressions into a consecutive narrative. The charm of the English people and the English countryside had taken hold of him, but he could have written humorously and yet admiringly of England, as he had of France, had the itinerant pattern been present for him to work from.

Even in the midst of his triumphs, however, he grew homesick, and when Livy vetoed a suggestion that she and Susy join him in England—a November crossing of the North Atlantic is no treat for a semi-invalid mother and a baby—he determined to come home and make plans for a longer visit, with his wife and child, the following year. He reached New York in November, laden with gifts for all his family and friends, and considerably taller in his own estimation than he had been three months before. England's treatment of him had been very different from New England's.

In proportion as Boston and Cambridge people thought themselves refined—so Howells summed it up—they questioned that quality which all recognize in Mark Twain now, but which was then the inspired knowledge of the simplehearted multitude. Longfellow made little of him, and Lowell less. Bret Harte these literati accepted, in spite of rudeness which suggested deliberation, as Mark Twain's seldom did; the only Cambridge pundits who wholeheartedly liked the humorist were the internationalized Francis J. Child and Charles Eliot Norton. In Boston the men of letters who immediately became his friends were Howells and Aldrich, and they, as the latter admitted, were only Boston-plated. But when Aldrich, one evening in the winter before Mark went to England, undertook to bring his friend home for dinner, trouble followed.

Mrs. Aldrich discovered her husband accompanied by a man in a long sealskin overcoat, and a sealskin cap which half concealed his shock of reddish-brown hair. Below the coat were yellowish-brown trousers and socks, and low black shoes. The man was obviously drunk, for he "showed marked inability to stand perpendicular, but swayed from side to side, and had also difficulty with his speech; he did not stammer exactly, but after each word he placed a period. His sentences were whimsical, and host and guest laughed loudly, with and at each other." Mrs. Aldrich was horrified at her husband's bringing such a man to meet her. The usual dinner hour came and passed, while the lady froze into stiffer and stiffer disapproval, and could bring herself neither to announce the meal nor ask this impossible being to share it. Not until after the unwanted stranger had at last taken the prolonged hint and departed unfed did Mrs. Aldrich learn who he was, and what she had done. What she had taken for intoxication was merely his natural manner. But neither she nor Mark Twain ever forgot that first meeting.

Nevertheless, some of high-brow America's myopia is understandable. Boston swallowed Bret Harte's rudeness, as it swallowed Matthew Arnold's, because it was expressed against a background of formal manners such as they understood, whereas Mark Twain's courtesy had a basic informality which was outside their experience. In his writing, moreover, these academicians saw first the residuum of the familiar, and subliterary, tradition of popular newspaper humor, and failed to realize how completely, even thus early in his career, he transcended the tradition. Because the English did not know the matrix, they found it easier to recognize the new birth. But for Mark Twain the English tour must have removed any doubts that still lingered as to his literary vocation. Undoubtedly it encouraged him to try the next step, of writing fiction.

CHAPTER X

ℕOVELS

A COMPLETE list of the books which authors' wives have prodded them into writing has never been compiled, but it would be long and variegated. A month or two after Mark's return from England his wife, and Charlie Warner's, plagiarized the scene which half a century earlier had launched Fenimore Cooper upon his literary career. One evening when the Warners came to dinner conversation turned upon some current novels which the wives had been enjoying. The husbands were scornful and captious, whereupon the situation developed with the inexorable logic of domestic syllogism. The wives wanted to know why, if the men disliked these books so much, they didn't write some better ones themselves. The men retorted, all right, they would, and then and there began to plan a novel to be written jointly. At intervals for years to come, Mark would plan collaborations with Howells and other friends, but this was the only joint enterprise ever carried through to completion.

Mark's approach to narrative writing, as has been mentioned, was curiously slow and timid. As early as 1868, on his return trip from California, he had sketched out an adventure story in which a French convict succeeded in escaping in a free balloon, to be picked up in a starving condition on the Illinois prairies twelve days later. (He returned to this fancy after a quarter-century in *Tom Sawyer Abroad*.) But the appearance of Jules Verne's *Five Weeks in a Balloon* made him abandon his plan, and if he had other story ideas during the next four years he had not tried to work them out. He had begun to think, however, that his family's long ordeal of deferred hope in the Tennessee land contained the material for a novel. He had never been in Jamestown, and had never seen the land, but he had heard too much about the place from his mother and Orion to have any doubts about his ability to portray the locale. He started at once, and before the first enthusiasm for the project waned turned out eleven chapters of *The Gilded Age*. Then Warner took over, and did twelve more chapters, in a similar burst of speed and enthusiasm. From that point on, their alternations were briefer, but the division of labor held fairly even. When the book was finished, Mark Twain had written thirty-two chapters out of sixty-three, and had shared three others with Warner. When it came to the closing chapters, each collaborator wrote his own version independently, both versions were read aloud to the council of wives, and their vote decided which should go into the book.

Looking back on the composition, Mark realized that it had been done "in the superstition that we were writing one coherent yarn, when I suppose, as a matter of fact, we were writing two *in*coherent ones." They had set out to write a comprehensive satire on the speculative fever and corrupt politics of the Grant administration during the postwar boom which collapsed in the panic of 1873 shortly before the book was published. But they were working in the heyday of Wilkie Collins, Sheridan Le-Fanu, and Mrs. Henry Wood—the day of the Three-Decker, with its crew of Missing Heirs who had "shipped as Able Bastards, till the Wicked Nurse confessed." In other words, these cavilers at the contemporary popular novel, when they began to plan one of their own, were wholly unable to free their minds from the stock pattern of stock Victorian fiction. Their social satire was to be expressed within the frame of such a plot as authors and readers alike were accustomed to.

Their underlying idea had a certain grandeur: to show how the speculative fever united the destinies and warped the lives of all sorts and conditions of men. It was a concept as valid and as spacious as the Chancery theme with which Dickens united the diverse groups who crowd the pages of *Bleak House*. But even Dickens achieved that coherence about a large central theme only the once, and neither Warner nor Mark Twain had Dickens' instinctive plot sense. They failed, because they had so much plot that it kept getting in the way of the theme, because they maltreated their characters to serve their plot, and because in their satire they lacked a sense of proportion and scattered their fire.

Mark's opening chapters are the best in the book. The picture of Obedstown, Tennessee, ranks high among his vivid portrayals of primitive communities; some of the river episodes anticipate the best chapters in *Life on the Mississippi*. The initial situation closely follows the actual history of the Clemens family's exodus to Missouri, and Colonel Sellers is a direct transcript of Uncle James Lampton. "The incidents which looked most extravagant . . . were not inventions of mine, but were facts of his life; and I was present when they were developed. . . . In fact, I was myself the guest who ate the turnips." That, indeed, is what ails Colonel Sellers as a character. "Truth," said Pudd'nhead Wilson, "is stranger than fiction, because fiction is obliged to stick to possibilities; truth isn't." James Lampton was a truth, but he was so improbable a truth that it is almost impossible to believe in him when he appears in a novel. But not content with the Tennessee land as a motive for daydreams and speculative frenzy, Mark also brought in the Salt River Navigation project, and started two themes of the Three-Decker on their way. First the Hawkinses adopted the orphan boy, Clay: the obvious intent was that this adopted child should become the stay of the family while their own son, Washington, wasted his time in dreams. Next they adopted the little girl Laura, left a waif after the steamboat explosion: she was booked as the Missing Heiress.

Then Warner began piling in his share of the plot, with Harry Brierly, Philip Sterling and the Bolton family. Again the unfulfilled purpose is evident. Philip and Harry were to point the old moral of the idle versus the industrious apprentice; Mr. Bolton was to illustrate the plight of the honest and benevolent man ruined by speculators simply because he was too honest to recognize cheats and too benevolent to refuse to endorse their notes. Ruth Bolton was to be Romola or Amelia in contrast to Laura Hawkins as Becky Sharp or Tessa. Once more the attempt was a failure, for Warner proved fully as incompetent as Mark Twain when it came to keeping subsidiary themes in motion. In order to create the Laura-Ruth contrast he had to begin by laying violent hands on Laura. Her seduction by Colonel Selby is supposed to motivate her change from an ambitious and thoughtful girl to a hard, calculating, revengeful woman. Thackeray might have made the change convincing; Tolstoi would have; Warner funked the job, and so far as making the reader believe in the change is concerned, his *scène à faire* might as well have been wholly off-stage, like the one in *Mourning Becomes Electra,* as the three-quarters off which he made it.

In the politics of the Grant era, when speculators and Congressmen vied with each other in converting public trusts to very private uses, a major theme for the social satirist lay ready. Both authors were equipped to handle it: Clemens by his months of experience as a Washington correspondent, Warner by the knowledge of the underside of politics which a newspaper editor cannot help acquiring. As a model for Senator Dilworthy they had Samuel C. Pomeroy of Kansas, who had recently failed of re-election because of vote-buying so flagrant and fragrant as to shock even the hardened nostrils of that postwar era. Simply to picture the tie-up between speculators, lobbyists and politicians—whereby government grants on a huge scale were obtained for the benefit of private individuals and corporations, and even philanthropic projects became the tools of selfish interests—would have driven home the indictment of a specific abuse as effectively as Dickens pilloried the workhouses or the Court of Chancery. But neither author was content to stop there. Mark hawked at everything from Washington society at large to illiterate bookstore clerks; Warner lugged in a railway survey, because he had worked on one himself in Missouri in the '50's, took pot shots at brutal railway employees, and ruined the closing chapters by having Laura shoot Colonel

Selby in order that he might criticize the American jury system and the insanity plea for murderers. In this last, however, Warner was certainly fully abetted by his collaborator, who had originally proposed to dedicate *Roughing It* to the late Cain, who had the misfortune to live in a dark age that knew not the beneficent insanity plea. In short, what might have been a high-powered bullet, piercing to the heart of a corrupt political system, became a charge of birdshot which peppered everything in sight but left no permanent scars. Yet even so, the title of the book has been accepted as the final description of the Grant era.

Both authors, moreover, got so tangled in their superabundant plot that they left unfinished ends hanging out on every side. Mark forgot Clay Hawkins from Chapter IX to Chapter LXI, when he rushed him home from Australia in time to comfort Mrs. Hawkins in her grief for Laura. Warner was as sketchy and unconvincing in depicting the Small-Bigler-Pennybacker speculations which ruined Mr. Bolton as he had been in handling Laura's seduction, failed to carry through whatever idea had originally been intended in Ruth Bolton's medical studies, and dropped his idle apprentice, Harry Brierly, without a word after Laura's acquittal. Even at the time the authors realized some of their shortcomings, and appended a note apologizing for their failure to find Laura's father. Yet with all its weakness the book became a best seller; within two months after publication it sold 40,000 copies, in spite of the panic of 1873.

But when the book was published Mark Twain was in England again. He and Warner had completed their manuscript in April, and early in May Mark, with Livy and Susy, departed for the longer visit which he had promised himself in the previous year. Before sailing they had commissioned Edward Potter to build them a house on the pleasant lot they had bought on Farmington Avenue—the house which became the scene and symbol of the happiest years of their lives. But there was business as well as pleasure in the trip. Mark had decided not to risk again the technical flaw in the English copyright of *Roughing It,* and planned to remain in England until *The Gilded Age* could be published there. And George Dolby's bait of lecture engagements in London was still on the hook, and this time Mark was ready to bite.

The first weeks in London were more like a royal levee than a pleasure trip. More literary celebrities were added to the previous list, and new acquaintances included Lord Houghton, Millais, Lewis Carroll, Sir Charles Dilke, and sufficient people of title to make a quorum at the House of Lords. Mark loved every minute of the homage and the luncheons and dinners, but before long the strain began to wear Livy down. After a couple of months Mark realized that if his wife was to have any peace and rest they would have to get out of London. They set out for the north, breaking their journey with a quiet visit to York. In Edinburgh, where they meant to live incognito, Livy broke down completely, but the illness brought them one of the pleasantest friendships of their lives. The physician they summoned was Dr. John Brown, author of *Rab and His Friends,* and what started as a professional relationship immediately turned into a personal one. The doctor romped with eighteen-months-old Susy, and frequently took the whole family with him in his carriage while he made his professional rounds. Though they never met again, they continued to correspond as long as the doctor lived, and when he died they mourned him as one of their own family.

The quiet month in Edinburgh restored Livy to the point where she was able to tour Ireland, make a country-house visit near Shrewsbury, and spend a fortnight in Paris. In London again, at the end of September, the social activity resumed, but Livy, though better in health, was thoroughly homesick, and the thought that they might have to stay at least another month on account of lectures and copyright was too much. Finally it was settled that Mark should give a week of lectures in London in mid-October and then take his family home. As soon as they were settled, he would return to perfect his copyright and resume his lecturing in the height of the London season. The first week of lectures was such an overwhelming success that even without the needs of copyright Mark would undoubtedly have returned to London. He sailed from Liverpool on October 21, saw Livy and the baby safe to Hartford, and was back in England again within a month. For his first lectures he had used the old Sandwich Islands script; now he shifted to *Roughing It,* and for two months filled the Hanover Square Rooms with Londoners who had never turned out with such sustained enthusiasm for any performance since Dickens had given his last public readings in those same rooms. George Dolby knew a good property when he saw one.

Back in America at the end of January, 1874, he succumbed briefly to the lures of James Redpath, and lectured several times in New England and New York. The new house, like all new houses, was costing more than the owners had expected, but despite the current depression the Clemenses had plenty of money. Mark's books kept on selling, and Livy's share of her father's estate—chiefly Pennsylvania coal-mining properties—was at this time worth nearly a quarter of a million. Their Hartford living had already assumed the lavish scale which marked it for the next fifteen years; they had so much company and so many activities that Mark found it almost impossible to do any literary work during the winters. Guests were constantly arriving and departing, but among them none was so welcome as William Dean Howells. The acquaintance first made in Fields' office at the end of 1869 had ripened into friendship, and in 1872 the two had begun the long correspondence which lasted the rest of Mark's life. Yet there always remained a touch of formality in their relationship: they were always "Clemens" and "Howells" with each other, whereas Clemens and Twichell were "Joe" and "Mark."

In April the family went to Quarry Farm, where in June Clara Clemens was born. Sue Crane had built her brother-in-law an outdoor study on a knoll far enough from the house to be completely quiet, and there Mark plunged into work, pausing only to gaze out over the Chemung valley and the ranges of hills beyond. The first work of the summer to reach the public was a dramatic version of *The Gilded Age*. This was forced upon him in May by the news that a popular actor, John T. Raymond, was producing in San Francisco a play founded on the novel. Mark and Warner had been foresighted enough to reserve the dramatic copyright, and immediately put a stop to the unauthorized performance, but after correspondence with Raymond, Mark agreed to prepare his own version—founded, it may be presumed, in spite of denials, upon the scenario which Gilbert Densmore had prepared for Raymond—and give Raymond the stage rights. Since Mark never succeeded by himself in writing an actable play, the supposition is reasonable that *The Gilded Age* in the theater owed its success to Raymond's stage sense. Even so, it was not a good play, though Raymond, playing Sellers as a low comedy part, made it a profitable one. But Howells' contemporary criticism, that Raymond debased the character, supports what Mark said about the actor in the *Autobiography:*

"The real Colonel Sellers was never on the stage. Only half of him was there. Raymond could not play the other half of him; it was above his level. That half was made up of qualities of which Raymond was destitute. For Raymond was not a manly man, he was not an honorable man nor an honest one, he was empty and selfish and vulgar and ignorant and silly, and there was a vacancy in him where his heart should have been."

Another incident of the summer gave Mark his first entry into the literary Valhalla of Americans in the later nineteenth century, the *Atlantic Monthly*. The servants at Quarry Farm were Negroes—John Lewis and his wife, the tenants who worked the farm, and Auntie Cord, the cook. Auntie Cord had been a slave in the prewar South; had been twice sold herself, and had had her children sold away from her. One evening she told the story of her life in Mark's presence, and the result was the little sketch which he called "A True Story," and which Howells delightedly accepted for the *Atlantic*. "I have not altered the old colored woman's story," Mark told the editor, "except to begin at the beginning, instead of the middle, as she did—and traveled both ways." His keen ear for dialect served him well in transcribing the Negro speech, and when it came time to read proofs he explained to Howells how he handled it: "I amend dialect stuff by talking and talking and *talking* it till it sounds right."

But his most effective work that summer was put into *Tom Sawyer*. What had started, abortively, first as a diary and then perhaps as a play he now took up as a story. The atmosphere and incidents of his Hannibal boyhood came crowding back to his memory as he wrote; he had only to set them down. In this, his first single-handed attempt at full-length narrative, he perfectly illustrated Howells' comment that "he was not enslaved to the consecutiveness in writing which the rest of us try to keep chained to. That is, he wrote as he thought, and as all men think, without sequence, without an eye to what went before or should come after. If something beyond or beside what he was saying occurred to him, he invited it into his page, and made it as much at home there as the nature of it would suffer him." *Tom Sawyer* violated every rule, past, present or future, of the "art novel." For Mark, nothing mattered except the effectiveness of the episode that was in his mind at the moment. By all the rules of art, for instance, the new boy, Alfred Temple, with whom Tom fought in the first chapter, ought thereafter to play a leading role in the book. Actually, he never again appeared in a major part, and only briefly in a minor one. When, at the close of the third chapter, Mark realized that his narrative required an older girl to fill the role which Pamela had taken in his own family, Tom's "cousin Mary danced in, all alive with the joy of seeing home again after an age-long visit of one week in the country." Mark hadn't needed her before, so naturally he hadn't thought of mentioning her membership in the household, any more than he thought of mentioning Huck Finn until he, in turn, was needed three chapters further along. The only thing in the book approaching a conventional plot was furnished by Injun Joe, and even the Injun Joe episodes were separated by long sections which had no connection with them. In fact, it took Tom's unprepared-for impulse to seek buried treasure to bring Injun Joe back into the story at all, and the half-breed's intended vengeance upon Widow Douglas was not built up to by the slightest hint earlier in the book. *Tom Sawyer,* in short, grew as grows the grass; it was not art at all, but it was life.

Its growth, however, was not completed in 1874. After driving along for weeks, with as many as fifty manuscript pages a day sometimes, Mark found at the beginning of September that his invention had run dry. Following what came to be his usual custom, he laid the manuscript aside to wait until he was again in the vein. Bliss wanted a new book for 1875, but with *Tom Sawyer* still incomplete he had to be content with the volume of miscellanies, *Sketches New and Old.*

Part of the mental block which made Mark lay *Tom Sawyer* aside may have been due to the aftereffects of an unpleasantness in August. He and Livy had gone to visit Jane Clemens and Pamela, who were still living in Fredonia, where they had settled when Mark was in Buffalo. The weather was hot; the trip prostrated Livy; Mark's temper flamed. A local banker, a friend of his mother's, came to call, and bored Mark, who apparently delivered himself of such a tirade that all present were staggered. By the time he got back to Elmira he was ashamed of himself: "I began to comprehend how much harm my conduct might do you socially in your village. I would have gone to that detestable oyster-brained bore and apologized for my inexcusable rudeness to him, but that I was satisfied he was of too small a calibre to know how to receive an apology with magnanimity." He even proposed that his mother and sister seek a home elsewhere, but the storm blew over, and Jane Clemens remained another decade in Fredonia before she went to spend her last years with Orion in Keokuk.

Their new house in Hartford was almost finished, and they were eager to be settled, but Livy's Elmira physician, observing the state in which she had returned from Fredonia, ordered her to rest for a month, so that it was nearly the first of October before they reached Hartford. Even then the new house was still full of workmen, and Mark was "bullyragged all day by the builder, by his foreman, by the architect, by the tapestry devil who is to upholster the furniture, by the idiot who is putting down the carpets, by the scoundrel who is setting up the billiard table (and has left the balls in New York), by the wildcat who is sodding the ground and finishing the driveway . . . by a book agent, whose body is in the back yard and the coroner notified." It was not an atmosphere conducive to literary work, and a request from Howells that Mark write something to start off the 1875 volume of the *Atlantic* brought the response, "It's no use—I find I can't. We are in such a state of weary and endless confusion that my head won't go."

He sent off that letter on the morning of October 24. In the evening he wrote another:

"Twichell and I have had a long walk in the woods, and I got to telling him about old Mississippi days of steamboating glory and grandeur as I saw them (during five years) from the pilot-house. He said 'What a virgin subject to hurl into a magazine!' I hadn't thought of that before. Would you like a series of papers to run through 3 months or 6 or 9?"

Howells, like Twichell and George Dolby, knew a good thing when he saw it. The result of the suggestion was a series of seven papers, which now form Chapters IV-XVII of *Life on the Mississippi.* Though Mark, as always, was humble before Howells' literary judgment, and authorized him to "cut it, scarify it, reject it—handle it with entire freedom," he was not afraid of the *Atlantic* audience, as Howells thought he was, or should be.

"It isn't the Atlantic audience that distresses me; for *it* is the only audience that I sit down before in perfect serenity (for the simple reason that it doesn't require a 'humorist' to paint himself striped and stand on his head every fifteen minutes). The trouble was, that I was only bent on 'working up an atmosphere' and that is to me a most fidgety and irksome thing, sometimes. I avoid it, usually, but in this case it was absolutely necessary, else every reader would be applying the atmosphere of his own [land] or sea experiences, and *that* shirt wouldn't fit, you know."

By this time, after family visits on both sides, the family humor of the Howells-Clemens correspondence was fully established, to bewilder earnest-minded readers of a later generation. Since both men were unusually happily married, it became a stock joke for both to pretend that their wives were termagants. In the very letter just quoted, Mark reported: "My wife was afraid to write you—so I said with simplicity, '*I* will give you the language—and ideas.' Through the infinite grace of God there has not been such another insurrection in the family before as followed this." Or, apropos of something in the "Old Times on the Mississippi" papers, Livy "lit into the study with danger in her eye and this demand on her tongue: 'Where is the profanity Mr. Howells speaks of?' Then I had to miserably confess that I had left it out when reading the MSS. to her. Nothing but almost inspired lying got me out of this scrape with my scalp. Does your wife give you rats, like this, when you go a little one-sided?" And Howells, before long, would be declaring that Mrs. Howells had charge of his sense of decency, and wishing that "she didn't brag so about her superior management of it," or reporting that "none but the pitying angels will ever know what Mrs. Howells said to me when she got me out of doors. She began by saying that I was always very lenient to *her* when she committed a blunder, and so she was not going to be hard on me. But I think the enormity of my crime must have grown upon her as she painted it to me. At any rate, I never wish to be *spared* again." People with unhappy homes do not write about them like this.

Howells and Aldrich delighted Livy by abetting her efforts to civilize Mark's attire. Despite his sealskin overcoat, and other lavish clothing, Mark still clung to the black "string" tie of his western days. His friends found it hard to bear, and each presented him with a conventional cravat. Mark reported that they had made Livy deeply and sincerely grateful. "For months—I may even say years—she had shown unaccountable animosity toward my necktie, even getting up in the night to take it with the tongs and blackguard it—sometimes also going so far as to threaten it. When I said you and Aldrich had given me two *new* neckties, and that they were in a paper in my overcoat pocket, she was in a fever of happiness until she found I was going to frame them; then all the venom in her nature gathered itself together,—insomuch that I, being near to a door, went without, perceiving danger. Now I wear one of the new neckties. . . ."

It was evidence of the delight Mark found in recalling old days on the river that he kept at the series of articles throughout the winter in Hartford. Above the library mantel in his new home he had placed Emerson's saying, "The ornament of a house is the friends who frequent it," and his friends entered without knocking, at all hours. As soon as he had settled in Hartford and had got on intimate terms with the Warners and Stowes, he was invited to join the Monday Evening Club, a discussion group which had been founded some years before by Dr. Stowe, Horace Bushnell and, among others, J. Hammond Trumbull, the prodigiously learned man who furnished the polyglot chapter mottoes for *The Gilded Age*. More than half the members were clergymen, whom Mark enjoyed arguing with. "The Facts on the Recent Carnival of Crime in Connecticut" was one of the papers he prepared for the Club, and as a rule he took pleasure in the meetings. But there were bores, even in the Club, and once, when one of these wound up his prosings with the conventional "piety ending," Mark commented that these tiresome damned prayer meetings might better be adjourned to the garret of some church, where they belonged.

As the spring of 1875 came on, Mark returned to the manuscript of *Tom Sawyer*, and found that his zest for the story had returned. The family did not go to Quarry Farm that summer, but despite the handicaps of working in Hartford he had finished the book at the beginning of July. He was anxious for Howells' opinion, and halfheartedly suggested the possibility of serializing the book in the *Atlantic,* though he doubted if such publication would be profitable. At the moment he did not think he had written a boy's book at all. "It will only be read by adults. It is only written for adults." Howells read the manuscript with enthusiasm, but did not agree about the audience that would like it: "I think you ought to treat it explicitly *as* a boy's story. Grown-ups will enjoy it just as much if you do; and if you should put it forth as a study of boy character from the grown-up point of view, you'd give the wrong key to it." Mark agreed, as he always agreed to Howells' criticisms, and accepted his revisions without question. Correcting and revising always irked Mark, so when he sat down "to the dreary and hateful task" he was delighted to find Howells' pencil marks scattered all along. "This was splendid, and swept away all labor. Instead of *reading* the MS., I simply hunted out the pencil marks and made the emendations they suggested. I reduced the boy battle to a curt paragraph; I finally concluded to cut the Sunday school speech down to the first two sentences, leaving no suggestions of satire, since the book is to be for boys and girls; I tamed the various obscenities until I judged that they no longer carried offence."

So much has been made of Howells' "expurgations" that they call for illustration. They were not all aimed at "obscenities." Thus Aunt Polly in her opening soliloquy had originally described Tom as "full of cussedness." Howells queried this, not because it was obscene but because to him it sounded Yankee; Mark substituted "the Old Scratch." At the end of Chapter III Howells wrote, "Don't like this chapter much. The sham fight is too long. Tom is either too old for this, or too young." The result was that Mark struck out fifty lines of manuscript. In the fifth chapter Mark's description of the poodle's antics after sitting down on the pinch bug had included the phrase, "with his tail shut down like a hasp." Howells wrote, "Awfully good but a little too dirty," and out it went. But the most famous correction of all was one which Howells neglected to make. In the closing chapter, Mark had made Huck Finn say of his life at the Widow Douglas', "They comb me all to hell." Finding that Howells had let the phrase stand, Mark's conscience rose up, and he asked if Howells had overlooked the strong word. Howells replied, "I'd have that swearing out in an instant. I suppose I didn't notice it because the locution was so familiar to my Western sense, and so exactly the thing that Huck would say. But it won't do for the children." It was Mark himself, rather than his wife, or Howells, who had the keenest eye and ear for verbal proprieties in print. He had read this chapter, "hell" and all, to Livy and to her mother and her aunt, and they had noticed it no more than Howells had. But in the book Huck was combed all to thunder, and juvenile morals were saved.

Far more has been made of the incident than it deserves. Every generation has its verbal taboos; even in this freer-spoken age, for instance, newspapers seldom use the words "rape" and "abortion." The Victorian age accepted certain conventions of expression, in print, and no doubt mentally made the necessary substitutions when a character in a book swore "by the Eternal," or ejaculated, "Curse you!" Stevenson, writing *Treasure Island,* complained of the hardships involved in depicting unprofane pirates—"Buccaneers without oaths— bricks without straw. But youth and the fond parient have to be consulted." And Mark Twain had no more doubts of the value and necessity of these taboos than he had of the institution of marriage. Before getting upset over the results, critics would do well to reflect that if a few changes in diction could make or ruin a book, it was no good to start with. In judging a writer's freedom of expression, the only fair comparison is with his contemporaries; hence it is with Howells himself, and with Anthony Trollope, not with Dos Passos and Hemingway, that Mark Twain must be compared. As further, unnecessary, proof of the universality of the taboo which Howells invoked, it was John Phoenix who told of the small boy, rebuked for picking his nose, who replied, "It's my nose, and it's Independence Day, and I'll pick thunder out of it." And Phoenix was not married to Olivia Langdon, nor edited by William Dean Howells; he wrote, moreover, for the dominantly male audience of California in the middle '50's.

The dilatoriness of engravers and other publishing delays kept back *Tom Sawyer* until the close of 1876, but when it appeared it was an immediate success with young and old. Within a few months after the English edition appeared, young Robert Louis Stevenson, discoursing on life and death and marriage in the pages of *Temple Bar*, quoted Tom's wish that he could die, temporarily, with the assurance that his readers would recognize the allusion without explanation. In America, Howells, as he had promised, set the sheep jumping in the right places by a laudatory review in the *Atlantic*, though there were stern moralists here and there who thought Tom a bad example to set before the young. It is not every year that a classic is born, and even Howells' closing statement, that Tom Brown and Tom Bailey are the only boys in books deserving to be named along with Tom Sawyer, today seems an understatement. It was Mark Twain's fifth full-length volume, but the first of his books which has stood the test of time as a coherent and appealing whole. He had reached full growth at last, thanks to Sam Clemens' boyhood in Hannibal.

CHAPTER XI

I N T E R R U P T I O N S

1875, which saw the completion of *Tom Sawyer,* was Mark Twain's fortieth year. His friend, John Hay, had said to him, in what must have been a moment of depression, that forty was the culmination of a man's life; he would never be so capable again. Hay was wrong, of course, as to both himself and Mark, but for several years Mark's literary output almost suggested that he was right. The story of the nine years which intervened between the completion of *Tom Sawyer* and the publication of *Huck Finn* at the end of 1884 is a record of abortive undertakings, half-finished manuscripts and second-best output.

In the spring of 1876 Mark succumbed to one of his periods of depression, and poured out his gloom in a long letter to Mrs. Fairbanks, who had written to Mark about the unhappy end of George S. Benedict, her husband's partner on the Cleveland *Herald.* After announcing his conviction that two or three years more would see the end of his ability to do acceptable work, Mark let himself go on meditations suggested by "Mother" Fairbanks' news:

"What a curious thing life is. We delve through years of hardship, wasting toil, despondency; then comes a little butterfly season of wealth, ease, and clustering honors.—Presto! the wife dies, a daughter marries a spendthrift villain, the heir and hope of the house commits suicide, the laurels fade and fall away. Grand result of a hard-fought, successful career and a blameless life: Piles of money, tottering age, and a broken heart. . . . It does seem as if Mr. Benedict's case is about the ordinary experience, and must be fairly expected by everybody. And yet there are people who would try to save a baby's life and plenty of people who cry when a baby dies. In fact, all of us cry, but some are conscious of a deeper feeling of content, at the same time—I am, at any rate. . . . What a booming springtime of life it is for Charley [Langdon]!— Fate has fixed things precisely right for him, to all seeming. I rejoice in his gladness and egg him on in his enthusiasms. Let him go it now when he's young! Never mind about that grisly future season when he shall have made a dazzling success and shall sit with folded hands in well-earned ease and look around upon his corpses and mine, and contemplate his daughters and mine in the mad-house, and his sons and mine gone to the devil. That is all away yonder—we will not bother about it now.

"I believe I haven't anything further of a hilarious nature to communicate. . . ."

The critics who attribute *What Is Man?* and *The Mysterious Stranger* to the disasters of Mark's later years have been too hasty. The black moods were part of his nature, part of the price he paid for his lightheartedness. Later in life, as troubles thickened the moods came oftener, but the troubles did not cause them, they merely intensified them and gave them point. In 1876 the gloom was profound while it lasted, but it was short-lived. Soon the family were at Elmira again for the summer, and Mark had plunged into work on a new book.

In the previous summer he had told Howells that perhaps it had been a mistake not to write *Tom Sawyer* in the first person, and added, "By and by I shall take a boy of twelve and run him on through life (in the first person) but not Tom Sawyer— he would not be a good character for it." This idea was probably still in his mind when he began *Huckleberry Finn*. As usual, the work went swimmingly at first. Then, as usual, came the slump. How far he had gone in his first draft is not on record, but as readers of the early chapters realize, Tom Sawyer is too much with them, and no doubt Mark began to suspect that merely to tell more of Tom's adventures from Huck's literal-minded point of view was thin and ineffective. At any rate, the manuscript was pigeonholed, to wait seven years for completion. For relaxation, Mark turned his attention to other things. He had been rereading Pepys' Diary, and had commenced the reading in the history of Elizabethan England which a year or two later furnished the background for *The Prince and the Pauper*. Well saturated in sixteenth-century turns of speech, he composed, as a letter to Joe Twichell, the *Fireside Conversation in the Time of Queen Elizabeth*—a title later shortened to *1601*. Mark's later story that he had written the sketch for the benefit of a magazine editor who had regretted that modern literature had no Rabelais was fiction. The sentences in his notebook which make the claim are among the many jotted down as parts of unwritten articles. The skit was done in a spirit of good dirty fun for the edification of a few chosen friends, and as such it served its purpose to admiration. Mark and Twichell read and reread it, and laughed themselves lame and sore in a secluded hickory grove. In due time copies found their way round the circle, and John Hay and others connived at private printings. Beyond demonstrating that Mark knew all the short and vulgar words, and had a robust man's pleasure in a tale of bawdry, *1601* is of small importance. It owes most of its fame to its surreptitious circulation.

The only work completed for publication that summer was "The Canvasser's Tale," which Howells took for the *Atlantic*— one of the literary grotesques which struck Mark when he was writing them as being immensely funny, and which sometimes Livy allowed to get past the home wastepaper basket. Back in Hartford in the fall, however, Mark undertook a dramatic collaboration with Bret Harte.

While Mark's star had been rising, Bret's had been sinking. The brilliant Western writer, whose trip from San Francisco to Boston in 1871 had been a triumphal procession, had gone from bad to worse. The *Atlantic Monthly*'s contract to pay ten thousand dollars for twelve contributions was a new high in American magazine fees. But Harte had furnished such mediocre material, and short-weight at that, that the contract had not been renewed. Having failed as a lecturer, Harte undertook

to write a novel, and Mark Twain had interested Bliss in its
publication by subscription. *Scribner's Monthly* paid six thousand dollars for the serial rights of *Gabriel Conroy,* and Bliss,
before the book appeared, had advanced the author the same
sum. But however much money Harte received, he was always
penniless and in debt. He had already tried his hand at a play,
Two Men of Sandy Bar. It had not gone well on the stage, except for the acting of C. T. Parsloe in the part of a Chinese
laundryman. Now Harte conceived what appeared a failure-
proof dramatic scheme. He would write a play for Parsloe with
a Chinese as the central character, thereby cashing in equally on
Parsloe's previous hit and on the popularity of "The Heathen
Chinee." To clinch success, he would get Mark Twain to help.

Whatever the earlier breach between Clemens and Harte
which the former had mentioned to Aldrich in 1871, it had been
healed, temporarily. Mark always remembered warmly the
friends of his Western days, and in this very year had written
a small preface for Dan De Quille's *The Big Bonanza,* a history of the Nevada silver mines, which he had persuaded Bliss
to publish, with profitable results. Moreover, the financial returns from the stage version of *The Gilded Age* had been satisfactory enough to whet his appetite for further dramatic effort.
He realized, however, his weakness in plot construction; Harte,
on the other hand, was technically adept. Accordingly, Mark
welcomed the proposed collaboration, and invited Harte to stay
with him while they wrote the play.

Bret had visited Hartford before, and had borrowed money
from Mark. When he arrived this time he announced that he
had only half finished a story, "Thankful Blossom," which he
had contracted to supply to J. R. Osgood in time for Christmas
publication, and that the manuscript must be in the mail the
next day. He worked all night, with the help of a couple of
bottles of Mark's whisky, and met the deadline. The potboiler
out of the way, the collaborators planned their play. Bret made
the scenario, to which Mark was to contribute certain characters, among them Scotty Briggs of the Buck Fanshaw episode

in *Roughing It*. For a fortnight they worked three or four hours a day, filling in the dialogue in Bret's scenario. The literary result of the visit delighted Mark; other things did not.

Bret had not pleased his host by "delivering himself of sparkling sarcasms about our house, our furniture, and the rest of our domestic arrangements," but Mark stood it until the last day. Then Harte uttered a witticism which seemed aimed at Livy. Whether or not Mark really said all the explosive things he set down in his *Autobiography* is beside the point; unquestionably he said plenty, and Harte never entered his home again. On the business side, however, they did not part company immediately. *Ah Sin* opened in Washington on May 7, 1877, and both authors attended the rehearsals, but before the opening night Mark was taken ill, and had to go home. Though first-nighters applauded cordially, Parsloe realized that the play was weak, especially in the last act. He urged Harte to patch it up, but Bret had gone into a sort of coma, and did nothing. Before opening in New York at the Fifth Avenue Theatre on July 31, Parsloe called additional rehearsals. Mark attended them faithfully for three weeks, but he was incapable of the kind of medication a drooping third act needed. On August 6 he called it, in a letter to Mollie Fairbanks, "that dreadful play of *Ah Sin*," but still had hopes of its success. But midsummer is no season in which to bring a weak play to Broadway. The critics were harsh, and the weather did the rest: *Ah Sin* and August closed together. The play had kept Mark from completely repudiating Harte despite his sarcasms against Livy, and despite a savage letter in March in which Harte accused Bliss of falsifying the royalty accounts of *Gabriel Conroy* in Mark's interest and with Mark's collusion. But when the curtain fell on *Ah Sin* it fell also on the friendship so gaily begun in San Francisco a dozen years before. On subsequent visits to England Mark was visited by many celebrities, but Bret Harte, American consul to Glasgow, was never among them. A fugitive anecdote, too characteristic to be wholly apocryphal, relates that at a literary banquet in Boston a speaker once launched into fulsome eulogy of Harte, concluding by turning to the glowering humorist and saying, "But you know Mr. Harte, don't you, Mr. Clemens?" "Yes," returned Mark in his most venomous drawl, "I *knew* the son of a bitch."

In fact, 1877 seemed a year of almost continuous disaster. The brightest spot in it was an excursion to Bermuda in the latter part of May, with Joe Twichell for company. Mark presumably needed to recuperate from the illness which had taken him away from the Washington opening of *Ah Sin,* but he was not too ill to have a good time. The literary result was a series of four "Rambling Notes on an Idle Excursion," which Howells accepted gladly for the *Atlantic,* thin though they were. Mark was still fascinated by the character of old Captain Ned Wakeman, whom Twichell had also met. He had already tried one or two drafts of the Captain's dream of Heaven— which he kept by him, unpublished, until 1907—and in the Bermuda notes introduced the Captain's exegesis of the story of Elisha and the prophets of Baal. But even with that purple patch, the papers seemed to Mark, when he read the proofs, oppressively and ostentatiously poor—an overstatement, but for once nearer the truth than Howells' commendation.

Summer work at Elmira, as already mentioned, was interrupted by the New York rehearsals of *Ah Sin.* His yearnings toward the theater still unabated by his agony over that unlucky play, Mark tried another drama single-handed. He wanted to call it *Balaam's Ass,* but when Livy objected he changed to *Simon Wheeler, Detective.* Under either, or any, title the play was bad. He wrote it in one prolonged rush of enthusiasm, boasting to Howells that its three hundred manuscript pages had been completed in forty hours of working time. But he had not conquered his perennial inability to contrive a coherent plot; the managers he submitted it to realized that not even Mark Twain's name on the playbills could make it act. Ultimately the manuscript joined the ever-growing collection of discarded or unfinished work in his pigeonholes.

At Elmira, too, he conceived the story for children which

finally took shape as *The Prince and the Pauper,* but during this season got little more than the general idea on paper. On his return to Hartford in the fall, he was elated by an invitation. On December 17, the publishers of the *Atlantic Monthly* were giving a contributors' dinner in honor of Whittier's seventieth birthday. The roster of fifty-odd guests was headed by Emerson, Holmes and Longfellow; Mark was asked to speak. His reputation as an after-dinner speaker was already high, and Howells, making the plans with the publisher, Mr. Houghton, thought he was ensuring a successful program. Mark determined to outdo himself in recognition of the honor. By long observation and slowly compacted experience he had reduced after-dinner speaking to a fine art of which he formulated the principles a few years later. He knew "that the best and most telling speech is not the actual impromptu one, but the counterfeit of it . . . that that speech is most worth listening to which has been carefully prepared in private and tried on a plaster cast, or an empty chair, or any other appreciative object that will keep quiet until the speaker has got his matter and his delivery limbered up so that they will seem impromptu to an audience. . . . A touch of indifferent grammar flung in here and there, apparently at random, has a good effect—often restores the confidence of a suspicious audience. [The speaker] arranges these errors in private; for a really random error wouldn't do any good; it would be sure to fall in the wrong place. He also leaves blanks here and there—leaves them where genuine impromptu remarks can be dropped in, of a sort that will add to the natural aspect of the speech without breaking its line of march."

Now a dazzling idea came to him for one of his favorite climaxes in which he could pretend that his pride went before a fall. He would tell how his use of his pen name caused him to be taken for an impostor. He labored over the speech, building up the situations, and packing sure-fire laughs into every line. In his California days he had, he began, sought a night's shelter in a miner's cabin in the Sierras. The miner received him coldly: "You're the fourth littery man that's been here in twenty-four hours—I'm going to move." Being asked to explain, the miner related how three tramps giving their names as Longfellow, Emerson and Holmes, had invaded the cabin the night before, eaten all his food, drunk all his whisky and played euchre dishonestly most of the night. When they departed Longfellow was wearing the miner's boots, with the avowed intention of using them to leave footprints on the sands of time. Their conversation, as the miner reported it, was studded with distorted quotations from their poems; to bring in the guest of honor, Emerson was alleged to have claimed the authorship of "Barbara Frietchie." Everything was planned to lead up to a surprise ending:

"I said to the miner, 'Why, my dear sir, *these* were not the gracious singers to whom we and the world pay loving reverence and homage; these were impostors.'

"The miner investigated me with a calm eye for a while; then said he, 'Ah! impostors, were they? Are you?' "

It was one of the funniest speeches Mark Twain ever wrote; it can be read aloud today—it has been, often, to undergraduates—and will convulse its audience with laughter. Before an audience composed of Howells, Aldrich, Twichell and other good companions it would have been a magnificent success. But Mark in preparing it had been wholly unconscious of the haloes with which literary Boston in its Indian Summer had surrounded the three ancients with whose names he was trifling. As soon as the speech reached the point where the miner named the poets and proceeded to describe them, a shudder passed round the table. "Mr. Emerson was a seedy little bit of a chap, red-headed. Mr. Holmes was as fat as a balloon; he weighed as much as three hundred, and had double chins all the way down to his stomach. Mr. Longfellow was built like a prize-fighter. His head was cropped and bristly, like as if he had a wig made of hair-brushes. His nose lay straight down in his face, like a finger with the end joint tilted up."

One guest laughed convulsively; the rest sat in frozen silence, except Emerson, whose mind was wandering in the sunny cloudland to which it withdrew more and more in his old age. Holmes feigned to be busily making notes of something; the rest gazed at their empty plates. Somehow Mark kept on to the end, and sat down amid a ghastly hush. Never before had any speech of his been so received; none would ever be so received again. Howells and Warner played the parts of Job's comforters, and Mark returned to Hartford bruised and sore and despairing. He wrote to Howells, "My sense of disgrace does not abate. It grows. I see that it is going to add itself to my list of permanencies—a list of humiliations that extends back to when I was seven years old, and which keep on persecuting me in spite of my repentancies." He proposed that Howells scrap the story which was to appear in the next issue: "I feel that my misfortune has injured me all over the country; therefore it will be best that I retire from before the public at present. It will hurt the *Atlantic* for me to appear in its pages now."

To Emerson, Holmes and Longfellow he sent abject letters of apology, which were graciously acknowledged, for these poets were gentlemen, and however fully they had shared the disapproval of the humor, they had no wish further to humiliate the penitent. Even the fact that F. J. Child and other people who had read the speech in the paper considered it masterly, could not soothe the author, any more than could Holmes' assurance from upstage that gentlemen of education and the highest social standing, and even one of the cleverest of Boston ladies, had been infinitely amused by it. Though the raw soreness gradually passed away, the sense of disgrace added a desire for flight to the plans which Mark was already making for the coming year.

Bliss had been urging him to prepare another travel book which might, they hoped, repeat the success of the *Innocents*. Mark decided to take his family to Germany, and spend at least a year in study, travel and writing. It was two years since *Tom Sawyer* had been published; three since it had been finished. In that interim he had brought no full-length writing to completion, and he felt that work in the home environment had become impossible. To his mother he declared, "I have a badgered, harassed feeling a good part of my time. It comes mainly of business responsibilities and annoyances, and the persecution of kindly letters from well meaning strangers. . . . The consequence is, I cannot write a book at home. This cuts my income down." But in his notebook he was franker: "To go abroad has something of the same sense that death brings. . . . I know you will refrain from saying harsh things *because* they can't hurt me, since I am out of reach and cannot hear them. This is why we say no harsh things of the dead." The wound of the Boston fiasco was slow to heal.

The Clemens family took seriously the educational possibilities of a year abroad. They engaged a German governess for the children, and both parents undertook to master the language—a task admirably calculated to evoke all Mark's latent reserves of profanity. With Clara Spaulding of Elmira, who had also shared the English tour of 1873, as company for Livy they sailed in April for Hamburg. The excursion began inauspiciously. The noises on shipboard tore at Mark's nerves, and Livy contracted a cold and sore throat which remained with her for weeks. They traveled by easy stages from Hamburg by way of Hanover and Frankfort to Heidelberg, where at last they found comfortable quarters and settled down. While his family continued their struggles with the language, Mark began collecting voluminous notes for the projected book. Everything from porcelain stoves to student duels was grist, and before long he had rented a private room to work in. But the language itself supplied the most fun. Mark informed Sue Crane that her sister would go to sleep murmuring, "Ich bin Ihnen sehr verbunden," and then wake up in the middle of the night to find that the sentence had become, "Ich Ben Jonson sehr befinden." He himself made immediate capital of his struggles by delivering an Independence Day address to the American students at Heidelberg in a weird mixture of German and English, sufficiently illustrated by his description of himself when he applied to Bayard Taylor, American Minister at Berlin, for a passport: "Geborn 1835; 5 Fuss 8½ inches hoch; weight doch aber about 145 pfund, sometimes ein wenig unter, sometimes ein wenig oben; dunkel braun Haar und rhotes Moustache, full Gesicht, mit sehr hohen Oren and leicht grau practvolles strahlenden Augen und ein Verdammtes gut moral character. Handlungkeit, Author von Bücher."

But all serious efforts at study ceased at the beginning of August when Joe Twichell joined them at Baden-Baden. Part of the plans made in Hartford had included this visit; Twichell was tired, and in need of rest and stimulus, and Mark was convinced that material for the new book would accumulate faster when he had a companion to discuss things with. They promptly set off on five weeks of splendid wayfaring. They called it a walking tour, but weren't fanatical about it. When they felt unambitious or there were stretches of dull country to cover they used any available means of conveyance, though they covered many more miles on foot than *A Tramp Abroad* would lead the guileless reader to believe.

After some trial heats in the Black Forest and back down the Neckar to Heidelberg, which occupied about ten days, they went by train to Lucerne, and devoted the remainder of their excursion to a pretty thorough exploration of the show places of the Alps. There was nothing sissified about some of their tramps. Seven hours on foot over the Gemmi Pass was solid pedestrianism, and so was the six-hour tramp, "up steep hills and down steep hills, in mud and water shoe-deep, and in a steady pouring rain," which brought them to St. Nicholas. Mark reported to Livy that he had been "as chipper and fresh as a lark all the way and arrived without the slightest sense of fatigue."

Twichell also was sending reports home. Mark, said his friend, "has coarse spots in him. But I never knew a person so finely regardful of the feelings of others in some ways. He hates to pass another person walking, and will practice some subterfuge to take off what he feels is the discourtesy of it.

And he is exceedingly timid, tremblingly timid, about approaching strangers; hates to ask a question." His regard for others included animals, and Twichell concluded his eulogy with a sweeping tribute modified by accuracy: "He is exceedingly considerate toward me in regard of everything—or most things." But what seems most to have impressed Twitchell was Mark Twain's childlike pleasure in trifles—making friends with a lamb on the Gorner Grat, picking wild flowers on the Gemmi to send to Livy, and throwing sticks and stones in the mountain torrents. Once, when Twichell set some driftwood afloat, Mark ran downstream after it "as hard as he could go, throwing up his hands and shouting in the wildest ecstacy, and when a piece went over a fall and emerged to view in the foam below he would jump up and down and yell. He said afterward that he hadn't been so excited in three months."

On September 9 Twichell started home, and thereafter the Clemens party began a leisurely sight-seeing tour from Switzerland into Italy. But Venice, Florence and Rome were all old ground for Mark, and he was bored. "Livy and Clara Spaulding," he told Twichell from Rome at the beginning of November, "are having a royal time worshiping the Old Masters, and I as good a time gritting my ineffectual teeth over them." The only concession he would make, after eleven years, was that he no longer considered the copies better than the originals. The responsibilities of travel always irked him, and serenity was hard to find. "I wish," he told Howells, "I *could* give those sharp satires on European life which you mention, but of course a man can't write successful satire except he be in a calm, judicial good-humor; whereas I *hate* travel, and I *hate* hotels, and I *hate* the opera, and I *hate* the old masters. In truth, I don't ever seem to be in a good-enough humor with anything to satirize it. No, I want to stand up before it and curse it and foam at the mouth, or take a club and pound it to rags and pulp. I have got in two or three chapters about Wagner's operas, and managed to do it without showing temper, but the strain of another such effort would burst me!" Invective or burlesque:

there was seldom a middle way between these when Mark's feelings were stirred, as he demonstrated at book-length in the *Yankee* a decade later. True satire calls for a cool head and a cool heart, and Mark's were inflammable.

They went into lodgings in Munich for the winter, where he tried to continue his book. It went slowly, though he sought to pad it out with yarns, later withdrawn for publication elsewhere, such as those two reversions to his California fondness for the humor of bad smells, "The Stolen White Elephant," and the yarn about the box of guns and the Limburger cheese. He told Howells in January that he was half done, and added, "I have given up writing a detective novel—can't write a novel, for I lack the faculty." He had reread his detective play, *Simon Wheeler*, and realized that " it was dreadfully witless and flat." The new book was labor and not fun, though by the end of January things were going better. He "tore up a great part of the MS written in Heidelberg,—wrote and tore up,—continued to write and tear up,—and at last, reward of patient and noble persistence, my pen got the old swing again."

But when they left Munich for Paris at the end of February the old swing had not carried him through. Throughout the wet and chilly spring in Paris he labored doggedly without zest. He and the family were thoroughly homesick, and tired of European hotels, and Mark confided to his notebook that "France has neither winter nor summer nor morals—apart from these drawbacks it is a fine country." American friends, including Aldrich and Frank Millet the painter, dropped in from time to time, other company was plenty, and at a dinner of the Stomach Club Mark delivered a speech so broadly humorous that even its title was suppressed by his biographer. Nevertheless, he disliked Paris, and so did his family, though they held on until July. Then, after nine days in Belgium and Holland, they went to England on the nineteenth. But in his nostalgic mood Mark could not recover even in London the honeymoon spirit of his earlier visits, and commented acidly alike on Charles Spurgeon's preaching and the snobbishness of the British press.

Finally, still pursued by chilly weather, they gave up, and sailed for home on August 23. Apart from the five golden weeks with Twichell, the tour had held little pleasure for Mark, with his hatred of railroads and hotels, and as a means to uninterrupted time for writing it had been no better than Hartford.

From New York they went straight to Quarry Farm, where in peace and sunshine Mark resumed his battle with his manuscript. He told Twichell that he had been knocking out early chapters for more than a year, "not because they had not merit, but merely because they hindered the flow of the narrative," and his purpose, avowed to Howells nine months earlier, was "to make a book which people will *read*." But instead of a book which would be read, he seemed to have one which could not be written. He carried the manuscript back to Hartford and struggled with it until the first week in January, when at last he struck. "I required 300 pages of MS and I have written near 600 since I saw you—and tore it all up except 288. . . . So I took the 288 pages to Bliss and told him that was the very last line I should ever write on this book. (A book which required 2600 pages of MS, and I have written nearer four thousand, first and last.)"

Work, to be sure, had been interrupted in November by a trip to Chicago to speak at the reunion of the Army of the Tennessee in honor of General Grant's return from his trip around the world. The audience's reception of the response to the toast, "The Babies," erased some memories of the *Atlantic Monthly* fiasco twenty-three months before. The success of a speech is in its hearers. What Mark said in Chicago lacked the uproarious fantasy of the Whittier birthday performance, but it was not delivered in a shrine before a quivering group of the devout. "My books are water; those of the great geniuses are wine. Everybody drinks water," Mark once confided to his journal. At the Grant banquet he had—in the metaphorical sense only—a water-level audience. His speech followed his established pattern. Beginning with pure fooling, it passed to more serious matters—in this instance, conventional flag waving—and ended with a surprise. After picturing the cradles throughout the land in which future admirals and historians and presidents were at that moment lying, he concluded: "And in still one more cradle, somewhere under the flag, the future illustrious commander-in-chief of the American armies is so little burdened with his approaching grandeurs and responsibilities as to be giving whole strategic mind at this moment to trying to find out some way to get his big toe into his mouth—an achievement which, meaning no disrespect, the illustrious guest of this evening turned *his* entire attention to some fifty-six years ago"—here came one of Mark's long pauses, while some of his listeners doubtless remembered that disastrous utterance in Boston—"and if the child is but a prophecy of the man, there are mighty few who will doubt that he *succeeded.*"

At five in the morning Mark, still too excited to sleep, wrote Livy that for two hours and a half he had been shaking hands and listening to congratulations. Sherman said, "Lord bless you, my boy, I don't know how you do it—it's a secret that's beyond me—but it was great—give me your hand again." And Grant had "sat through fourteen speeches like a graven image, but I fetched him! I broke him up, utterly! He told me he laughed till the tears came and every bone in his body ached." People who think that Mark Twain hated his business of humor have a good deal to explain away in his elation at the success of his speeches. If ever a man had a noble good time when his fun went over, it was Mark Twain. He delighted in analyzing, with a degree of attention which he never gave to his written work, the technical refinements by which he gained his effects.

But one of the things which ailed *A Tramp Abroad* was that he worked too hard for his fun. He felt, to begin with, that he must avoid the charge of merely repeating the pattern of the *Innocents.* He undertook, therefore, to make the new book as different as its material would warrant. Though he could not, as he told Howells, write satire, he could write burlesque, and in *A Tramp* he tried it on a larger scale than ever before. The title itself was burlesque: the narrator and his companions never walked, but were supposed never to be conscious that they were not doing what they set out to do. The entire book, likewise, was meant as burlesque, with three main themes—foreign study, particularly the German language; the conventional book of travel and mountaineering; art and art criticism. Chapters of fact and straight information were to be interspersed, and the plan allowed ample scope for digression into anecdotes having small connection with the main themes or even with Europe.

The success of the burlesques was in inverse ratio to their length. The most amusing passages in the book are those relating to Mark's struggles with the German language. "You always seemed to me," Howells commented on this very point, "a man who liked to be understood with the least possible personal inconvenience." Like most of Howells' judgments of his friend, it was shrewd. Mark compensated for his astonishing command of his own language by an almost complete inability to express himself in any other. He could get the hang of German or French or Italian in private, but in public, under the stress of immediate need his lines of communication usually broke down. Once when he endeavored to explain something to a couple of Germans, the Teutons listened to the end, and then exclaimed, reverently, "Gott in Himmel!" The neophyte's sense of bewilderment with a foreign tongue was first-rate material for humor, and in developing it Mark admirably employed his safest and kindest humorous device of making himself out a bigger ass than the reader would have been in similar circumstances.

On the other hand, the travesty of travel and travel books was labored. Mark thought it magnificent fun to equip the pedestrians with alpenstocks and sun helmets for their tramp up the Neckar valley, but the device leaves the reader cold. The undertaking to supply a series of legends for that unstoried valley was better in conception than in execution. The average guidebook legend is so inane that parody is as difficult as burlesquing the ritual of a college fraternity. He even reverted to a trick of his San Francisco days in parodying the jargon of fashion writers. The longest of the burlesques, the ascent of the Riffelberg, showed Mark painting himself striped and standing on his head every fifteen minutes in the effort to be funny. That some then popular Alpine books consistently overplayed their accounts of peril and suspense gave the chapters a point at the time which they have lost with the passing of the originals. But that very fact indicates inherent weakness in the episode. First-grade parody transcends and embalms its originals; one need not have read Ouida in order to relish *Zuleika Dobson*. Moreover, the device of having the travelers always miss the sunrises and the best scenery is overworked through repetition.

The comments on art were predestined to recall the fresher and more impudent utterances in the *Innocents*. Mark's efforts to vary the trick by including crude sketches of his own, which he described in the jargon of the critics, were only a qualified success. The frontispiece, concocted by pasting an advertisement across the lower part of Titian's "Moses," was the crudest of slapstick. But he thought it frightfully funny at the time.

A notable lack in *A Tramp*, as compared with the *Innocents* and *Roughing It*, was the scarcity of vivid character sketches. One remembers the inanely garrulous American on Lake Lucerne, the veterinary student at Heidelberg, and one or two others, but one searches the book in vain for the counterparts of Scotty Briggs and Mr. Ballou, Jack, the Poet Lariat and the Doctor. Mark disliked too many of the people he portrayed; his most attractive study is the young woman in the Lucerne hotel who led him on when she suspected his claim that he remembered her.

Even the interpolated episodes and digressions too often suffer from the same malady of overwriting. The incident on which he based his hunt for his missing sock in the vast hotel room in Heilbronn, for instance, was far funnier as he told it at the time to Twichell than as he elaborated it. He had finally captured the sock without making any noise at all, but when at last it was in his hand he rose too quickly, and upset the washstand. "Livy screamed, then said, 'Who is that? What *is* the matter?' I said, 'There ain't anything the matter—I'm hunting for my sock.' She said, 'Are you hunting for it with a club?' " It is sometimes a mistake to try to improve upon "the undoctored incident that actually occurred."

And yet—Chesterton's phrase, about the best of his work being found in the worst of his works, recurs. For the book contained phrases and passages that were Mark Twain at his best. When he said that Albert Smith's lectures on Mont Blanc "made people as anxious to see it as if it owed them money," he expressed the thing as he alone could. And were one asked to choose from all Mark Twain's works the most perfect example of the genuine Western tall story, patiently and skillfully built up from a matter-of-fact prelude to a sustained climax, the choice would probably come down at last to Jim Baker's blue-jay yarn. Whenever Mark's memory went back to the Sierras or the Mississippi, to Jim Gillis or Jim Wolf (who appeared in *A Tramp* as Nicodemus Dodge), everything was sunny blue. There his fancy played freely and without strain. As he grew older his increasing resentments against the irritations of the moment made it harder for him to turn them immediately to literary account, as he had done a decade or so earlier. Only when his mind could roam at will in a past simplified and made peaceful by distance could he take his ease in his writing. His day of making reportorial books according to contract was almost over. Only the latter half of *Life on the Mississippi* and—under the urgent need of paying his debts—*Following the Equator* were still to come in the genre which created his first fame. But the five years after his return from Europe were the years which established, once and for all, his right to a place among the greatest of American writers.

CHAPTER XII

HIGH NOON

THOUGH Mark Twain claimed, with considerable truth, that his interest in his books ceased as soon as they went to press, he took pleasure in the praise which Howells in the *Atlantic* bestowed on *A Tramp,* especially in its recognition of what the reviewer, in a letter a few months subsequent, called "the bottom of fury" in Mark's fun. But the particular phrase was applied to another book, for even before the last pages of *A Tramp* had gone to Bliss, Mark was embarked on a fresh project.

As early as November 23, 1877, he had set down in his notebook the idea for a story:

"Edward VI and a little pauper exchange places by accident a day or so before Henry VIII's death. The Prince wanders in rags and hardships and the pauper suffers the (to him) horrible miseries of princedom, up to the moment of crowning in Westminster Abbey, when proof is brought and the mistake rectified."

About three months later he confided to Mrs. Fairbanks that he was writing "a historical tale of 300 years ago, simply for the love of it—for it will appear without my name—such grave and stately work being considered by the world to be above my proper level." But the European interlude had interrupted him before he was fairly started, though he had apparently made a fuller plot outline than was usual with him. Historical fact required him to confine the action to the three weeks between Henry's death and Edward's coronation, and imposed a salutary restraint upon his propensity for digression and expansion. By the time *A Tramp* was off his hands he was eager for the new work.

The winter had gone well with him. The public triumph of the Grant speech had been followed by a smaller one in Boston which had meant even more to the speaker. Invited again to address an *Atlantic Monthly* dinner, he had delivered a graceful little tribute to Oliver Wendell Holmes which partly effaced the memory of his previous "mistake." Now, with the incubus of *A Tramp* off his shoulders, he wrought diligently at *The Prince and the Pauper*, trying the successive chapters on the home audience as they were completed.

Susy was eight, and Clara six, in 1880. From babyhood they had been accustomed to demand stories of their father—extempore tales suited to their ages and interests. When they were small they would descend upon him with an order for a story about the latest thing they had heard of, whether they knew what it was or not. Some years later, for instance, the baby required a story about a "bawgun strictor" and a plumber though until the tale developed she was not sure what a boa constrictor was. A favorite game was a story bringing in, in their proper order, all the pictures and ornaments about the mantelpiece in their Hartford library. The task sometimes strained even Mark's powers of improvisation. "These bric-a-bracs were never allowed a peaceful day, a reposeful day, a restful Sabbath. In their lives there was no Sabbath. In their lives there was no peace. They knew no existence but a monotonous career of violence and bloodshed." But now the children were old enough to form part of the jury for *The Prince and the Pauper*, which was intended for boys and girls.

The 1880's were not afraid to include such facts of life as suffering and death in tales for children, and plenty went into the new story. "My idea," Mark told Howells, "is to afford a realizing sense of the exceeding severity of the laws of that day by inflicting some of their penalties upon the King himself and allowing him a chance to see the rest of them applied to others." It was, in fact, the first fruit of his growing sense of the inequalities of the English social and economic system, which had been intensified on his latest visit. And the home audience heartily approved. "I have even," he continued to Howells, "fascinated Mrs. Clemens with this yarn for youth. My stuff generally gets considerable damning with faint praise out of her, but this time it is all the other way. She is become the horse-leech's daughter and my mill doesn't grind fast enough to suit her. This is no mean triumph."

Work on the book continued at Quarry Farm that summer, with an interlude occasioned by the birth of Jean Clemens. Mark was proud of the new baby, but the sight of his children, in moments of darkness, intensified his sense of Time's winged chariot hurrying near. He broke off a letter to Twichell, in which he had been commenting harshly upon Daniel Webster's youthful letters, then recently published:

"Well, we are all getting along here first-rate; Livy gains strength daily, and sits up a deal; the baby is five weeks old and—but no more of this; somebody may be reading *this* letter 80 years hence. And so, my friend (you pitying snob, I mean, who are holding this yellow paper in your hand in 1960,) save yourself the trouble of looking further; I know how pathetically trivial our small concerns will seem to you, and I will not let your eye profane them. No, I keep my news; you keep your compassion. Suffice it you to know, scoffer and ribald, that the little child is old and blind, now, and once more toothless; and the rest of us are shadows, these many, many years. Yes, and *your* time cometh!"

But the completion of *The Prince and the Pauper* that summer helped to involve its author in nearly two decades of worry and disaster over publishing. His relations with the American Publishing Company were strained, and the strain was intensified by the results of his contract for *A Tramp Abroad*. At Orion's suggestion he had insisted on half profits, instead of the previous royalties, and the returns were so satisfying that he immediately concluded that he had been swindled on his earlier books. While he was in this mood Elisha Bliss, the only man who might have talked him out of it, died. Frank Bliss, Elisha's son, succeeded to the directorship, but Mark had no confidence in his capacity to push the business. Other publishers were constantly making offers, and just now Mark was ill-advised enough to listen to James R. Osgood of Boston, formerly a partner in the fine firm of Ticknor and Fields, but now set up independently. Mark liked Osgood; the fact that he had no experience in the highly specialized work of subscription publishing did not dawn upon the author until too late.

Osgood's first plan was to issue Mark's two new stories about boys as a single volume. *The Prince and the Pauper* was finished; the other story was *Huckleberry Finn,* which was still a long way from completion, though Mark had worked at it occasionally during the past summer at Elmira. Osgood's astonishing proposal Livy promptly vetoed. She was right, even though her reason—that *The Prince* was the better story—was wrong. But by the time Howells had added his praise of *The Prince* to Livy's, Osgood was ready to make a separate volume of it, and illustrate it lavishly. Too lavishly, for one of the numerous things which Elisha Bliss had known, but Osgood did not, was that cheap engravings meant a big saving in production costs, and most subscribers wouldn't know the difference anyway. Under the triple handicap of an inexperienced publisher, high manufacturing costs, and a new style unfamiliar to Mark's readers it is scarcely surprising that the book, in comparison with its predecessors, was a commercial failure. Its failure, in turn, pushed Mark another step along the road to becoming his own publisher, though the final decision did not come until after he had given Osgood another chance—or two chances, if one counts the little volume containing "The Stolen White Elephant" and some other inconsequential sketches.

The Prince and the Pauper stands among Mark Twain's books in about the same relation to *Tom Sawyer* and *Huck Finn* as *The Black Arrow* stands among Stevenson's in comparison with *Treasure Island* and *Kidnapped.* It has good touches: the skill with which Miles Hendon's gradual transition from mockery to affection in his relations with the outcast Prince is handled; the hermit, driven insane by Henry's rape of the monastic foundations; Mother Canty's recognition of her son. But too much of the drama savors of the melodrama of the Victorian stage; too much space is devoted, for a children's book, to attacks upon old oppressions and inequalities; time and events have exposed the weakness of Mark's underlying assumption that the modern world is in all respects better than the ancient one. Pessimistic as he was in his opinions of the damned human race, Mark still accepted unquestionably the nineteenth-century dogma of progress. In common with most of his contemporaries he identified material conveniences with moral growth, sometimes grotesquely, as when in 1889 he could think of nothing to congratulate Walt Whitman upon except the fact that he had seen the development of steam transportation, the telegraph, the telephone and the electric light.

After completing *The Prince and the Pauper* he was too busy with other enterprises to do much consecutive writing. The book did not appear until the end of 1881, more than a year after it was finished. In the interim Mark bubbled with ideas, few of them sensible, and none of them carried out. He planned to start a subscription for erecting a monument to Adam. He wrote part of a burlesque book of etiquette. He tinkered some more with *Captain Stormfield's Visit to Heaven,* and had a notion for a sort of companion piece:

"Write the Second Advent, with full details—lots of Irish disciples—Paddy Ryan for Judas and other disciples. Star in the East. People want to know how wise men could see it move while sober. John interviewed."

Such memoranda convince the reader of the need for Livy's firm hand. So far as recorded, this particular notion never got past the notebook stage, but others, such as "The Undertaker's Love-Story," were written while the inspiration was hot, and had to be cooled by the critic on the hearth.

The range of Mark Twain's activities and interests during these years leaves the reader wondering where he found the time. The Hartford house was usually so full of guests that the harassed Livy yearned for the seclusion of Quarry Farm, yet in the midst of his financial, social and political embroilments, Mark still found time for his children and for reading. Besides the storytelling, already mentioned, it was the family custom to encourage the youngsters to perform charades and little plays, and their father devoted hours to the elaboration of a historical game begun at Quarry Farm, which was intended to impart dates painlessly, and make them stick.

Of his own reading Mark had recorded in the 1870's, "I like history, biography, travels, curious facts and strange happenings, and science. And I detest novels, poetry and theology." The affirmation was accurate; the negation too sweeping. Anything which straightforwardly reported life attracted him: in the early days of their marriage, for instance, he vexed and puzzled his wife by his delight in P. T. Barnum's autobiography, and his travel books are filled with illustrations of his avidity in seeking out and absorbing even obscure volumes relating to the subjects in hand. A few books he read and reread nearly every year, among them Lecky's *History of European Morals*, Pepys' *Diary*, Suetonius' *Lives of the Caesars* and Carlyle's *French Revolution*. Of these favorites, Pepys appealed because of his direct and uninhibited transcript of life, the others, for their capacity to dramatize the characters and ideas of the past. The interest in oddities and curiosities was partly a holdover from his newspaper days, partly an expression of his perennial love for the grotesque. When Rudyard Kipling interviewed him in 1889, Mark mentioned that he had just been reading an article in the *Britannica* on pure mathematics, and astronomy so fascinated him that he once, to help his comprehension of the distances involved, went to the labor of computing for himself the length of a light-year. He kept abreast of all current discoveries in science, and sometimes went off the deep end in accepting conclusions which were not yet validated.

His aversions, however, had their qualifying exceptions. Actually, he might be said to have loved theology, as an unfailing target for his derision, and his avowed dislike of novels and poetry was far from absolute. His use of them for purposes of

parody and burlesque shows that he had read most of the standard popular poets of his day. An early favorite, among individual poems, was Seba Smith's "The Burial of Moses," a
restrained example of the more rhetorical Victorian style. The
same delight in full-voiced poetry made him, forty years later,
applaud Kipling's "Bell Buoy." When the *Rubaiyat* became
popular in America in the 1880's, he was among its fervent
admirers, and during the same years he succumbed to the lure
of the Browning societies, and devoted careful preparation to
the oral rendition of *Men and Women,* the *Dramatic Lyrics* and
Parleyings. "I used to explain Mr. Browning," he wrote in
1887, "but the class won't stand that. They say that my reading imparts clear comprehension,—but they say the poetry
never gets obscure till I begin to explain it. . . . Put me in the
right condition and give me room according to my strength, and
I can read Browning so Browning himself can understand it."
Unquestionably, it was Browning's skill in the portrayal of
character that attracted him; the poems were additions to the
gallery of people whom he more frequently found in history and
biography.

Pretentiousness, overwriting, inaccuracy of expression he detested in whatever literary form he encountered them. In later
life he so turned against the sentimentality of Dickens as to
declare that he had never been able to read him, though in fact
he had, in his youth. Goldsmith and Jane Austen he sometimes
reread, for the pleasure of hating them all over again—he felt as
much out of place, he once declared, among the latter's characters as a barkeeper would in heaven. Yet he read and admired
all of Howells' novels—because he admired Howells, but also
because of the simple and lucid style in which they were written. If he had ever known Jane Austen personally, he would
have liked her books, too, as he liked Sarah Orne Jewett's and
Grace King's. In 1888, after popular persecution had forced
him to read *Robert Elsmere,* he tried a course of novel-reading,
but it did not amuse him, and he dropped it. His interest was
always in the style, rather than the story—in the technique of

an art in which he himself had no technique beyond lucidity. In the early 1880's, however, reading and writing were the least of Mark's activities. He had a hand in everything from education to gambling. He helped at least two Negro students through college, and financed the young sculptor, Karl Gerhardt, through three years of study in Paris. He planned for Osgood a *Library of American Humor* which Howells was to edit with the help of Charles H. Clark of the Hartford *Courant*. And almost any inventor or stock salesman found in him the same predestinate sucker who had dabbled in Nevada mines a couple of decades before. But only one of these wildcat schemes, prior to the Paige typesetting machine, came close enough to his literary career to call for mention. Dan Slote interested him in backing a new engraving process which was to revolutionize the arts of book illustration and diemaking. Before the invention was perfected it was already obsolete, because of the half-tone and other photoengraving techniques which were in every way simpler, cheaper and more satisfactory. But while Mark's enthusiasm was still high he brought Charles L. Webster, who had married Pamela's daughter, Annie Moffett, to New York to manage the business for him. Young Webster was energetic, and though he did not make a success of the engraving process, he discovered, and reported to Mark, that Dan Slote had been making far more than he was entitled to out of the Mark Twain Scrapbook. The result, after a threat of litigation, was a new contract which guaranteed the inventor one-third of the profits on all sales. That was the first result and the least important. A second one was that when Dan Slote died, early in 1882, Mark considered him a pickpocket and swindler. But the most far-reaching result was that the episode gave Mark an exalted idea of Charley Webster's business ability, and thereby paved the road for the Charles L. Webster Publishing Company and ultimate bankruptcy.

But he was not through with Osgood yet, nor was Osgood through with him. No sooner was *The Prince and the Pauper* off the press than Osgood had a new idea. The papers on "Old

Times on the Mississippi" were still buried in the *Atlantic* files, though a Canadian pirate or two had reprinted them without permission. In themselves these chapters were not enough to make a volume, so Osgood proposed that Mark undertake a complete tour of the navigable length of the river, from New Orleans to Minneapolis, and embody his observations in a second section of the book. Osgood, who was good company, offered to go along, and to complete the party they took a stenographer who was to record notes and impressions while they were fresh. The idea of revisiting the river had been in the back of Mark's mind for years, but always something had come up to thwart his plans. Now he was full of enthusiasm, and doubtless had completely forgotten that in September 1881 he had given Mrs. Fairbanks a graphic account of the exhaustion produced by a leisurely trip from Elmira to Fredonia and back—an account which ended with the cheery opinion that physically he was older at forty-five than some men are at eighty.

All that mood had passed, certainly, when he found himself on the river again. A scheme for traveling incognito promptly broke down because his face was as familiar to every reader in the country as his drawl was to the old-timers he encountered in the pilothouses. He had taken his trip just in time to see the sunset of the steamboating empire. Horace Bixby, George Ritchie and one or two other old friends were still active and successful as pilots, but the sight of an almost empty river, where it was a sensation to have two steamboats in sight at once, impressed Mark's imagination. Except for the towboats with their strings of coal barges, the railroads had almost destroyed the once booming river traffic. "The romance of boating is gone now," he noted. "In Hannibal the steamboatman is no longer a god. The youth don't talk river slang any more." Persons who take seriously Mark's occasional nostalgia for his piloting days apparently forget the decline and fall of steamboating. The imagination boggles at the effort to picture him clinging to a dying trade while other ways of life were booming.

If the war had not taken him off the river when it did, disgust with a drooping business would have done so within a few years, but perhaps too late for him to find his full capacities as a writer.

He observed with a keen eye the mechanical improvements in the river trade during his twenty-year absence—the beacons that marked the channel, the dredging of the snags and other deathtraps for steamboats, the searchlights which had removed from night navigation most of the perplexities which the beacons had not solved. But the old free and easy ways were gone; officers of the boats were in uniform, and the pilots were employees instead of potentates.

In New Orleans he spent some happy days with G. W. Cable, then at the height of his fame as a portrayer of the Louisiana Creoles, and with Joel Chandler Harris, who had made a special trip from Atlanta to join the party. In the course of his sightseeing, Mark renewed his acquaintance with the French Quarter, and collected facts and statistics for his book. Yet when they left for the return trip upriver, he felt that the main purpose of his visit was but lamely accomplished. He had hoped to hunt up and talk with a hundred old steamboat men, but had got so pleasantly involved in social life that even his reminiscent chats with Horace Bixby were too brief to satisfy either man.

The upper reaches of the Mississippi, above Keokuk and Muscatine, were new ground, and Mark's plans called for visits to the booming new cities which the settlement of Minnesota and the Dakotas had brought into existence since the war. On his way north he spent three days in Hannibal, "examining the old localities and talking with the grey-heads who were boys and girls with me. . . . I have been clasping hands with the moribund—and usually they said, 'It is for the last time.' " John Garth and his wife, who had been Helen Kercheval and a boyhood sweetheart of Sam Clemens, were his hosts for the three days, and then he completed his itinerary, against an increasing tide of homesickness.

The contract with Osgood called for completion of the manuscript in time to get the book out for the Christmas trade. But deadlines always benumbed Mark's faculties, and domestic crises added their share of hindrance. In mid-June, when they were on the point of starting for Elmira, Jean came down with scarlet fever, the other children soon followed, and Mark himself was taken ill, though not with scarlet fever. When at last they got to Quarry Farm, the *Library of American Humor,* which continued to be a millstone about his neck, interfered further with the book. The deadline was passed before they returned to Hartford in October, but the book still lacked thirty thousand words of completion, and to Howells, now visiting in London, Mark reported the desperation which beset him:

"The spur and burden of the contract are intolerable to me. I can endure the irritation of it no longer. I went to work at nine o'clock yesterday morning, and went to bed an hour after midnight. Result of the day, (mainly stolen from books, tho' credit given,) 9500 words, so I reduced my burden by one third in one day. It was five days work in one. I have nothing more to borrow or steal; the rest must all be written. It is ten days work, and unless something breaks, it will be finished in five."

As readers of the book notice, he had been reading the historians of the river, and all the available accounts by early nineteenth-century travelers. The reading was even more extensive than appears in print, for a chapter and a half of detailed comment on Dickens, Marryat, Harriet Martineau and other English critics was ultimately discarded. His borrowings, however, were not limited to these sources. The manuscript reveals that the flowery passages of description, which he put in the mouth of the old gentleman who had traveled with a panorama, were actually lifted bodily from an advertising booklet put out by a railroad company: the descriptions were simply clipped and pasted in. But Mark's books seldom came to a natural end, even without a deadline. He got tired, after a while, and stopped.

While he was still struggling with his manuscript he had been drawn dangerously nearer the lodestone of personal publishing. Though Osgood was still his publisher, he called Charley Webster from the graveside of the Kaolatype engraving process to organize and direct the New York office from which the canvassing of the sales was to be conducted. And he also, by one of the shrewd touches of business acumen which occurred even in his wildest dreams, recorded his pen name as a registered trademark, with the result that to this day none of his writings, whether still covered by copyright or not, can appear with "Mark Twain" on the title page without the consent of his estate.

It is a commonplace of criticism that the two parts of *Life on the Mississippi* are inharmonious, but the reason for the incongruity is not always recognized. The material for the first part of the book was mainly the chapters on piloting which he had contributed to the *Atlantic* in 1874. To complete the first half of the book Mark added three prefatory chapters about the early history of the river, including in them a whole section from the still unfinished manuscript of *Huck Finn* as the best description he could give of the ways of the keelboat and raftsmen. This chapter was never restored to its proper place in the book it was written for. He also added an inferior chapter about cutoffs and the improvident pilot, Stephen, and the three vivid and accurately biographical chapters about Pilot Brown, the *Pennsylvania* disaster and Henry Clemens' death. These completed the narrative of his apprenticeship in the spirit of the earlier work. But this first part remains highly selective in detail and point of view. Its theme is the romance of the river and of piloting; the sordid commercialism of the great days has no more place there than obstetrics or sociology would have in *Tom Sawyer*. Curiously enough, he had nothing whatever to say about his experiences as a licensed pilot. Even with the additional chapters the first half of the book leaves him still a cub. So far as his published writings are concerned, the two years during which some critics suppose him to have been happiest are a biographical blank.

The second half returns to the reportage of the *Innocents* and

A Tramp Abroad. Though he embroiders and digresses, his primary concern is with things seen and heard, and whether as reporting or as satire, the chapters are notably better than most of *A Tramp.* Three-dimensional characters are present again, as in *Roughing It*—Uncle Mumford, the salesmen of oleo-margarine and cottonseed oil, the New Orleans undertaker, the practical joker who tried to feed Mark misinformation about steamboats, they all live and breathe. And though the abundant facts and statistics now have nothing to commend them save a faint historical boredom, the social criticism is still good for a fight south of the Mason and Dixon line.

Mark Twain, Howells thought, was the most desouthernized Southerner he had ever known, and the strongest literary proof of the statement is in this book and in *Huck.* The much-discussed but seldom read chapter that Mark deleted dealt with the postwar attitude of the South toward slavery; it was not nearly so scathing as his published arraignment of Southern ideas of delicacy, refinement, womanhood, religion and propriety, as illustrated by shootings and stabbings performed by Southern gentlemen. He had graduated forever from the roses-and-magnolia legend of the prewar South; what most blunted his criticism, perhaps, was his fondness for seeking a single tangible explanation for, a personal villain behind, any phenomenon he disliked. In this case the villain was Sir Walter Scott. The syllogism was plain: the Southern type of sentimentality, as expressed in print, bore a strong resemblance to the sentimentality of Scott's romances of chivalry. Ergo, Scott was the father of all that Mark disliked in the unrealistic utterances of the South. As a piece of reasoning it was on a par with his later acceptance of the maunderings of the Baconians; straight ridicule of the obsolete verbal flowers, without lugging in Sir Walter, would have been more effective in laughing the fashion out of court.

The weakest part of the book is the interpolated narratives, of which the longest and most labored is the story of the vengeance of Ritter, the Austrian. Later on, when Mark told about the mendacious carpenter in Hannibal, who had filled his boyish ears with yarns about the terrible destruction he wrought upon every man who bore the name of Lynch, he recognized that the man had been talking melodramatic blather, probably borrowed from *Nick of the Woods*. Yet he did not recognize that Ritter's story was precisely the same sort of melodramatic blather, and adding to it a farcical postscript about the treasure which they could not find in the town of Napoleon, because Napoleon had been washed away, did not redeem the situation. But it helped to fill out the book to the contract length, and that was the main consideration.

For the desperate burst of energy he had reported to Howells in October had not finished the job after all. A week later he was at a standstill.

"I never had such a fight over a book in my life before. And the foolishest part of the whole business is, that I started Osgood to editing it before I had finished writing it. As a consequence, large areas of it are condemned here and there and yonder, and I have the burden of these unfilled gaps harassing me and the thought of the broken continuity of the work, while I am at the same time trying to build the last quarter of the book. However, at last I have said with sufficient positiveness that I will finish the book at no particular date; that I will not hurry it; that I will not hurry myself; that I will take things easy and comfortably, write when I choose to write, leave it alone when I so prefer. The printers must wait, the artists, the canvassers, and all the rest. . . . I ought to have finished it before showing it to anybody, and then sent it across the ocean to you to be edited, as usual. . . ."

Some of the unfilled gaps and broken continuity still appear in the finished book. The chapter entitled "Tough Yarns" contains only one tough yarn, but in the manuscript it contained three. Two of them were discarded because they were overly gruesome; a paragraph in the discussion of cremation about the profitable amount of soap recoverable from the ashes was deleted for the same reason. The pilot who tried to lie to Mark about his adventures was originally allowed to tell an admirable tall tale about having been blown up nine times in boiler explosions. Three times in five years he was flung through the roof of the same cabin in Walnut Bend. The third time the owner was annoyed because the pilot had fetched the cook along, and moved away. The passage was excellent humor, but it had to come out because the expertness of its telling marred the dramatic climax when the pilot, calling Mark Twain by name, told him to do his own lying, since he was handier at it.

Not until January 1883 did he finally get the manuscript off his hands. Even when he was busiest, or because he was busiest, other projects tempted him. Besides the ever-present *Library of Humor* he and Howells were playing again with the notion of dramatic collaboration. At the moment, in the winter of 1882-1883, their idea was a play built round the character of Orion Clemens, and Mark kept forwarding to Howells his brother's perennially hopeful letters, as material to work on. "This immortal and unteachable misjudgment, is the immortal feature of this character, for a play; and we will write that play." What Mark never realized was his kinship with his brother in everything save the spark of literary genius. That constant enthusiasm for new projects, at which Mark sometimes laughed and sometimes raged, was himself, enlarged and a trifle distorted, but recognizable. No character who ever lived ought to be easier to understand than Mark Twain, for most of his salient traits can be isolated from their literary wrappings and studied analytically in his brother and his children. He was just entering upon the decade in which his Orion Clemens traits were to have their fullest expression, and there is a certain wry appropriateness in the fact that two of his most cherished projects dealt, the one with Orion, the other with a revival of Colonel Sellers, otherwise Uncle James Lampton. Over the contriving of this second play, in the fall of 1883, Mark and Howells laughed themselves stiff and sore, the humorist's goadings inspiring his friend to flights of mad extravaganza wholly unlike his usual mild and serene self. It was a shock to them both when Raymond, to whom they offered it, returned the play with the blunt statement that this Colonel Sellers was not a dreamer but a lunatic. How right the actor was, any reader of *The American Claimant,* the book in which the plot of the play finally reached print, can see for himself. But before the spirit of Colonel Sellers finally swept Mark away on his quest of illusory pots of gold he had a creative interval in which he completed his masterpiece.

CHAPTER XIII

HUCK FINN

By the time he reached Quarry Farm in June 1883, Mark's brain was seething with ideas for new stories and additions to old ones. To this summer belongs the dismal Second Advent notion, already quoted, besides a projected tale about the life of castaways in the interior of an iceberg, a modern improvement for Captain Stormfield's Heaven by which heaven was to be heated with hot-air registers connected with hell, and the theme later worked out as "The £1,000,000 Banknote." But what really mattered was that Mark took out the half-finished manuscript of *Huckleberry Finn* and fell to work.

Since he had laid the book aside seven years before, it had been his literary stepchild. But his trip down the river had revived and sharpened old memories, and to fill out *Life on the Mississippi* he had studied and borrowed from the pigeonholed manuscript. Now he found himself in the vein, and was soon telling Howells and Orion that he was turning out copy at the rate of three or four thousand words a day.

"I haven't piled up MS so in years as I have done since we came here to the farm three weeks and a half ago. Why, it's like old times, to step right into the study, damp from the breakfast table, and sail right in and sail right on, the whole day long, without thought of running short of stuff or words. . . . I expect to complete it [*Huck*] in a month or six weeks or two months more. And *I* shall like it, whether anybody else does or not. It's a kind of companion to Tom Sawyer. . . ."

This was the halcyon season when Susy was writing her charming biography of her father, and she and Clara joined their mother in the daily editing of their father's latest pages.

217

"The children always helped their mother to edit my books in manuscript. She would sit on the porch at the farm and read aloud, with her pencil in her hand, and the children would keep an alert and suspicious eye upon her right along, for the belief was well grounded that whenever she came across a particularly satisfactory passage she would strike it out. . . . The passages which were so satisfactory to them always had an element of strength in them which sorely needed modification or expurgation, and was always sure to get it at their mother's hand. For my own entertainment, and to enjoy the protests of the children, I often abused my editor's innocent confidence. I often interlarded remarks of a studied and felicitously atrocious character purposely to achieve the children's delight and see the pencil do its fatal work. I often joined my supplications to the children's for mercy, and strung the argument out and pretended to be in earnest. They were deceived, and so was their mother. It was three against one, and most unfair. But it was very delightful, and I could not resist the temptation. Now and then we gained the victory and there was much rejoicing. Then I privately struck the passage out myself. It had served its purpose. It had furnished three of us with good entertainment, and in being removed from the book by me it was only suffering the fate originally intended for it."

The *Autobiography* records no more charming picture of the Clemens home life than this, and none has been subject to more misunderstanding. In the more melodramatic interpretations, Livy is cast for the role of the Oriental slave-trader who furnishes eunuchs for the Sultan's harem. No critical iconoclasm is too extreme to be imputed to her by critics who, in pursuit of their theories, have been willing to make every exertion short of the labor of ascertaining the facts. Less than five years after *Huck Finn* was written all that remained of the manuscript was given by a local book collector to the Buffalo Public Library, where it has been on exhibition ever since. From it can be gathered a pretty exact notion of how Mark Twain revised and how much his domestic censorship actually amounted to.

The extant manuscript begins in the middle of Chapter XII, breaks off at the end of Chapter XIV, and resuming with Chapter XXII is complete from there to the end. Such strong scenes as the Shepherdson-Grangerford feud, the camp meeting, and the shooting of Boggs are missing, but present are the attempt to lynch Colonel Sherburn, "The Royal Nonesuch," the whole Wilks episode, and Huck's struggle with his conscience over surrendering Jim. In more than nine hundred places the manuscript differs textually from the book, the changes ranging from single words to whole paragraphs added or deleted. Some of the changes were made at first writing, or almost immediately afterward; others indicate the direction taken in passages rejected and destroyed; still others must have been made in proof. But most important of all are certain penciled marginalia, some of which Livy may have written—her handwriting closely resembled her husband's—which reveal the precise nature and extent of the criticisms offered at those family readings.

But whatever their date, nature or extent, all the revisions are of the same sort. They are not the dilution of grim realism to make it meat for babes; they are the work of a skilled craftsman removing the unessential, adding vividness to dialogue and description, and smoothing incongruities. By Mr. DeVoto's reckoning thirty-seven of the nine hundred corrections are the sort that Livy is reputed to have demanded, but most of these are trifling alterations of single words.

The only clear evidence of change of plan in a main section of the story scarcely supports the theory of censorship. When Huck and Tom arrived at Silas Phelps' plantation, their creator originally intended them to find there a boy and a girl about their own ages, named Phil and Mat. Fragmentary deleted passages on renumbered pages show that Mark Twain had developed this idea to the point where Tom passes himself off as Sid. By then, however, Mark must have realized that Tom and Huck, unaided, were going to furnish quite as many complications as the story would hold. Accordingly he destroyed the two older children, leaving only the brood of youngsters too small to share in the excitement, but he neglected to revise downward the ages of their parents, who thus appear in the story as somewhat elderly to have so young a family.

The overwhelming majority of the changes are in detail. Thus, when Huck and Jim visit the wrecked steamboat Huck talks down Jim's fears by expatiating on the untold riches, in five-cent cigars and other precious things, of steamboat captains. This whole long speech was added overleaf in the manuscript to replace the unimaginative sentence, "Steamboat captains is always rich, and have everything they want, you know." Some of the best phrases were afterthoughts that must have been inserted in the proof. The King's "soul-butter and hogwash" was first only "humbug and hogwash." Later on, when the King has "to brace up mighty quick, or he'd 'a squshed down like a bluff bank that the river has cut under," the simile was an afterthought; in the manuscript he "kerflummoxed." Again, the mob tears down Sherburn's fence, and begins "to roll in like a wave." When the Colonel appears with his shotgun, the book says, "The racket stopped, and the wave sucked back." For the last phrase the manuscript has only, "the crowd fell back," and the description in the next paragraph of the Colonel's laugh, "not the pleasant kind, but the kind that makes you feel like when you are eating bread that's got sand in it," replaces, "not the kind of laugh you hear at the circus, but the kind that's fitten for a funeral—the kind that makes you feel crawly."

Many substitutions were dramatic. The first thoughts might be picturesque, but were out of character. When Huck first summed up Mary Jane Wilks he said, "She _was_ the best girl that ever was! and you could depend on her like the everlasting sun and the stars, every time." The speech would have been right in the mouth of the Playboy of the Western World, but not in Huck's. It was changed in proof to "She _was_ the best girl I ever see, and had the most sand"; and a sentimental reference to "the big friendly river stretching out so homelike before us" was deleted entirely. Huck, telling Jim of the ways and works

auction passage, this one shows Mark composing as he wrote, with only the vaguest general plan in mind.

In the earlier adventure on the wrecked steamboat changes were made both in manuscript and proof. At first writing, when Huck and Jim board the wreck, "rip comes a flash of lightning out of the sky, and shows us a skiff tied to the skylight pretty close beyond the door, for all that side was under water." This was struck out at once; it destroyed both the surprise of finding the ruffians on the wreck and the suspense when the raft went adrift. But later in the chapter the manuscript elaborated the plans of Bill and Jake for silencing their treacherous companion, Jim Turner: they gagged him, and were going to leave him bound in the expectation that the wreck would soon break up and drown him; if it didn't, they would come back before daylight and dump him in the river with a rock tied to him. But all these details were struck out in the proofs, probably because they merely complicated the action without intensifying it.

In this passage, too, occurs the first of the penciled marginalia. These are few in number, and mostly of a character unlike what Mark's description of Livy's censorship implies. When Huck cuts the skiff loose the note says, "Provide him with a knife." One can almost hear Susy or Clara, remembering the equipment with which Huck had escaped from his father's shack, interjecting, "But, papa, he hasn't any knife!" At any rate, whoever made the suggestion, the note explains why Huck found, among the junk in the wrecked house floating downriver in Chapter IX, "a bran-new Barlow knife worth two bits in any store."

Several such notes appear on the pages telling of the flight after the Wilks fiasco. When the crooks plot to sell Jim, Huck said the Duke "found fault with every little thing, and he even cussed Jim for being a fool and keeping his blue paint and King Leer clothes on, and made him take them off and wash himself off; and yet it warn't no fault of Jim's, for nobody hadn't ever told him he might do it." This passage was scored through, and the note says, "This is lugged—shove it back yonder to where they escape lynching and regain raft." Here the words are unmistakably Mark's: he had noticed the weakness, and jotted or dictated the correction. But he failed to act upon it, and the reader never learns when or how Jim shed his "sick Arab" make-up. The next note, however, was used. When Huck, trying to find what the scoundrels have done with Jim, arrives at the Phelps plantation the penciling says, "Has good clothes on." Hence in the previous chapter, when Huck leaves the raft, the book shows him donning his store clothes, instead of "some old rough clothes" which he wore in the manuscript. As he goes ashore in the canoe, one note says, "the skiff being new and worth advertising"; another, "Go back and burn the skiff when they escape lynching"; a third, "Go back and put old clothes on after escape from lynching." These, like a couple during Tom's elaborate schemes to free Jim, were not used. When Tom told Huck about famous escapes the pencil wrote "Edmond Dantes" in the margin, but the book still keeps the manuscript reading of, "them prisoners in the bottom dungeon of the Castle Deef." When the boys are working every night in Jim's shack, a marginal note says, "They always take along a lunch," but it was not written into the story, and so far as the reader knows, the night work was done without extra nourishment.

The sole marginal note which accords with Mark's description of Livy's censorship occurs on the leaf where Huck describes the King's make-up in "The Royal Nonesuch." It is the single, sufficient word, "scandalous." Of course no one acquainted with fraternity initiations and other gatherings where Greek phallic comedy survives has ever been in doubt as to the sort of show the King provided for the male population of Bricksville, Arkansas. If Livy were to come down hard on anything in the book, this was the passage to be suppressed. Keen interest therefore attaches to the changes Mark made in obedience to that word.

He altered the title of the "play" to "The Royal Nonesuch." Throughout the manuscript it bore the name Jim Gillis had given it when he told the story in the Tuolumne hills—"The Burning Shame." A single phrase was deleted: the King originally "said he judged he could caper to their base instincts; 'lowed he could size their style." The description of the King's make-up was twice modified. "Stark naked" was softened to "naked." In the book Huck adds, "And—but never mind the rest of his outfit; it was just wild, but it was awfully funny." In the manuscript he said, "And—but I won't describe the rest of his outfit, because it was just outrageous, although it was awful funny." And that is the sum of the changes made in what is probably the bawdiest scene Mark ever conceived for publication. Out of the vast laboring mountain of charges that censorship destroyed his virility, emerges this tiny and ineffectual mouse. Livy, instead of appearing as the abhorred fury with the shears, proves to have been armed with nothing heavier than buttonhole scissors.

To be sure a few other changes, possibly in the interests of decorum, were made without marginal proddings, but the complete list is neither long nor impressive. In most instances, other considerations than prudery may have dictated them, as when "drunk," used twice in one paragraph, became "tight" and "mellow." "Rotten eggs," similarly, became "sickly eggs," but since "rotten cabbages" stands in the same sentence, the alteration merely avoided repetition. The kings who "hang" round the harem in the book, were allowed to "wallow" in the manuscript; smells "too rancid" for Huck were toned down to "too various," and "the signs of a dead cat being around" replaced "the smell of a dead cat." In several places Mark modified his unhappy fondness for seeking humor in decay, death and viscera. Jim, made up as the sick Arab, "didn't only look like he was dead, he looked considerably more than that." Realism would have gained little had the phrase been let stand as "he looked like he was mortified." It would be a questionable improvement to describe unappetizing meat as "a hunk of your old cold grandfather" instead of the "hunk of old cold cannibal," which again was second thought. And was it better to say that conscience "takes up more room than a person's bowels," instead of "all the rest of a person's insides"?

A very few alterations considered the feelings of the churchly. Huck first said that the King, rigged out in his store clothes, looked as if "he had walked right out of the Bible"; this became "the ark," but the King still might be "old Leviticus himself." "Judas Iscarott" was softened to "Judus"; the King looked up toward the sky instead of the Throne. Two of Tom's jibes were altered, "mild as Sunday School" becoming "mild as goose-milk," and "Sunday-schooliest ways" changing to "infant-schooliest." On the other hand, when Huck trusted "to Providence to put the right words in [his] mouth when the time come," Mark changed "Providence" to "luck" in the manuscript, but restored his first thought in the proof. And once an inadvertently written "damn" was immediately changed to "dern." Susy's biography describes her mother as marking pages—presumably in the proofs—on which changes were to be made. Doubtless some of these alterations, therefore, are hers and not her husband's.

In the Wilks episode the manuscript allowed the King and Duke to be more goatish toward Mary Jane and her sisters than the book did. Their first welcome had included the statement that, "Soon as he could, the duke shook the hair-lip and sampled Susan, which was better looking. After the king had kissed Mary Jane fourteen or fifteen times, he give the duke a show, and tapered off on the others." And Huck, getting Mary Jane away before the showdown, had asked, "Do you reckon you can face your uncles, and take your regular three or four good-morning smacks?" The first passage was deleted; the second softened. But the motive was chiefly esthetic. Mary Jane was a heroine—Huck's ideal of spirited young womanhood. The passages were out of harmony with his feelings.

Out of all the hundreds of changes one phrase alone may be sincerely regretted, as a masterly specimen of Mark's command of invective. When the scoundrels quarreled, after the Wilks fiasco, the Duke's denunciation of the King originally ended as here italicized: "You wanted to get what money I'd got out of the 'Burning Shame' and one thing or another, and scoop it *all, you unsatisfiable, tunnel-bellied old sewer!"* No pencil mark stands against the passage in the manuscript, but perhaps it may be classed as one of those "remarks of a studied and felicitously atrocious character" inserted to draw Livy's fire, and deleted when they had served their purpose. It is a pity that Mark lost his nerve.

Detailed study of the manuscript of his greatest book, in short, reveals no evidence of blighting censorship. The revisions show a skilled craftsman at work and show, too, that here as always he plunged at his writing with little preliminary planning, improvising as he went and frequently running into blind alleys. *Huck Finn* owes part of its superiority over *Tom Sawyer* to the fact that for its main outline it has only the familiar journey motif which always made Mark's thoughts flow most freely. As has been said, he simply took a clever and uninhibited boy, and let the whole world of the Mississippi happen to him. The great river itself bears Huck on from one experience to another, with none of the makeshift transitions that link Tom's adventures. After *Tom Sawyer* was finished Mark thought that he had perhaps made a mistake in not writing it in the first person; in *Huck Finn* he rectified that mistake, and gave the book the autobiographical form which is almost indispensable in successful picaresque romance.

American literature contains no other gallery of character studies comparable with the pageant of *Huck Finn*. The criticism brought against the first part of *Life on the Mississippi,* that it gives only the romance of the pilot's life, cannot apply here. The whole life of the river, as it was lived in the decades preceding the Civil War, marches past. Huck's odyssey takes him through all the levels of Southern society, from such brutal and squalid outcasts as old man Finn to the Grangerfords. And whatever Huck sees, whether it be brutality, cowardice, chicanery, or loyalty and courage, he reports objectively, calmly, without passion and without moralizing. People who think that

Mark Twain suppressed the slavery chapter in *Life in the Mississippi* for fear of offending Southern readers and spoiling his sales have apparently never read *Huck*. One cannot indict a nation or a region, though it has been tried, but the community traits which made the Civil War on the Southern side are displayed coolly, and at full length. The Grangerfords are the cotton aristocracy of the valley, the class to which Jefferson Davis, for example, belonged, and it was these hotheads, not the old aristocracy of Virginia, who made the war. Old man Finn, in his tirade against the free Negro who could vote in Ohio and who couldn't even be sold in Missouri unless he stayed there six months, counterattacks the growing tendency to sentimentalize the memory of the South's "peculiar institution" in a way that makes Mrs. Stowe and Simon Legree seem shrill and ineffective. But the last word on slavery is not put in the mouth of drunken old Finn; it is spoken by kindly, bustling Mrs. Phelps, when Huck is trying to think up explanations for his delay in reaching the place he didn't know he was coming to. The passage has often been quoted, but no matter:

"It warn't the grounding—that didn't keep us back but a little. We blowed out a cylinder-head."

"Good gracious! anybody hurt?"

"No'm. Killed a nigger."

"Well, it's lucky; because sometimes people do get hurt."

The Phelps family are a step below the Grangerfords in the social scale; as Mark explained, their plantation is his uncle John Quarles' farm, moved down to Arkansas. But Colonel Sherburn, like the Grangerfords, is an aristocrat. He cold-bloodedly shoots down the drunken Boggs, because he had sworn he would do it the next time Boggs got abusive, and when a gentleman made a promise he kept it. Yet with his ruthlessness the Colonel has the aristocrat's proud courage which enables him by sheer force of character to rout the lynching mob. Mark evenhandedly records the merits as well as the defects of the social system he portrays.

Below the Grangerfords and Sherburn and the Phelpses,

again, comes the Wilks family—well-to-do small-town trades-people, whose way of life is subtly differentiated from the gentry's. The daughters of this family have not studied art or music; they do not compose elegiac verses, and their parlor lacks the steel engravings, the basket of plaster fruit and the crockery dogs and cats and parrots which the Grangerfords had brought back from some excursion to New Orleans or even faraway Philadelphia. And below the Wilkses, again, is Mrs. Judith Loftus, the backwoods wife, shrewd and observant, frankly and lavishly inquisitive, but quite unperturbed at being alone in her cabin at night while the menfolks are out hunting for runaway Jim. But it is useless to call the roll any further; a cross section of America is here, and not all the foolishness of Tom Sawyer at the beginning and the end of the book can dim its brilliance.

Yet when the book came from the press—in December 1884 in England, and February 1885 at home—America was placidly unaware that a masterpiece had been born. Abroad, Stevenson told John Addington Symonds that the whole story of a healthy boy's dealings with his conscience was incredibly well done—and Stevenson, as Scot and Presbyterian, should have known. But in America Howells was no longer on the *Atlantic*, to set the critical sheep jumping; Huck had a meager and lukewarm reception from the high-brows, while some of the godly were scandalized. The public library at Concord, where Bronson Alcott was still exuding Transcendental philosophy, made itself conspicuous for a moment by banishing Huck from its shelves because he was a bad example for youth. This advertisement naturally stimulated the sales, though they needed no stimulation. Forty thousand copies had been subscribed for in advance of publication, and the great public, which cares nothing about high-brow criticism, but knows whether a book is entertaining or not, gave Huck a place of honor which he has never lost.

Among the discerning people who knew a masterpiece, however, was Joel Chandler Harris, and Mark wrote to thank him for his good word about Huck, "that abused child of mine who has so much unfair mud flung at him. Somehow I can't help believing in him, and it's a great refreshment to my faith to have a man back me up who has been where such boys live, and knows what he is talking about." Doubtless few early readers recognized the bottom of fury in Mark's fun, but their uncritical approval came nearer the truth than the Concord School of Philosophy had brought the local librarians.

Yet in that publishing triumph were the seeds of future trouble. Mark Twain had taken the last step on the road he had been following; he had become his own publisher. Though neither *The Prince and the Pauper* nor *Life on the Mississippi* had exactly fallen dead from the press, the sales had been disappointing in comparison with those which Bliss had achieved for the earlier books. So now that Charley Webster had an efficiently organized staff of canvassers, Mark had determined to finance his young nephew-in-law and set up a complete subscription publishing house. One of his first steps after putting up the money was to seek a remedy for the greatest weakness of Bliss's and Osgood's books—the poor quality of the illustrations. The merits of some humorous drawings which E. W. Kemble had contributed to *Life* caught his eye, and he engaged Kemble to illustrate *Huck*, with the result that it was the first of Mark's important books in which the illustrations were not a pain to any sensitive eye.

If Charley Webster had made a failure of selling *Huck Finn*, it might have been better for the author, in the long run. Now Mark had a publishing house on his hands, a house equipped for quantity production. To keep it running and make it pay it was necessary to find books for it to publish. The demands of the business were constantly diverting Mark's attention from his proper literary vocation, and he had the misfortune to begin his general publishing business with a success unprecedented in trade history. He secured the contract for General Grant's *Memoirs*.

CHAPTER XIV

SLIPPERY PLACES

HERO worship and business acumen combined to fire Mark's enthusiasm when he heard in November 1884, just before *Huck Finn* came from the press, that General Grant had decided to write his memoirs. Following the failure of Ferdinand Ward's Wall Street bucket shop, into which he had been inveigled after retiring from the presidency, the General was penniless and ailing. In his desperate need for funds he had undertaken to prepare two or three articles for the *Century Magazine*'s notable series on the battles and leaders of the Civil War. When Mark Twain learned that Grant had decided to continue the work begun in those articles the General was already considering a contract which the Century Company had offered him.

Mark lost no time in visiting Grant, and on being told that Century was unwilling to guarantee that Grant's book would earn as much as the $25,000 which Sherman's *Memoirs* had brought in under the Scribner management, he exploded. Century, he declared, didn't know a good thing when it saw it. His own book would be out in a few weeks, and by the time Grant's was ready the Webster Company would be the best organized subscription firm in the country. If Grant would give his book to Webster, Mark was ready then and there to draw his personal check for $25,000, not as payment in full but as a mere trifling advance on the total royalties to be.

All the business was not settled at one interview, of course, but the upshot was that Mark got the contract, and everybody was happy except the Century Company and Grant himself. The General couldn't believe Mark's prophecies about sales, and regarded him as a good neighbor about to bankrupt himself for friendship's sake. He was right about the bankruptcy, in the long run, but his *Memoirs* were not responsible for it, except as one of the links in the chain of events which built up and then destroyed the firm of Webster and Company. As to the value of Grant's book, Mark's business judgment was vindicated as few men's has ever been. Over three hundred thousand sets were sold, at prices ranging from nine to twenty-five dollars a set; on February 27, 1886, the Webster Company drew Mrs. Grant a check for $200,000—the largest royalty payment that had ever been made in the history of publishing.

A new firm never got off to a faster start than Webster and Company. But in that tremendous initial success lay the seeds of its ultimate collapse. The Grant book had had everything needed for sensational sales: the country, twenty years after Appomattox, was ready to study the causes and events of the Civil War; Grant was the greatest of the surviving military leaders, and public sympathy with the bankrupt old man, heroically finishing his book as he lay dying of cancer, gave it an emotional sales appeal which transcended even its historical interest. But almost any subsequent book was bound to be an anticlimax. Webster secured and published McClellan's memoirs and Sheridan's, and sold them at a profit, but the big bonanza in Civil War material was over. And then, in the same year in which that astonishing royalty check was drawn for Julia Grant, Mark and Webster thought they had discovered the book which would make even their first success seem small-time stuff.

They would publish the life of Pope Leo XIII, to be written by a Catholic prelate of distinction and with the sanction and blessing of His Holiness himself. There is no quainter episode in the life of Mark Twain, freethinker and rabid hater of all ecclesiastical establishments, than the enthusiasm with which he plunged into this enterprise. But the same fever infected even the bystanders. All one had to do was to calculate the number of Roman Catholics in the world, figure the percentage of sales on the basis of the Grant results, and be convinced forthwith that even Colonel Sellers could scarcely overestimate the number of millions there were in it. Howells, with other usually levelheaded people, was as enthusiastic as Mark himself. And everything went well in the negotiations. Charley Webster went to Italy, in almost royal state, was granted an audience with His Holiness, and received the formal approval he sought. The firm outdid itself in preparations for vast sales, even to simultaneous publication in six languages.

All they had neglected in their calculations were the facts that more Catholics were poor than rich, that outside the United States, England, France and Germany the majority were illiterate, and that even among the literate the percentage of readers was not high. Furthermore, most literate Catholics had precisely the same reading tastes as their Protestant or agnostic neighbors; a biography, even of the Pope, had to have something besides piety to recommend it. On the whole, it was a high tribute to Webster's salesmen that the book actually showed a profit, though in comparison with the dreams that had launched the undertaking, the profit was minute. Nevertheless, for the first five years of its existence, the Webster company was a well-to-do concern, and its later troubles belong in a later chapter. Had Mark confined his business speculations to publishing, he would not have got into very serious trouble.

But it was in 1885, when *Huck Finn* was prospering and the Grant *Memoirs* were going to press, that Mark encountered the man and the invention which were his ruin. James W. Paige came along with plans for a typesetting machine which would revolutionize the printing business. All that was needed was a few thousand dollars to build a demonstration model. For Mark Twain, onetime printer and now a publisher, the hook scarcely needed bait. And perhaps it should be underscored that in this speculation, as in some others, Mark's basic judgment was sound—as sound as John Clemens' when he bought the Tennessee land. In the rapid increase of machinery in the printing industry there was one archaism: however swift and accurate the power press, all the type still had to be set by hand, as

Sam Clemens had set it in the Hannibal *Journal* office a generation before. A mechanical process which would quicken typesetting to the same tempo as the other stages of printing was
due, and overdue. Mark's misfortune was to find the wrong invention and the wrong inventor. It was the Kaolatype engraving
process all over again—before the new method could be perfected, a better and cheaper one came on the market.

Even as it was, there would have been a comfortable and
partial success for the Paige machine if Paige, like his backer,
had not been a dreamer and a perfectionist. The original plans
called for a machine which would merely set the type, leaving the
spacing and justifying of the lines to be done by hand. Had
the machine been put on the market in this state it would have
anticipated the Mergenthaler linotype by several years. But
before the first experimental machine was finished Paige had
worked out refinements by which he expected to make it perform all the processes, including sorting the type. It is useless
to detail the long series of tinkerings and rebuildings which finally produced a machine so delicate and complicated that it failed
to stand up under the stress of continuous high-speed operation.
Mark's chance for a fortune from the invention came, not from
Paige, but from the offer which the backers of Mergenthaler's
invention made him of a half-interest in their machine in exchange for a half-interest in his. He refused the offer, because
his faith in Paige blinded him to the merits and the threat of
the linotype. The details of the long struggle, the constant
deferring of hope, have no place in the story of his life as a
literary person. But the fact that from 1885 until 1891 Mark's
attention was centered on the work in progress in the Pratt
and Whitney factory in Hartford explains the dearth of completed writing during those years. It also explains the lavish
output of second-best work in the years immediately after 1891.
Milton turned aside from his vocation to write clumsy pamph-
lets because he was a son of the Puritan revolution; Mark
Twain turned aside from his to promote an invention, because
he was a son of the machine age. Yet it was the romantic dream,

more than the potential millions, which drew him. Mark Twain loved the openhanded living which money bought, but his interest in the money itself was much more as a safeguard for his family's future than for power or display. The great inventions of the nineteenth century fascinated him more as exhibitions of ingenuity than as sources of wealth.

Mark's diversion from his true work, however, did not come consciously, nor all at once. Even before *Huck Finn* was published, he had embarked on other projects. He tried again to dramatize *Tom Sawyer*, but concluded at last that one might as well try to dramatize a hymn. In January 1884 he was full of enthusiasm for a serious novel, in which he intended to make use of his knowledge of Hawaii. He explained it both to Mrs. Fairbanks and to Howells, but it was to the latter that he gave the full statement of the underlying theme:

"Its hidden motive will illustrate a but little considered fact in human nature; that the religious folly you are born in you will *die* in, no matter what apparently reasonabler religious folly may seem to have taken its place meanwhile, and abolished and obliterated it. I start Bill Ragsdale at 12 years of age, and the heroine at 4, in the midst of the ancient idolatrous system, with its picturesque and amazing customs and superstitions, 3 months before the arrival of the missionaries and the erection of a shallow Christianity upon the ruins of the old paganism. Then these two will become educated Christians, and highly civilized. And then I will jump 15 years, and do Ragsdale's leper business. . . ."

But though he had stacked his billiard table with all available books about Hawaii the task of converting the theme into action apparently proved too much; the novel took its place in his ever-growing collection of unwritten or unfinished works. Its interest lies in its deterministic theme, for it was during the 1880's, when everything seemed prosperous for Mark, in family and fortune alike, that he worked out the details of the philosophical theories which he increasingly expressed in his last years. It is a dogma of the critics that his pessimism was the fruit of his personal disasters in the 1890's; actually, all that the disasters did was to confirm, and give edge and poignancy to ideas which had been formulated long before.

Upon the foundations of Calvinistic determinism, which were laid for him in the Presbyterian Sunday school in Hannibal and from which he had long ago removed the Calvinistic superstructure of Revelation and Grace, he erected a determinism based partly on Lecky's *History of European Morals*, partly upon his own interpretation of nineteenth-century science. In his notebooks of the 1880's the following idea is stated more than once:

"Special Providence! The phrase nauseates me—with its implied importance of mankind and triviality of God. In my opinion these myriads of globes are merely the blood corpuscles ebbing and flowing through the arteries of God and we are but animalculae that infest them, disease them, pollute them; and God does not know we are there and would not care if He did."

His low opinion of human nature was fortified by his almost annual rereading of Suetonius, Pepys and Saint-Simon, but Mark was too sensitive and high-strung to need literary confirmation of his frequent rages against life and mankind. Even in his happiest years he did not lack for pain to keep him awake. Any celebrity, especially if he is known to be prosperous, receives a daily grist of begging letters, for instance, which uncover all the seamiest sides of human nature. With this particular irritation it became Mark's habit, with Livy's encouragement, to pour out his rage in a long and inflammable reply, which he then put aside to cool. When it and he were cool, he would write a second letter, which got mailed and usually settled the matter. But sometimes the first draft was sent, and the result was trouble, for while his rage lasted, Mark was capable of neither mercy nor justice. The Hingston incident is as good an illustration as any. In London, in 1872, he deliberately and publicly cut E. P. Hingston, whom he had known and liked in Nevada when Hingston was Artemus Ward's manager, because Hingston had written a laudatory introduction for Hotten's piratical edition of *The Innocents Abroad*. Afterwards, of course, his conscience smote him, but the subsequent pangs of the attacker's conscience do little to mollify the victim of the attack.

In January 1882 he devoted three weeks to collecting material for a scathing biography of Whitelaw Reid, because he had been told that Reid's paper, the New York *Tribune*, had been making almost daily attacks upon him. At the end of three weeks he was at last calm enough to act on Livy's suggestion that he verify the report of the attacks before continuing his counteroffensive. He then discovered that they consisted of "one discourteous remark of the *Tribune* about my *book*—not me—between Nov. 1 and Dec. 20; and a couple of foreign criticisms (of my writings, not me) between Nov. 1 and Jan. 26! . . . And my three weeks' hard work have got to go into the ignominious pigeonhole. Confound it, I could have earned ten thousand dollars with infinitely less trouble." Apropos of this very incident Howells said, "You could offer Clemens offences that would anger other men and he did not mind; he would account for them from human nature; but if he thought you had in any way played him false you were anathema and maranatha forever. . . . He went farther than Heine, who said that he forgave his enemies, but not till they were dead. Clemens did not forgive his dead enemies; their death seemed to deepen their crimes, like a base evasion, or a cowardly attempt to escape. . . . He was generous without stint; he trusted without measure; but where his generosity was abused, or his trust betrayed, he was a fire of vengeance, a consuming flame of suspicion that no sprinkling of cool patience from others could quench; it had to burn itself out. . . . In his frenzies . . . he would not, and doubtless could not, listen to reason. But if between the paroxysms he were confronted with the facts he would own them, no matter how much they told against him."*

But his rages had often nobler targets than individuals who

---

*From *My Mark Twain* by William Dean Howells. Copyright 1910 by Harper & Bros., 1938 by Mildred Howells and John Mead Howells.

had somehow offended him. The sense of the brevity of life and its inevitable end in ignoble senility and decay, which he had expressed in his letter to Twichell when Jean was a baby, was never far from his mind in his quieter moments. During this decade, for example, he heard from his boyhood friend, Will Bowen, of some bereavement Bowen had just suffered. Bowen's letter had come just as Mark was setting out to attend a wedding, and the thought of it, and the reflections it suggested, ran through his mind in the midst of the gaiety.

"Here was the near presence of the two supreme events of life: marriage, which is the beginning of life, and death,·which is the end of it. I found myself seeking chances to shirk into corners where I might think, undisturbed; and the most I got out of my thought, was this: both marriage and death ought to be welcome; the one promises happiness, doubtless the other assures it."

It was from this decade that Howells preserved the memory of the effect Mark's appearance had upon Matthew Arnold— the memory which ends, "He glimmered at you from the narrow slits of fine blue-greenish eyes, under branching brows, which with age grew more and more like a sort of plumage, and he was apt to smile into your face with a subtle but amiable perception, and yet with a sort of remote absence; you were all there for him, but he was not all there for you."* And it was on such thoughts as he had expressed to Will Bowen that his mind was oftenest absent.

But what most stirred his nobler rages was the sight and thought of oppression and injustice. Hereditary rank and privilege especially roused him, for Mark was an American republican of the simple old school which had believed that the whole world would be free when men had hanged the last king in the guts of the last priest. He was not blind to the existence of oppression and injustice at home—he approved, for instance, the efforts of the Knights of Labor to organize industrial workers—but whatever of the sort existed in America seemed

---

*From *My Mark Twain* by William Dean Howells. Copyright 1910 by Harper & Bros., 1938 by Mildred Howells and John Mead Howells.

to him pallid and inconsequential compared with what was recorded of the European past in the pages of Carlyle and Pepys, Saint-Simon and Lecky. And the first notion of a story which might embody some of his thoughts on these subjects came to him in a comic notion he jotted down in 1883:

"Dream of being a knight errant in armor in the Middle Ages. Have the notions and habits of thought of the present day mixed with the necessities of that. No pockets in the armor. Can't scratch. Cold in the head—can't blow—can't get a handkerchief, can't use iron sleeve. Iron gets red-hot in the sun—leaks in the rain, gets white with frost and freezes me solid in winter. Make disagreeable clatter when I enter church. Can't dress or undress myself. Always getting struck by lightning. Fall down and can't get up."

The notion was not original. Three years before, Charles Heber Clark ("Max Adeler") had published a story called "The Fortunate Island," in which an American professor found himself in a land inhabited by descendants of the Arthurian peerage, whom he astounded by his knowledge of nineteenth-century mechanics. Mark did nothing with the notion then, but in the fall of the next year, when he was on a reading tour with G. W. Cable, Cable gave him a copy of Sir Thomas Malory, whom he had never read. Malory fascinated him, and made him rage and laugh at the same time. In the summer of 1886 he began the story which became *A Connecticut Yankee in King Arthur's Court*. What he then expected it to be, he told Mrs. Fairbanks in November of that year. "The story isn't a satire peculiarly; it is more especially a *contrast*." He intended, he continued, to bring out the salient features of Arthurian times and his own, by constantly juxtaposing them. Only two or three chapters were then written, and he was in no hurry to finish. "I expect to write three chapters a year for thirty years; then the book will be done. I am writing it for posterity only— my posterity; my great-grandchildren. It is to be my holiday amusement for six days every summer for the rest of my life." He had no intention, he added, of besmirching or belittling Malory's great and beautiful characters—"I am only after the *life* of that day, that is all; to picture it; to try to get into it; to see how it feels and seems."

Such abstemiousness of composition, of course, was impossible for Mark when he really got interested in an idea. He returned to his manuscript during 1887, at Quarry Farm, and the following fall brought it home to Hartford almost finished. Though a couple of years earlier he had announced confidently that he did not expect to publish any more books, by the end of 1888 he had changed his mind, and was under pecuniary pressure besides. The Webster Company, from which Charley Webster had had to retire because of a nervous breakdown, was not doing too well, and needed a Mark Twain book to bolster its sales. And the Paige machine was swallowing several thousand dollars of Mark's money a month, and still was not finished. The Clemens household was costing about $35,000 a year to maintain, and it may have been at this time that Mark and Livy held the review of their expenses which Robert Barr reported. According to Mark, after going over every item, they could find no places where they could economize, except by canceling their subscription to *Harper's Magazine,* and using a cheaper brand of toilet paper. But the machine, adding itself to the other distractions of winter in Hartford, prevented the completion of the *Yankee,* even though Mark for a time borrowed study-room in Twichell's house while workmen were busy in his own.

And still he was thinking out his "philosophy." Some of the conclusions he had put into a paper, "What is Happiness?," which he had read before the Monday Evening Club as early as 1883. That paper summarized what may be called the social aspect of his determinism. During 1887 or 1888 he wrote into the *Yankee* a broader statement—one completely out of character for the man who was supposed to be expressing it:

"Training—training is everything; training is all there is *to* a person. We speak of nature; it is folly; there is no such thing as nature; what we call by that misleading name is merely heredity and training. We have no thoughts of our own, no opinions of our own; they are transmitted to us, trained into us. All that is original in us, and therefore fairly creditable or discreditable to us, can be covered up and hidden by the point of a cambric needle, all the rest being atoms contributed by, and inherited from, a procession of ancestors that stretches back a billion years to the Adam-clam or grasshopper or monkey from whom our race has been so tediously and ostentatiously and unprofitably developed. And as for me, all that I think about in this plodding sad pilgrimage, this pathetic drift between the eternities, is to look out and humbly live a pure and high and blameless life, and save that one microscopic atom in me that is truly *me:* the rest may land in Sheol and welcome for all I care."

So much were these ideas in his mind that they came out in a casual interview with a total stranger in the summer of 1889. Rudyard Kipling, twenty-four years old and en route to London after "seven years hard" on Anglo-Indian newspapers, made a special pilgrimage to Elmira to seek out the man whom he had learned to love and admire fourteen thousand miles away. Kipling was still wholly unknown outside of India, and brought no credentials or letters of introduction. But he found Mark in a friendly and expansive mood. After they had agreed heartily on the subject of international copyright, Kipling asked whether Tom Sawyer married Judge Thatcher's daughter, and whether they were ever to hear of Tom as a man.

"I haven't decided," was the reply. "I have a notion of writing the sequel to Tom Sawyer in two ways. In one I would make him rise to great honor and go to Congress, and in the other I should hang him. Then the friends and enemies of the book could take their choice."

Kipling protested, because to him Tom Sawyer was real.

"Oh, he *is* real. He's all the boy that I have known or recollect; but that would be a good way of ending the book, because, when you come to think of it, neither religion, training, nor education avails anything against the force of circumstances that drive a man. Suppose we took the next four and twenty years of Tom Sawyer's life, and gave a little joggle to the circumstances that controlled him. He would, logically and according to the joggle, turn out a rip or an angel."

"Do you believe that, then?"

"I think so. Isn't it what you call Kismet?"

"Yes; but don't give him two joggles and show the result, because he isn't your property any more. He belongs to us."

The things a man says, when he talks with a stranger, are the things uppermost in his mind, the things he has said before to other people. Mark Twain had therefore, to repeat, formulated the complete theory, later written out as *What Is Man?*, in the full tide of his good fortune and happiness, in the decade when the majority of his fellow writers, honoring his fiftieth birthday, had awakened to the fact that Mark Twain was something more than just another funny man, and even Oliver Wendell Holmes, the last of the Brahmins, had written congratulatory verses. It was life, not personal misfortune, that inspired his savage arraignment of life; the fierce indignation which consumed his heart sprang from sources deeper than bankruptcy and bereavement.

Much of that fierce indignation he poured into the pages of the *Yankee,* ready at last for the printer about the time he talked with Kipling. For his own good, and the good of the Webster Company, Mark determined to make a handsome book of it. The same alertness which had led to his engaging Kemble as illustrator of *Huck Finn* brought to his attention the work of Dan Beard, whose founding of the American Boy Scouts was still a long way in the future. He gave Beard a free hand in choosing the subjects and treatment for his illustrations, but sought to explain the nature of his narrator:

"This Yankee of mine has neither the refinement nor the weakness of a college education; he is a perfect ignoramus; he is boss of a machine shop; he can build a locomotive or a Colt's revolver, he can put up and run a telegraph line, but he's an ignoramus, nevertheless."

In that characterization of his hero, Mark unconsciously exposed the first of the artistic blemishes in his book. In giving the idea he had started with, he also revealed how far he digressed from it at times. Doubtless the idea for the Yankee came from some of the expert machinists he had talked with so often over the Paige machine in the Pratt and Whitney shops. But in writing the book he proved wholly incapable of the sort of artistic selection which had held the narrative and the comprehension of events in his masterpiece down within recognizable distance of the intellectual and emotional limitations of twelve-year-old Huck. One of the passages of philosophy incongruously put in the Yankee's mouth has already been quoted, but most of his comments on State and Church and chivalry are almost equally incongruous. In the course of the story, moreover, it appears that this Connecticut ignoramus has read Casanova and Saint-Simon and Lecky, and even shares his creator's exasperated fascination with the German language. He is more like Elihu Burritt, the literary blacksmith, than like any possible foreman at Pratt and Whitney's; but most of all, of course, he is like Mark Twain. Projecting himself back into his own boyhood, Mark could lay aside enough of his mature acquirements to give an air of reality to the stated characteristics of his creations; he could not project himself into a mature person of different background from his own without trailing inappropriate clouds of his own glory after him.

But the mixture of Mark Twain himself with the Yankee is the least of the book's mixtures. Far more annoying is its mixture of the Mark Twain who loved grotesquerie and extravaganza for their own sakes with the Mark Twain who hated the cowardice and injustice of the damned human race. The starting point of the book, the dream of the discomforts of traveling in armor, corrupted the whole scheme. Fierce indignation against oppression constantly slides off into slapstick farce. In his effort to have his Yankee mechanically up to date the author laid even his farce open to the danger of becoming swiftly outmoded—within a couple of years or so after Lancelot and his knights rode to the rescue on high-wheel bicycles, for instance, the introduction of the "safety" made the episode, even on its slapstick level, somewhat more archaic than Malory himself.

But the basic weakness of the book, the weakness which almost destroys its satiric value, is Mark's complete incapacity for understanding history in terms of institutions. For all his wide reading, he never got beyond thinking of it in terms of individuals—such individuals as he had met on the river. Again it is needless to elaborate; it is enough to mention the Roman Catholic Church as it appears in the pages of the Yankee. As an embodiment of economic and political power Mark realized and hated it; as a spiritual force, for any end save terror and oppression, it scarcely exists in his pages except in the one scene where the courageous young priest stands by the girl who is executed for the theft of a piece of cloth. To him, the Church was still the "awful ecclesiastical swindle" he had called it in Florence in 1867. That its power over the minds of simple folk was due to anything more than terror and chicanery he seldom even suspected, any more than he stopped to consider what would have happened to his Yankee, or any stranger in medieval Europe, who was not baptized and who did not attend Mass and confession.

What he thought, even of the institutions with which he was more directly acquainted, depended, moreover, rather upon his momentary mood than upon any deep and settled convictions. While the book was at press, for example, he rejoiced in the revolution which dethroned the genial Dom Pedro as Emperor of Brazil, and had no doubt that by the act of proclaiming a republic instead of a monarchy Brazil had become a free country. Yet this was the same Mark Twain who a dozen years before had declared his hatred of all shades and forms of republican government and had prophesied—humorously, it is true—the coming of a monarchy in the United States. Consistency was never Mark's strong point, but without an underlying ideal of the good state, effective satire of institutions is impossible. The most ironic element of all in his book the author never realized. The Yankee talked constantly of establishing an Arthurian democracy, but what he actually established was a dictatorship, with himself in the title role.

The chief accomplishment of the *Yankee*, in fact, was some immediate empty laughter from the bulk of his American readers, and the temporary estrangement of many of his admirers in England, who relished neither the burlesquing of the Arthurian story nor the gibes at British institutions, including the royal grants which Parliament had to vote for each of Queen Victoria's lengthy family. Though Mark regretted the things he had left out, which burned in him and kept on multiplying till the saying of them would require a library, and a pen warmed up in hell, it would have done no good artistically had he put them in, unless he had taken out the extravaganza and told the whole tale on the bitter level of the King's and the Boss's experience as slaves.

The book did not even accomplish its immediate purpose of relieving financial pressure on its author. The Webster Company was getting out of its depth in promoting the massive Stedman and Hutchinson *Library of American Literature,* which was being sold on the installment plan, and Mark was drawing heavily on his company's funds to keep up his Hartford establishment and continue to finance Paige. Nearly two hundred thousand dollars, including most of Livy's liquid capital, had gone into the machine, and when at last it was approximately complete it was too late. The capital necessary for manufacturing the machines in quantity proved shy and at length unobtainable. In trying to interest capitalists, moreover, Mark had been obliged to relinquish his original contract with Paige, which had given him complete control of the invention, and now he saw the dream of wealth which had absorbed his best energies for most of a decade slowly begin to fade.

Personal losses, too, were added to the financial ones as the decade ended. His brother-in-law, Theodore Crane, died in the summer of 1889, and his death broke the old happy circle at Quarry Farm. During the next year Jane Clemens died, at the age of ninety, and shortly afterward Livy's mother followed.

At the beginning of 1891 Mark, in his fifty-sixth year, found himself, for the first time in twenty years, dependent upon writing for his whole livelihood, unless his publishing business could be pulled out of the red and once more made the going concern it had been in the days of *Huck Finn* and the Grant *Memoirs*. Though he had forfeited the control of the Paige machine he had not wholly abandoned hope that it might be profitable to him; he retained a minority interest, and perhaps Paige could enlist capital where Mark had failed. But anyway, the Webster Company would go to town on the *Library of American Literature*—rebounding from despair, Mark foresaw sales of a million sets. Meanwhile, however, the Company would need more funds, and so would its backer.

He pulled out of their pigeonholes various unfinished articles, finished them, and sold them to magazines. Among the manuscripts thus unearthed was the play about Mulberry Sellers which Mark and Howells had had so much fun with eight years before. Now he set to work to turn the play into a novel, and in spite of rheumatism in his shoulder completed most of the work within three months and disposed of the serial rights for twelve thousand dollars. In his old way, he fattened the book by incorporating in it various fragments of essays, including a defense of the irreverent American press against Matthew Arnold's strictures. No interpolations, however, could make *The American Claimant* any more incoherent than it was by nature. Raymond's criticism applied just as truly to the book as it had to the play: Colonel Sellers is no longer a dreamer, he is a lunatic, and a tiresome lunatic at that. Not even the flight of fancy—"Mulberry Sellers wafts you a kiss across the universe"—with which the book ends can redeem its absurdities. Of all Mark's stories it is the one which the reader lays aside with the least regret.

It had not even the merit of appreciably lessening the financial stringency. Long before the manuscript was completed, the Clemenses had decided upon drastic curtailment of their expenses. They determined to go to Europe for an indefinite stay.

There they could live on a scale less lavish than the Hartford establishment demanded until Mark's business entanglements were unraveled. They closed their house, and found other jobs for the coachman, Patrick MacAleer, who had been with them since their honeymoon days in Buffalo, and for George Griffin, the Negro butler who had come once to wash windows and had stayed eighteen years. When the day of departure came, June 6, 1891, Livy was the last to leave the house, which she never entered again. The golden day was over. The journey on which they were setting out was a journey deeper and deeper into the shadows. Of the four members of his family who sailed with him that day on the *Gascogne* only one would be alive when it came Mark Twain's turn to make the last journey of all.

CHAPTER XV

I*N* EXILE

THOUGH his dislike of travel had grown with the years Mark Twain was not gloomy or disheartened at the outset of his exile. His frontier training had taught him not to cry over spilt milk, but in 1891 he was far from convinced that the milk was irrevocably spilt. Though Charley Webster was dead, after a long illness, the firm was seemingly well managed by Fred Hall, who shared some of his employer's irrepressible optimism Just give the *Library of American Literature* a chance to get going, with two or three smaller books on the side to bring in immediate returns, and the firm would be riding high again. All that the Clemens family foresaw was a year or two of residence abroad, much in the style of their 1879 sojourn.

The summer passed pleasantly enough. Mark was treated for his rheumatism, first at Aix-les-Bains and later at Marienbad, and they attended the Wagner festival at Bayreuth. Before sailing Mark had contracted with William M. Laffan to write six travel letters at a thousand dollars apiece, for the New York *Sun,* and these experiences furnished him with the material for quickly fulfilling half the undertaking. He also considered the possibility of doing still another travel book, and in September took a trip in quest of material. Leaving his family at Lausanne, he spent ten happy days drifting down the Rhone from its source to Arles, accompanied only by a courier and the boatman. The courier was Joseph Very, whom Mark had impulsively recommended by name in *A Tramp Abroad,* but whom, before the present trip had continued very long, he was ready to offer to Satan as a gift. But it was a restful trip—too restful, for he took few notes, saw few sights and concluded, rightly, that the material was too slight to turn into literature.

In October the whole family established themselves in Berlin for the winter. So far as leisure for writing was concerned, the move was a mistake, though he described the big new city in an article fittingly called "The German Chicago." Berlin proved almost as full of social distractions as Hartford, and distractions of a more impressive sort. Mark discovered that he was almost as well known in Germany as he was at home. Dinners at the American Embassy brought him acquaintance with various members of the German nobility, and before the winter ended he was a dinner guest of the Kaiser's, which prompted Jean to remark that pretty soon there wouldn't be anybody left for him to get acquainted with but God. Apparently his fulminations against hereditary rank had temporarily burned themselves out; at any rate he recorded in his notebook an incident which should have made the author of the *Connecticut Yankee* see red. Spending a few days at a village in the Hartz Mountains, the Clemenses were invited to a reception in honor of Fürst vom Stolberg-Wernigerode, "the proudest unroyal prince in Germany, and the richest." The village doctor and his wife were not in society, for he was a baker's son, but were allowed to attend the reception. After Mark and Livy had shaken hands with the Prince, "the doctor's wife put out her hand and the Fürst let on that he didn't see it. Poor thing, instead of taking warning, she raised her hand *higher*, imagining that he hadn't seen. He *ignored* it. It was tragic. She had a cry that night." And that is all he says, except to add what charming people the Prince's sister and niece were. But at King Arthur's court, or Queen Victoria's, instead of the Fürst vom Stolberg-Wernigerode's, the episode would have been good for at least a page of invective.

However much Mark basked in the social climate of Berlin its physical climate was bad for him. His rheumatism continued to plague him at intervals, and he was in bed for a month with one of the attacks of bronchitis which were the bugbear of his final years. At the first of March they went to Mentone for a month, and thence to Italy, where the family enjoyed themselves as before with sight-seeing. In Florence they made arrangements to rent the Villa Viviani for the following winter. Finally, in June, Mark established his family at Bad Nauheim for the summer, and dashed back to America on the first of many attempts to find out what was wrong with his business. During the next two or three years he crossed the ocean a dozen times, as affairs grew steadily worse. This first trip was typical of most of the others. The Paige machine was still unmanufactured; Fred Hall was still optimistic about the future of the Webster Company, though it was slowly dawning on him and Mark alike that if the *Library of American Literature* continued to sell it would break them. Because it was offered on long-term installment payments, the more sets they sold the deeper they went into the red. Agents' commissions and manufacturing charges had to be paid in full when the sales were made, and the slow dribble of monthly payments from the purchasers was not enough to balance the cash outlay. But in the summer of 1892 Mark was still ready to believe that the business had a future, though the sales of *The American Claimant,* which Webster had published in May, were disappointing.

By the middle of July, Mark was back in Bad Nauheim. His rheumatism was better, and he turned vigorously to the business of making books. On the eastward trip he had written a magazine article, "All Kinds of Ships," which, like the six newspaper articles of the previous year, showed that he could still do first-rate work in the humorous-descriptive vein which had first made him famous. At Nauheim his first undertaking was the story eventually called *Tom Sawyer Abroad.* It was not his first effort to revive his most popular characters: four summers before, he had begun *Tom and Huck among the Indians,* but had bogged down after a few chapters were drafted. This time he found the work flowing smoothly, and he piled up two hundred and eighty pages before the first enthusiasm waned. Mary Mapes Dodge had been begging him for a serial for that finest of all children's magazines, *St. Nicholas,* and had offered $5,000 for the serial rights. This story, Mark concluded, would do.

It is always a risk for an author to revive characters with whom the public has become familiar in their original settings. Unfavorable comparisons are inevitable. The surprising thing is that in *Tom Sawyer Abroad,* and the later *Tom Sawyer, Detective,* Mark did not do worse, especially when one recalls Dickens' disastrous attempt to revive Sam Weller and his father. Actually, when Huck and Tom and Jim get to arguing, long passages in *Tom Sawyer Abroad* are fully as good as anything in *Huck Finn.* The weakness of the story is in its machinery, literally. When a romancer endows his characters with a machine or any other form of power which transcends normal experience, he is in trouble at once. He has to find uses to which the extraordinary power can be put, and he has to find a plausible ending for the story. The problem has staggered abler plot builders than Mark Twain ever was, including Jules Verne and H. G. Wells. To put the boys, about the year 1850, into a navigable balloon of incredible speed and carrying capacity, was just the sort of fantasy that Mark could never resist. But having got them there, the difficulty of contriving adventures commensurate on the one hand with their limited capacities, and on the other with the unlimited power at their disposal, was more than he could manage. The story does not end; it peters out. Only the perennial simplicity of Jim, and the literalness of Huck, keep it from total failure.

Still at Nauheim, Mark embarked on a second story before *Tom Sawyer Abroad* was finished. This he conceived as a farce, to be called *Those Extraordinary Twins.* Grotesques had an unending fascination for him. In planning this story he harked back to an extravaganza about the original Siamese Twins which he had written in 1869. Along with some topical matters, such as the statement that the Twins had enlisted on opposite sides in the Civil War, and had taken each other prisoner at Seven Pines, the early sketch had contained many of the ideas for the later undertaking. In particular, Chang was represented as a strong advocate of temperance, and a member of the Good Templars, but unfortunately Eng sometimes got drunk, and that made Chang drunk, too, though his temperance principles were unshaken. "All just men were forced to confess that he was not morally, but only physically drunk. By every right and by every moral evidence the man was strictly sober; and, therefore, it caused his friends all the more anguish to see him shake hands with the pump and try to wind his watch with his night-key." That Mark returned to this notion, after a lapse of twenty-three years, illustrates once more the continuity of his mind and his humor, in their weaknesses as well as their strength. But what was good enough for a magazine skit was incapable of expansion to book length.

He carried the half-finished manuscript with him when the family moved to the Villa Viviani at the end of September, and continued to work at it. Presently some subordinate characters moved forward to take the spotlight away from the twins, and by the end of the year Mark reported to Fred Hall that the story was finished. "The last third of it suits me to a dot. I begin, today, to entirely re-cast and re-write the first two-thirds—new plan, with two minor characters, made very prominent, one major character dropped out, and the Twins subordinated to a minor but not insignificant place." He had, in fact, begun to write *Pudd'nhead Wilson*.

No franker statement of his own methods of narrative writing exists than Mark's preface to *Those Extraordinary Twins*. Confessing himself a man without the novel-writing gift, he described such a man's difficulties when he tried to build a novel: "He has no clear idea of his story; in fact he has no story. He merely has some people in his mind, and an incident or two, also a locality. He knows these people, he knows the selected locality, and he trusts that he can plunge those people into those incidents with interesting results. So he goes to work. To write a novel? No—that is a thought which comes later; in the beginning he is only proposing to tell a little tale; a very little tale; a six-page tale. But as it is a tale which he is not acquainted with, and can only find out what it is by listening as it goes along telling itself, it is more than apt to go on and on and on till it spreads itself into a book."

In the present case, he continued, he found the story changing from a farce to a tragedy in the middle. After a while he realized that it was really two stories instead of one. He pulled out the farce and developed the tragedy, but decided to print part of the farce as a sample of what it had started to be. Yet so far as the plot was concerned, he was unaware of what it had turned into. Negotiating for sale of the serial rights, he told Hall that whereas *The American Claimant* had contained nothing new, "the fingerprints in this one is virgin ground—absolutely *fresh*, and mighty curious and interesting to everybody." He did not realize that the plot was the oldest of the Victorian situations—the Rightful Heir changed in his cradle for the child of the Wicked Nurse. The nurse's motive—the dread of being sold down the river—was unusual and convincing, but the only novelty in the plot was the provision of something other than the conventional strawberry mark as the means whereby the substitution was finally discovered. His readers, however, were so used to the strawberry-mark theme that the conventionality impressed them no more than it did the author.

The truly original element in the story Mark Twain seemingly overlooked. It had come naturally to him, as part of his inheritance from slavery days in Missouri, and he presented it simply, without heat or underscoring. The moral overhead of slavery, by which slave women became their masters' concubines and bore them slave children, was a dangerously realistic theme to handle in the still prudish closing years of the Victorian age. But simply because he handled it without heat, as a fact of nature, Mark Twain got away with it. Remembering Wales McCormick's jesting advances to Ament's mulatto girl, he remembered also how the girl's mother had made only perfunctory objection: it was the privilege of the dominant race to exercise the *droit du seigneur* if it chose. Into his presentation of the theme he also worked his conviction that it is training—"conditioning" is the modern slang—not innate quality, which makes a free man or a slave. The conclusion of the story is as grimly realistic as the tragedy of Roxy. Whatever Mark Twain had omitted from *Life on the Mississippi* about the South's attitude toward its peculiar institution, he more than made up for now. It is, in short, the fearless and dispassionate handling of the ticklish theme of miscegenation, and neither its Victorian plot nor the hocus-pocus of the fingerprints, which entitles *Pudd'nhead Wilson* to a place among Mark Twain's works that falls only a little short of Tom and Huck. But though the author failed to see the true originality in his plot, he unquestionably knew that he was using the story to illustrate his deterministic philosophy. "Training is everything," he said in one of the chapter mottoes. "The peach was once a bitter almond; cauliflower is nothing but cabbage with a college education." Tom Driscoll is one thirty-second Negro; thirty-one thirty-seconds of his personality are the product of training and environment, but the one thirty-second is his soul. And Valet de Chambre, all white, is in speech and thought a slave, because he was reared a slave.

Furthermore, the picture of Dawson's Landing added another notable canvas to Mark's gallery of community portraits, which had begun with Obedstown, Tennessee, and in which Hadleyburg and Eseldorf were still to come. In this book, too, Mark gave the growing bitterness of his humor fuller expression than even in the chaotic pages of the *Yankee*. The sayings from Pudd'nhead Wilson's Calendar, which served as chapter mottoes, were nothing new in Mark's writing, but hitherto they had been slipped into the body of his text, where the casual reader scarcely noticed them. For years he had been jotting down similar ideas in his notebooks. The novelty in *Pudd'nhead Wilson* was that Mark at length let these remarks stand on their own merits as epigrams, instead of seeking places where they could be worked into the narrative. They range from the crisp aphorism—"Nothing so needs reforming as other people's habits," or, "It is difference of opinion that makes horse-races"—to distilled bitterness. "Why is it that we rejoice at a birth and grieve at a funeral? It is because we are not the person involved." "Whoever has lived long enough to find out what life is, knows how deep a debt of gratitude we owe to Adam, the first great benefactor of our race. He brought death into the world." The black moods were deepening; life itself, not the institutions that as targets had contented Mark Twain in the *Yankee,* was the object of his scorn, though the climax of his personal troubles was still four years in the future.

Not even *Tom Sawyer Abroad, Those Extraordinary Twins,* and *Pudd'nhead Wilson* exhausted the amazing spate of work which began at Nauheim and continued in Florence. Half a dozen articles and sketches reached completion, among them *Adam's Diary* and the *Defence of Harriet Shelley* which was inspired by Edward Dowden's labored attempt to whitewash the darkest episode in the poet's career.

Than this latter, Mark Twain never wrote a more brilliant piece of prose. It crackles and scintillates with wit, but wit controlled and directed into a masterpiece of destructive analysis. Though more can be said against Harriet than Mark was willing to admit, his demolition of Dowden's specific charges has stood. Shelley's latest and most scholarly biographer, Newman Ivey White, follows Mark Twain almost word for word in dismissing most of the Dowden accusations as frivolous and disingenuous. Moreover, as a dissection of the "literary cake-walk" style of formal Victorian biography the essay is a permanent joy, and in its characterizations of Shelley and his circle it surpasses the work of most of the Shelley scholars. Of all the English poets, Shelley, it would seem, was the one whom Mark Twain was least likely to understand. But he did. Shelley "was so rich in unselfishness, generosities, and magnanimities that he made his whole generation seem poor in these great qualities by comparison. . . . He never had any youth. He was an erratic and fantastic child during eighteen years, then he stepped into manhood, as one steps over a door-sill." Mrs. Boinville's "unwholesome prairie-dogs' nest" of a literary circle, and Godwin's menagerie above "his little debt-factory of a book-shop" have never been better described. "Godwin was not without self-appreciation; indeed, it may be conjectured that from his point of view the last syllable of his name was surplusage. He lived serene in his lofty world of philosophy, far above the mean interests that absorbed smaller men, and only came down to the ground at intervals to pass the hat for alms to pay his debts with, and insult the man that relieved him." Or Mary Godwin, "a child in years only. From the day that she set her masculine grip on Shelley he was to frisk no more." It seems a pity that Mark Twain did not give more time to literary biography. He would have livened it up, and cleared away some of the fog of special pleading.

But this essay was a mere by-product. In the same letter to Fred Hall which announced the completion of *Pudd'nhead Wilson,* Mark described another project:

"I am writing a companion to *The Prince and the Pauper,* which is half done and will make 200,000 words; and I have had the idea that if it were gotten up in handsome style, with many illustrations and put at a high enough price, maybe the L.A.L. canvassers would take it and run it with that book."

The "companion" was the *Personal Recollections of Joan of Arc.* From the day when he had first learned of her existence, from a stray leaf of print blowing about the streets of Hannibal, the story of the French heroine had fascinated Mark Twain. As he grew older and bitterer, Joan attracted him more and more. With her faith and courage and simplicity she seemed one of the few characters in history who could in any wise justify the existence of the human race—even as Livy and Susy Clemens, and Howells and a few others, were its justification among his contemporaries. The idea of telling her story as a companion piece to *The Prince and the Pauper* had apparently come to him while he was writing the latter book, but though he made a few notes, and did some general reading, the project was one of the many swallowed by his all-engrossing interest in Paige's machine. Now, in the early spring of 1893, he carried

Photograph by J. G. Gessford, New York City

MARK TWAIN IN 1904

the narrative on steadily as far as its first great climax, the raising of the siege of Orleans. Then all work stopped for a while. The long death struggle of his business interests reclaimed his entire attention, except for some revisions of *Pudd'nhead Wilson.*

He made another flying visit to America in April 1893. Paige was still optimistic, but unremunerative; the Webster affairs, however, were damping even the buoyancy of Fred Hall. The great financial panic of 1893 was beginning; banks were restricting credit and calling notes. By the time he was back in Europe and had moved his family from Florence to Munich for the summer Mark was in his usual mood in regard to a losing game—he wanted to cut his losses and quit. His letters to Hall were filled with futile suggestions, such as selling the *Library of American Literature* to meet the more pressing debts of the firm, and then starting a magazine "of an entirely unique sort." But he was worried, even panicky, most of the time; he spent sleepless nights walking the floor, and when he tried to work he was likely to find himself adding up his debts and his income on the margins of his manuscripts.

In such a mood he naturally got little done. He gave *Pudd'nhead Wilson* its final revision, and sent off his article on Harriet Shelley; otherwise the summer was almost a total loss so far as writing went. At times he clung to the illusory hope that the machine, in which Paige was now trying to interest Chicago capitalists, might yet pull him out of the hole, but he could hold that thought only intermittently. By the end of August he could stand the strain no longer. The business depression was cutting down even the income which Livy received from her share in her father's coal business, and Hall's reports made clear the folly of any longer regarding the *Library of American Literature* as an asset. All he hoped for now was that the Webster Company might pay its debts to outsiders. "In very prosperous times we might regard our stock and copyrights as assets sufficient, with the money owing to us, to square up and quit even, but I suppose we may not hope for such luck in the present condition of things." But he had to see for himself. Establishing the family once more in lodgings for the winter, this time in Paris, he returned to New York and settled himself in a single room at the Players Club, of which he was a charter member. Though he did not know it, his financial savior was on the way.

One evening early in October a friend introduced him to Henry H. Rogers of the Standard Oil Company. Though many people—including some of Mark Twain's critics—regarded Rogers as a buccaneer, he was a charming person to everyone except his business rivals, and had neither the dullness nor the sanctimoniousness of his partner, John D. Rockefeller. Rogers had long admired Mark's books, and he and the author took to each other at once. Though their first evening together was wholly social, before long Rogers, on a hint from the friend who had introduced them, was probing the tangle of Mark's business affairs. He began with the machine. On the reports of the experts whom he set to investigating it he had hopes, and bade Mark in the meantime stop walking the floor. But before long the experimental test of the machine under working conditions proved that it was too complicated to stand the strain, and at long last the dream was laid aside.

Without Rogers Mark's last years might have been very black indeed. The financier next looked into the affairs of Webster and Company, and on his advice the firm made an assignment for the benefit of its creditors, on April 18, 1894. In the midst of Rogers' investigations George Warner, Charles' brother, came to Mark with word of a book by a prominent man which would go like wildfire and put Webster and Company on its feet again—"a book that arraigns the Standard Oil fiends, and gives them unmitigated hell, individual by individual. It is the very book for you to publish; there is a fortune in it." Mark wanted to say, "The only man _I_ care for in the world; the only man I would give a damn for; the only man who is lavishing his sweat and blood to save me and mine from starvation and shame, is a Standard Oil fiend. If you know me, you know whether I want the book or not." But he did not say it, for George Warner was an old and well-meaning friend. He only said that he didn't want any book; he wanted to get out of publishing, and all other business.

Had Rogers not represented him at the meeting, Mark Twain would have come out stripped of everything he possessed. The creditors wanted him to make over to them his copyrights, and even the Hartford house. The author, oppressed with the sense of debt, might have yielded, but Rogers was not to be bullied. He pointed out that $60,000 of the firm's indebtedness was owing to Olivia Clemens, and that the Hartford house belonged to her. For her, as preferred creditor, Rogers secured the assignment of the copyrights. In the midst of the depression, they were worth little, but they had been remunerative once, and they could become so again. The terms finally agreed upon gave the creditors an immediate settlement at about fifty cents on the dollar, and had Mark Twain chosen to take advantage of the bankruptcy laws, that would have been all. But he refused to take advantage; sooner or later, he declared, he would pay every cent his firm owed.

Not that he was completely penniless, even at this nadir in his fortunes. Livy reminded him that in addition to whatever he could earn comfortably by writing, they still had an income of about $6,000 a year from her property, and that she could make further economies until their expenses fitted their funds. Though she felt that there was something disgraceful about business failure she did her best to be cheerful, and concurred heartily in her husband's resolve that all debts should be paid in full.

Pending the results of the final tests of the Paige machine, however, Mark made no immediate move toward payment. The bankruptcy had brought him a profound sense of release from an intolerable burden, and his energies turned once more to his writing. On his way back to his family he wrote, on the steamer, his article on "Fenimore Cooper's Literary Offenses," which, as a piece of criticism, is almost as good as the defense of Harriet Shelley. It falls short of the earlier essay only because Mark failed to restrain his propensity to burlesque. Not content with exposing Cooper's real clumsinesses and improbabilities, he exaggerated them. The Clemenses spent the summer at Étretat, in Normandy, and there Mark resumed work on his *Joan of Arc*. His first spurt carried him past the account of the Battle of Patay; then the news of the final failure of the Paige machine put him off for a time. When they once more settled in Paris for the winter he went steadily on, and by the end of April *Joan* was completed.

Harper's Magazine accepted it at once for serial publication, but at Mark's insistence it was published anonymously. He was sure that a main reason for the comparative failure of *The Prince and the Pauper* had been its immediate publication over his name: people had expected a humorous book and, not getting it, had been disappointed. *Joan,* he declared, was written for love; he did not care whether it sold or not, but he wanted it judged on its merits, and not as one of Mark Twain's ventures into unfamiliar fields.

Though he later believed that he had been twelve years collecting the material for the story, and two years writing it, the version given to Henry Rogers at the time it was completed tells how he actually worked:

"The first two-thirds of the book were easy; for I only needed to keep my historical road straight; therefore I used for reference only one French history and one English one—and shoveled in as much fancy work and invention on both sides of the historical road as I pleased. But on this last third I have constantly used five French sources and five English ones and I think no telling historical nugget in any of them has escaped me."

That frank confession reveals one reason why *Joan* is artistically almost as much of a failure as the *Yankee*. The latter failed through its excess of burlesque and irreverence; *Joan* failed through excess of reverence, and lack of invention. Dramatically, the Sieur Louis de Conte is less convincing than the Yankee. Having undertaken to tell the story in the first person,

Mark Twain was unable to cope with the problem of back-ground—the difficulty which besets, for instance, the novelist who attempts epistolary narrative. The Sieur de Conte keeps going into details about things—everything from the dirt floors of the Domremy cottages to the complex rivalries of English, French and Burgundians—which any genuinely contemporary chronicler would have taken for granted. And for all his scorn of Sir Walter Scott, Mark's fondness for piling up descriptions of arms and costumes is more like Sir Walter than it is like Froissart.

But having unwittingly taken Sir Walter as his model for the more directly historical portions of the book, Mark shows up badly in comparison. The loyal Howells put his finger on the central weakness of *Joan:*

"I am not at all troubled when he comes out with a bit of good, strong, downright modern American feeling; my suffering begins when he does the supposedly medieval thing. Then I suspect that his armor is of tin, that the castles and rocks are pasteboard, that the mob of citizens and soldiers who fill the air with the clash of their two-up-and-two-down combats, and the well-known muffled roar of their voices have been hired in at so much a night, and that Joan is sometimes in an awful temper behind the scenes; and I am thankful when the brave Sieur Louis forgets himself again."*

For Mark's imagination, so magnificent on the level of the thoughts and acts and feelings of American individuals, could not visualize and transfer convincingly to paper the clash and spirit of medieval combat.

"We suffered repulse after repulse, but Joan was here and there and everywhere encouraging the men, and she kept them to their work. During three hours the tide ebbed and flowed, flowed and ebbed; but at last La Hire, who was now come, made a final and resistless charge, and the bastille St. Loup was ours."

---

*From *My Mark Twain* by William Dean Howells. Copyright 1910 by Harper & Bros., 1938 by Mildred Howells and John Mead Howells.

Let those two sentences stand as sufficient specimens of the battle pieces throughout the book. They aren't even as convincing as the stage combats to which Howells likened them. The epic style was beyond Mark's grasp. He might better have treated his theme from the level of modern prose, after the manner of G. B. Shaw or John Erskine, but his reverence for the Maid prevented him.

Again the comparison with Sir Walter or Mark's other aversion, Fenimore Cooper, is inevitable. A novelist must not revere his women too highly if he wants to make them convincing human beings. Mark's Joan is too bright and good; she is always so sure of herself and her mission that her battles lack suspense. When she is on trial Mark's ignorance of the importance of ideas and institutions in history, already noted in the *Yankee,* combines with his reverence for her character to obscure the issues. He never understood, as Bernard Shaw understood, that from its own point of view, and in its age, the prosecution had a case. Joan is merely a pure and beautiful girl being foully done to death under the forms of law by a pack of revengeful and sadistic persecutors. When all is said, she is Susy Clemens.

Only in the minor characters does the story come to life—for they are Missouri farmers or bullies from the river and the mines, transplanted to Lorraine and Picardy. The Paladin boasting of his exploits, and the "boys" kidding him, are familiar figures, however unmedieval. They are the same boys who went grailing from Camelot; the same who staged a mock hold-up on the divide between Gold Hill and Virginia City. And though Mark thought his story so grave and stately that none would recognize its authorship, it must have been a very inattentive reader who got through the first installment in *Harper's* without being able to name the writer. Joan's menagerie, for instance: the squirrel sitting on her shoulder, "turning a rocky fragment of prehistoric chestnut-cake over and over in its knotty hands, and hunting the less indurated places, and giving its elevated bushy tail a flirt and its pointed ears a

toss when it found one—signifying thankfulness and surprise—
and then it filed that place off with those two slender front teeth
which a squirrel carries for that purpose and not for ornament,
for ornamental they never could be, as any will admit that have
noticed them"—only one author could have written that description, and scores of others in which Mark shovels in his
fancy work and invention on both sides of the historical road.

Uneven and inadequate as the romance is, Mark loved it
best of all his books, because he loved Joan. But by the time it
was finished it was evident that writing alone was never going
to lift the burden of the Webster debts. With the last hope of
the Paige machine gone Mark turned, in February 1895, to the
old expedient which had freed him in the past, the lecture platform. On a flying visit to New York, he made the preliminary
arrangements with J. B. Pond, and then, with the encouragement
of his old friend Sir Henry Stanley, in London, he mapped out
an ambitious campaign. He would lecture his way round the
world.

So far as the direct returns from the platform were concerned,
he could have stayed right in the United States and Canada,
and cleaned up. But he was nearly sixty; he dreaded the platform more than ever, and his plan was that a tour round the
world would yield material for a new travel book, dealing with
places and people he had never seen or written about before.
A year on the road, followed by a fresh book, ought to pay off
all his obligations, if the book could be sold as largely as the
Innocents and *Roughing It* had sold. The cash results of the
combination would probably equal those of two or three years
straight lecturing in the home market. He had resumed business relations with his old firm, the American Publishing Company, with *Pudd'nhead Wilson,* though Harper's was to handle
Joan and *Tom Sawyer, Detective;* the new book of travel was
planned for the subscription market.

For the lecture tour in Australia, New Zealand, India and
South Africa, Mark put himself under the management of R. S.
Smythe, who had proved his quality as a manager of Stanley

and other celebrities. One of Mark's numerous experiences in "mental telegraphy" came when his letter to Smythe, proposing the tour, crossed one in which the manager suggested the same scheme. Undaunted by an overheard conversation in a New York club, in which a businessman, after inquiring how old Clemens was, had remarked that men who fail in business after the age of fifty rarely regain their feet, he laid his plans for the comeback.

The family returned to America in May and went to Quarry Farm for two peaceful months while Mark prepared his lectures, completed his business arrangements and cursed a carbuncle which threatened to upset his plans. Neither Mark nor Livy could face the thought of his taking the long journey alone; the winter of 1893-1894, which Mark had spent at the Players Club while his family stayed in Paris, had been the longest separation of their married life, and they did not intend to repeat it. But they could not take all the family as well. Jean was too young; Susy dreaded ocean travel, and hoped that by living quietly for a year or so with her aunt, Sue Crane, she might achieve the robust health which her singing teacher had told her she must have if her perfect soprano was ever to win the place it deserved in grand opera. So Clara was the chosen companion, and the eldest and the youngest were left behind in Elmira when Mark and Livy and Clara set out on the first stage of the long road which he need never have traveled if he had not dreamed great dreams. Their last glimpse of Elmira was Susy's radiant figure, blowing kisses after the train that was taking her parents away from her forever.

CHAPTER XVI

TRIUMPH AND DISASTER

To BEGIN a transcontinental lecture tour in mid-July seemed as foolhardy as the *Quaker City* pilgrims' summer visit to Palestine. Originally Mark had planned to set out in September, but the later start would have delayed his Indian tour until the beginning of the hot season, so he elected to do his grilling in his own country. They sweltered their way across the continent by a zigzag northern route, ending in Vancouver thirty-three days after leaving Elmira. Before sailing Mark used a false newspaper report that he was lecturing for his own benefit as the occasion for a public statement:

"I intend the lectures as well as the property for the creditors. The law recognizes no mortgage on a man's brain, and a merchant who has given up all he has may take advantage of the laws of insolvency and start free again for himself. But I am not a business man, and honor is a harder master than the law. It cannot compromise for less than 100 cents on the dollar, and its debts never outlaw. From my reception thus far on my lecturing tour I am confident that if I live I can pay the last debt within four years, after which, at the age of sixty-four, I can make a fresh and unincumbered start in life. . . . I meant, when I began, to give my creditors all the benefit of this, but I am beginning to feel that I am gaining something from it, too, and that my dividends, if not available for banking purposes, may be even more satisfactory than theirs."

After all expenses were paid this first month of the tour left a balance of five thousand dollars to be remitted to the fund which Henry Rogers was managing. But the first lap of the ocean trip brought keen disappointment. Mark was booked to lecture in Honolulu, and had looked forward to revisiting the islands which had done so much for his nascent fame, nearly thirty years before. But there was a cholera epidemic; no one was allowed to land. Mark could only gaze at Oahu, "just as silky and velvety and lovely as ever," and declare that if he could he would go ashore and never leave. They crossed the equator on September 5—Mark averred that Clara kodaked it—and were in Sydney on the sixteenth.

Smythe had made his preparations well and all Australia, seemingly, turned out. Within the first fortnight after his programs began Mark was able to remit £437 to Rogers, and despite a second carbuncle, which kept him abed in Melbourne for a week, he enjoyed himself thoroughly. When the larrikins in Sydney and Melbourne recognized him on his way back from his lectures and shouted, "Good night, Mark!" he swelled with pride. A few years before, he had had an argument with Howells, who had declared that Mark was famous; Mark had insisted that he was merely well known. Now he began to think Howells was right, though final conviction did not come until two or three years later, when a Viennese police officer recognized him and let him through the lines that were guarding the streets for a royal procession.

Mark passed his sixtieth birthday, and Livy her fiftieth, in New Zealand. For a man of his age and for a woman whose health had always been frail the New Zealand journey had many of the features of a nightmare. They were tossed about in inadequate and overcrowded steamers; they became used to giant cockroaches scuttling across their faces at night; they landed at open roadsteads in baskets and surfboats. Yet they suffered no ill effects, though Mark welcomed the sunny peace of the voyage from Australia to India during the first fortnight in January. On that voyage he made one of his periodical efforts to control his profanity. He swore off and told Livy he had done so: "I was on deck in the peaceful dawn, the calm and holy dawn. Went down dressed, bathed, put on white linen, shaved—a long, hot, troublesome job, and no profanity. Then started to breakfast. Remembered my tonic—first time in three months without being told—poured it into a measuring-glass, held bottle in one hand, it in the other, the cork in my teeth—reached up and got a tumbler—measuring-glass sprang out of my fingers—got it, poured out another dose, first setting the tumbler on washstand—just got it poured, ship lurched, heard a crash behind me—it was the tumbler, broken into millions of fragments, but the bottom hunk whole—picked it up to throw out of the open port, threw out the measuring-glass instead—then I released my voice. Mrs. C. behind me in the door: 'Don't reform any more, it isn't any improvement.' "

Two months of crisscrossing India, from the tropic heat of Ceylon to the snows of Darjeeling, from Bombay to Calcutta and through the Northwest Provinces, were a continual delight, despite Mark's persistent bronchial cough and despite the discomforts of Indian railways. The barefoot silence of the Indian servants wore upon Mark's irritable nerves at times, however, and he noted the parallels between the position of the subject peoples of India and his own memories of Missouri slavery. But it is needless to rehearse the details of that tour—it is all in *Following the Equator,* which ranks with the *Innocents* as the most directly factual of Mark's travel books.

Black moods were frequent, however, and it was Livy who had to do the encouraging. She and Clara alone knew what went on behind the scenes, for when he was with people, her husband always seemed cheerful. But when he was down he could see no prospect of any good thing to come, and believed that they must spend the rest of their lives in poverty. He did not want to return to America, but Livy sagely attributed his feelings to the grind of travel, and hoped that when he was settled at his writing in some quiet English village his cheerfulness would return. The platform which had furnished one of his recurrent nightmares was taking its toll. Writing, she knew, was the work he loved; it was certainly with her active approval that he abandoned the notion of further lecturing, once the circumnavigation was completed.

En route to South Africa, Mark relaxed and read endlessly, even to the extent of rereading *The Vicar of Wakefield* and Jane Austen, that he might abuse them all over again. South Africa was still seething with the excitement which had followed the Jameson Raid, but it had no effect on Mark's audiences. Almost the only person of distinction whom he did not meet was Cecil Rhodes. Perhaps it was as well that he did not. His opinion of Rhodes, as he recorded it in his book, was sound though scathing; the flattery of a personal meeting might have clouded that judgment.

The notebooks of the trip are full of philosophizing. The sight of millions of "heathen," the sound of hundreds of missionaries of all denominations, roused all the latent antagonisms which dated back to the missionary sermons he had endured as a boy in Hannibal. His opinions are neither startling nor especially original, but they further confirm the fact that his "philosophy" was already full-fledged before the final disasters came upon him. His reading of Sir John Lubbock's study of ants prompted him to an elaborate mockery in which he demonstrated that the insects would join any church with sugar in it. If he were going to construct a God, he declared, he would have Him as dignified as the better sort of men in regard to bestowing His favors, and "there would not be any hell—except the one we live in from the cradle to the grave." And he was grim on the subject of anniversaries. They "are very well up to a certain point, while one's babies are in the process of growing up: they are joy-flags that make gay the road and prove progress; and one looks down the fluttering rank with pride. Then presently one notices that the flagstaffs are in process of a mysterious change of some sort—change of shape. Yes, they are turning into milestones. They are marking something lost now, not gained. From that time on it were best to suppress taking notice of anniversaries."

The long voyage brought them to England on July 31, 1896. Though Mark originally planned to spend the winter lecturing either in the larger cities at home or for a season in London, he was sick of the platform, and wanted to write his travel book while the impressions were fresh. They took a house at Guildford, in Surrey, and made ready to greet Susy and Jean, who, with Katie Leary, were to sail from New York on August 12. But on that day came a letter saying that Susy was slightly ill, and that the sailing had been postponed. Livy and Clara were alarmed, and hurriedly prepared to return to America. They sailed on August 15. Three days later a cablegram told the solitary father that Susy was dead.

She had, they learned later, been unwell for some time, but she, like her parents and the Howellses, had become a temporary convert to "mental healing," and did not consult a doctor. She had been overworking at her singing; serious illness developed while she was paying a farewell visit to the Warners in Hartford. A doctor, summoned at last, diagnosed nervous exhaustion from overwork, and prescribed rest and quiet. She was moved, with faithful Katie Leary in attendance, to her own room in the old Hartford home. She grew rapidly worse, and on August 15 the doctor recognized the malady as meningitis. Three days of blindness and delirium followed, and then came the end.

When their ship reached quarantine the captain called Clara to his cabin and showed her a paper containing the news. One year, one month, and one day—so the bereaved father despairingly reckoned up the time—from the time they had left Elmira, Livy and Clara returned, on the same train and in the same car. Their last sight when they left had been Susy waving good-by from the platform; now Susy was waiting mute in her coffin in the old Langdon home. To his wife Mark poured out his grief in a tortured letter:

"I loved Susy, but I did not know how deeply before. Still, while the tears gushed, I was able to say: 'My grief is for the mother—for myself I am thankful.' My selfish love aside, I would not have it otherwise.

"You will see her. Oh, I wish I could see her and caress the unconscious face and kiss the unresponding lips—but I would not bring her back—no, not for the riches of a thousand worlds. She has found the richest gift that this world can offer. I would not rob her of it. Be comforted, my darling—we shall have *our* release in time. Be comforted, remembering how much hardship, grief, pain she is spared, and that her heart can never be broken now for the loss of a child. . . . How lovely is death; and how niggardly it is doled out.

"She died in our own house—not in another's; died where every little thing was familiar and beloved; died where she had spent all her life till my crimes made her a pauper and an exile. How good it is, that she got home again."

Mark had borne his financial losses with a stoical fortitude, in the spirit of the Nevada miners who, when one hopeful enterprise went awry, turned to the task of rebuilding, with no time wasted in useless repining. But this blow struck through all his defenses. He harassed his soul with regrets for the unspoken word of love and praise:

"Sometimes in those days of swift development in Paris her speech was rocket-like; I seemed to see it go up and up and up, a soaring, streaming, climbing, stem of fire, and finally burst in the zenith and rain colored sparks all around. And I felt like saying, 'You marvelous child!' But never said it. To my sorrow I remember it now. But I came of an undemonstrative race."

He filled notebooks with every vivid memory of Susy's character he could recall; he collected every tragic detail of her delirium and death. And Susy, as he described her, was a quickened feminine version of himself, intense, careless of time and money, not industrious except in the things in which she was gifted; living on the heights most of the time, but occasionally plunging into the depths, "yet through all her seasons of unhappiness there were outbursts of happiness—exaltations of it."

When Livy and Jean and Clara rejoined him, and they had hidden themselves and their grief away in the house they had taken in a quiet corner of Chelsea, he raged against himself, against life, against "whatever brute or blackguard made the world." The honorable motive that had sent him around the world held no comfort now; his voice would lose its drawl as he rehearsed the steps of their tragedy:

"Do you remember, Livy, the hellish struggle it was to settle on making that lecture trip around the world? . . . I, almost an old man, with ill health, carbuncles, bronchitis and rheumatism, I with patience worn to rags, I was to pack my bag and be jolted around the devil's universe for what? To pay debts that were not even of my making. And you were worried at the thought of facing such hardships of travel, and *she* was unhappy to be left alone. But once the idea of that infernal trip struck us we couldn't shake it. Oh, no! for it was packed with sense of honor—honor—honor—no rest, comfort, joy—but plenty of honor, plenty of ethical glory. And as a reward for our self-castigation and faithfulness to ideals of nobility we were robbed of our greatest treasure. . . . You want me to believe it is a judicious, a charitable God that runs this world. Why, I could run it better myself."

But for Mark there was one anodyne for his pain—work. The debts were still there; money was still needed; the book he had planned must be written. In the last week of October he flung himself into the task and labored at it doggedly, while for Livy there was no release except in the cares of the home. Holidays came and passed without notice. They did not celebrate Thanksgiving; they only remembered that "seven years ago Susy gave her play for the first time; that was the last Thanksgiving jollification we ever had in our house." And on Christmas morning, "we three sat and talked as usual, but the name of the day was not mentioned. It was in our minds, but we said nothing."

Yet during this black autumn Mark Twain interested himself fruitfully in behalf of Helen Keller, and by his intercession with Mrs. Henry Rogers secured the fund which enabled the girl to complete her education. Meanwhile he continued to pour out his sorrow to such understanding friends as Howells and Twichell. To the former he wrote, early in 1897, that he had become indifferent to nearly everything but work; he stuck to that, "without purpose and without ambition; merely for the love of it." And then followed a paragraph of acute self-analysis:

"This mood will pass, some day—there is history for it. But it cannot pass until my wife comes up out of the submergence. She was always so quick to recover herself before, but now there is no rebound, and we are dead people who go through the motions of life. Indeed I am a mud image, and it will puzzle me to know what it is in me that writes, and has comedy-fancies and finds pleasure in phrasing them. It is a law of our natures, of course, or it wouldn't happen; the thing in me forgets the presence of the mud image and goes its own way, unconscious of it and apparently of no kinship with it. I have finished my book, but I go on as if the end were indefinitely away—as indeed it is. There is no hurry—at any rate, there is no limit.

"Jean's spirits are good; Clara's are rising. They have youth —the only thing that was worth giving the race."

But to add to their griefs Jean had developed epilepsy during the adolescent year she had spent in Elmira. Medical science then, as now, was almost helpless against the disease, but for the present Jean continued her studies at home. For the second time in their married life Mark and Livy shut themselves away from the world, as they had in Buffalo in the months after Jervis Langdon's death and Langdon Clemens' birth. But then part of their seclusion had been concession to convention, part the necessity of Livy's health. Now they were well in body, but too bruised in spirit to wish for society. "I did know," Mark told Joe Twichell, "that Susy was part of us; I did *not* know that she could go away; I did not know that she could go away, and take our lives with her, yet leave our dull bodies behind."

One fruit of his voluntary seclusion was a sensational report in a baser American newspaper that Mark Twain was dying in poverty in London, deserted by his family. Part of the story grew from an honest confusion between the humorist and a cousin; the rest was invention. Presently a callow reporter found his way to the house in Tedworth Square and naïvely sent in the cable his agency had received from New York: "If Mark Twain very ill, five hundred words. If dead, send one thousand." And the mind that even in its grief had comedy-fancies and took pleasure in phrasing them, sent back the perfect answer: "James Ross Clemens, a cousin of mine, was seriously ill two or three weeks ago in London, but is well now. The report of my illness grew out of his illness; the report of my death was an exaggeration."

As usual, Mark had spoken hastily when he told Howells at the end of February that his book was finished. He said in his notebook on April 13 that he finished the book that day, and said so again on May 18. That time it was really true. Livy, in her desolation, apparently read the manuscript with more attention than she had been able to give to some of the previous books; at least, she wrote out more of her comments. Much has been made of her objections to such words as "stench," "offal," and "breech-clout," and Mark's rejoinder that "you are steadily weakening the English language, Livy." Not so much has been made of another note of hers: "I hate to say it, but it seems to me that you go too minutely into particulars in describing the feats of the aborigines. I felt it in the boomerang-throwing." Mark's rejoinder there was to relegate the material to a special appendix and later discard the appendix. Against her objection to a handful of "strong" words should be set Livy's realization that her husband's unfailing delight in technical processes was likely at times to lead him into boresome minutiae. He once wrote a five-hundred word letter to tell Joe Twichell how to strop his razor. Livy had the wit to recognize and the courage to say that the details which sometimes enthralled her husband might conceivably weary his readers. Neither have the results of her criticisms always been examined. When she wrote, "I don't like the 'shady-principled cat that has a family in every port,' " her husband replied, "Then I'll modify him just a little." Hence, on the voyage from Sydney to Ceylon, the book says that one of the ship's cats "goes ashore, in port, in England,

Australia, and India, to see how his various families are getting along, and is seen no more until the ship is ready to sail." The modification strongly resembles what happened in *Roughing It* to the note about Kanaka fornication.

But the book was finished at last, though it might be more accurate to say of *Following the Equator,* as of *A Tramp Abroad* and some other volumes, that it was merely stopped. To be sure, it carried the travelers through to the end of their journey, but a better ending lay in the final sentence of the penultimate chapter, which had dealt faithfully with Cecil Rhodes: "I admire him, I frankly confess it; and when his time comes I shall buy a piece of the rope for a keepsake." As a whole the book ranks much below the *Innocents,* but it is better than *A Tramp.* Mark Twain at sixty could not hope to recapture the zest of experience which went into his first book; *Following the Equator* shows often that it is the work of a weary man. It contains a higher percentage of quoted matter than any of its predecessors—Mark's old printer's habit of looking for "fat" to fill out his pages more quickly, coupled with his literary habit of reading all the available books about the subject of the moment. Yet its very weariness saves it from the labored burlesque of *A Tramp.* It is full of bitter wisdom, of which the Pudd'nhead Wilson chapter-mottoes are only a small part. The journey had shown Mark among many other things the seamy side of empire-building: he had had few illusions about white civilization before he started; he had none when he ended. Scattered through the book, moreover, are his considered judgments on a variety of subjects, including his own art. "Americans are not Englishmen, and American humor is not English humor; but both the American and his humor had their origin in England, and have merely undergone changes brought about by changed conditions and a new environment." In that one sentence he summed up the great tradition of which he himself was the culmination.

With the book at last out of the way the Clemenses went into society a little more, and stayed on in London for Queen Victoria's Diamond Jubilee on June 22. Mark got a lot of fun out of writing a description of it for the American newspapers, using figures snipped out of fashion plates as portraits of the visiting royalty. "He laughed like a child" over his fancies, his daughter remembered. Then they went to the Continent again, to a pension on Lake Lucerne, where they had once been so happy. The black shadow followed, though they were slowly growing used to living under it. When August 18 came, the first anniversary of Susy's death, they could not even comfort each other. Livy spent the day alone at a little village up the lake; Mark spent it alone under the trees on the mountainside, writing a memorial poem. Verse was not his natural medium; the lines halt, their intention only partly fulfilled, but deep emotion shows beneath the imperfect expression.

He tried other writing, seeking themes to voice his desolation. In 1893, when the avalanche of business ruin was gaining momentum, he had written to Sue Crane: "I dreamed I was born and grew up and was a pilot on the Mississippi and a miner and a journalist in Nevada and a pilgrim in the Quaker City, and had a wife and children and went to live in a villa at Florence—and this dream goes on and on and sometimes seems so real that I almost believe it is real. I wonder if it is? But there is no way to tell, for if one applies tests they would be part of the dream, too, and so would simply aid the .deceit. I wish I knew whether it is a dream or real." Now he tried to work the idea into a story: a man dreams that he has lost his wife and children, and waking from his dream and confronted by his living family, believes that this is the dream, and that the disaster was the reality. The story, like most of the stories he began during the next few years, was not finished; he could not find the symbol to supply his literary framework—the Melancholia to preside over his City of Dreadful Night.

In the autumn they moved on once more, to Vienna, where Clara was to study music with Leschetizky. But the shadow moved with them behind all the social gaiety, as years before, for an evening, Mark Twain had carried in his heart when he went to a wedding the news of Will Bowen's bereavement. And before the year was out death struck away another of his links with the past: on December 11 Mollie Clemens cabled that Orion was dead. Mark replied immediately in words which might better have stood as his final tribute to his gentle brother:

"It is ten in the evening. We sent our cablegram of sympathy half an hour ago and it is in your hands by this time, in the wintry mid-afternoon of the heaviest day you have known since we saw Jenny escape from this life 33 years ago, and were then too ignorant to rejoice at it.

"We all grieve for you; our sympathy goes out to you from experienced hearts, and with it our love; and with Orion, and with Orion I rejoice. He has received life's best gift.

"He was good—all good and sound; there was nothing bad in him, nothing base, nor any unkindness. It was unjust that such a man, against whom no offence could be charged, should have been sentenced to live 72 years. It was beautiful, the patience with which he bore it.

"The bitterness of death—that is for the survivors, and bitter beyond all words it is. We hunger for Susy, we suffer and pine for her; and if by asking I could bring her back, I could stoop to that treachery, so weak am I, and so selfish are we all. But she and Orion are at peace, and no loyal friend should wish to disturb them in their high fortune...."

Again the thought was not new. More than three years before, on hearing of A. W. Fairbanks' death, he had told his old friend, "I am sorry for you—very very sorry—but not for him nor for anybody who is granted the privilege of prying behind the curtain to see if there is any contrivance there that is half so shabby and poor and foolish as the invention of mortal life." The difference between these earlier words and the later ones is simply that between theory and fact, conjecture and experience. The heart knew its own bitterness now, where before the bitterness had been only in the mind. And that nothing might be lacking in the circle of family griefs, Jean was heartbroken when the news came that George Griffin, their Negro butler during the happy years in Hartford, was also dead.

Nevertheless, that winter of 1897-1898 was not wholly black. *Following the Equator* had been published in November, and although the day of the subscription book was almost past, Mark Twain's name and the widespread public sympathy with his effort to clear himself of debt had brought initial sales as good as those of *Roughing It*. All royalties were paid over to the fund which Henry Rogers was managing, and before the year was out the work of payment had commenced. Mark had refused tempting offers from Pond to lecture in America, believing that his book, aided by strict economy, would be sufficient to discharge the claims without the ordeal of another long campaign on the platform. The event proved him right. By the end of January 1898 he was clear of debt, after less than four years, instead of the five he had calculated on. There was even a balance on hand, which Rogers, by judicious investment, ran up before long into a sizable nest egg for a new fortune. "The burnt fool's bandaged finger went wabbling back to the fire" more than once; Mark could never resist a plausible-sounding speculation, but thanks to Rogers he never again endangered the major part of his capital, though he was fully prepared to do so in backing a carpet loom invented by an Austrian, until Rogers investigated the possible market and put a damper on Mark's enthusiasm.

With the lifting of the burden of debt came a fresh inclination to write. During the two years spent in Vienna, Mark did most of the work on *What Is Man?*, talking out the ideas at such length and so often that even the patient Livy, despite her conviction that her husband's utterances at home should not be curbed, was moved to protest. She would not listen to the successive chapters of the treatise as they were completed; they made her too melancholy. "The truth always has that effect on people," her husband retorted. He had planned the book as long ago as 1886, in the brave days of happiness; writing it now released the bitterness which filled his heart. He was Job, without Job's faith. He cursed God with fervor, but he could not die.

During the summer in Switzerland he had, by his own computation, started three books and thirteen magazine articles wrong, and had only succeeded in making two brief sketches come out as he wanted them to. Now, however, things came readily; he did half a dozen successful articles during 1898, among them the first of his examinations of Christian Science. To this last, despite his ridicule of the financial acumen of the Founder, Mark brought an open mind. He, like Howells, had experimented with "mental healing" of a non-Eddy sort—once even carrying the thing to the point of persuading himself and all his nearsighted family to leave off their glasses until headaches and eyestrain forced the abandonment of the venture. And he and Livy remembered how she, as a girl, had been restored to health by a faith healer when she seemed helplessly bedridden. But what increasingly fascinated him about Mrs. Eddy was her organizing skill, and he fell an easy victim to the mathematical fallacy—which even professional statisticians like Roger Babson are not immune to—that the rate of growth of a new cult will continue without interruption. That there is a law of diminishing returns in religious cults, as in every other human enterprise, never dawned upon him; he proved by strictly accurate figures that by 1920 the Christian Scientists would have a clear majority in Congress, and would be able to make theirs the established church of America if they so desired.

But among his Vienna writings in 1898 two stories were notable. Both expressed his bitterness about the damned human race, though only one was finished at this time. The short story, as an art form, was not Mark's métier, but in "The Man That Corrupted Hadleyburg" he came near to perfection. What he wrote to Howells about the never-completed "Which Was the Dream?" turned out to describe accurately the Hadleyburg story: "All of the first half of the story—and I hope three-fourths—will be comedy. . . . I think I can carry the reader a long way before he suspects that I am laying a tragedy-trap."

For the story is a tragedy-trap, and not merely for the Richardses who suffer the penalty of their undetected lie. It traps the reader, too, and at the end leaves him, if he is honest with himself, saying, "There, with or without the grace of God, go I." Hadleyburg is a community as vividly realized as Obedstown, Tennessee, Dawson's Landing, Missouri, or Bricksville, Arkansas, but it is also a place where the whole damned race is at home.

Of the other story, the first definite note was made in September 1898:

"Story of little Satan Jr. who came to Hannibal, went to school, was popular and greatly liked by those who knew his secret. The others were jealous and the girls didn't like him because he smelled of brimstone. He was always doing miracles—his pals knew they were miracles, the others thought they were mysteries."

By the following May, he told Howells that now he was able to put aside his potboiler pen, and do what he had wanted to do—"write a book without reserves—a book which should take account of no one's feelings, delusions; a book which should say my say, right out of my heart, in the plainest language and without a limitation of any sort. I judged that would be an unimaginable luxury, heaven on earth. It is under way now, and it *is* a luxury! an intellectual drunk. Twice I didn't start it right, and got pretty far in it, both times, before I found it out. But I am sure it is started right this time. It is in tale-form. I believe I can make it tell what I think of Man, and how he is constructed, and what a shabby poor ridiculous thing he is, and how mistaken he is in his estimate of his character and powers and qualities and his place among the animals. So far I think I am succeeding. I let the madam into the secret day before yesterday, and locked the doors and read to her the opening chapters. She said—

" 'It is perfectly horrible—and perfectly beautiful!'

"Within the due limits of modesty, that is what I think."

The tale, of course, was *The Mysterious Stranger,* and the

laying of the scene in Hannibal, instead of a medieval village, was one of the false starts. The original plan was presumably spacious: the book might have continued until Satan had shown the boys all the kingdoms of the world and their abominations. At bottom the design differed only slightly from the *Yankee*. The survey of human cruelty and stupidity was the same; Father Adolph was blood brother to the ecclesiastics of King Arthur's court; the astrologer was Merlin. Even the Protestant gibe about the foundling asylum connected with the priory and nunnery was repeated from the earlier book. The difference was not in the material nor in its structure; it was in Mark Twain. Ten years before, he was still a Victorian optimist at heart, believing in the dogma of progress and in salvation by material betterment. Now he was certain that earth and high heaven ailed from their prime foundation; the human race and its Maker were too mean and paltry for any redemption, here or hereafter. But composition bogged down before long, and the final chapters were not written in time to receive Livy's extorted word of praise. It was the last flame of Mark's purely creative energy, and its blaze consumed his world.

The overshadowing dread of leaving his wife and children in poverty had been lifted; Mark was able to sleep of nights as well as anyone. At the end of 1898 Livy computed for him that besides their house and furniture in Hartford, their income from British and American copyrights represented a capital value of $200,000 and that they had $107,000 cash in the bank besides. On hearing the news, Mark averred that he went out and bought a box of six-cent cigars; he had been smoking 4½-centers before. But the brief peace of this Indian Summer did not last. Jean's affliction had not yielded to treatment, and during the summer of 1899 her father took her to Dr. Kellgren's sanitarium in Sanna, Sweden, in hopes that osteopathic treatment would avail where others had failed. Mark was converted for a time to the new therapy, as he had been in the past to mental healing, and one reason why the Clemenses chose London instead of Vienna as their home during the winter of

1899-1900 was the opportunity to continue Jean's treatments there. At last, however, hope faded.

England was in the midst of the Boer War, and Mark was torn between his sense of justice and his sense of civilization. "My head," he said, "is with the Briton, but my heart and such rags of morals as I have are with the Boer"—and he explained why, in strangely prophetic words: "For England must not fall; it would mean an inundation of Russian and German political degradation which would envelope the globe and steep it in a sort of Middle-Age night and slavery which would last till Christ comes again."

As always, London offered too many distractions to allow of much literary work. An essay on Joan of Arc, heatedly withdrawn after the editor, Douglas Murray, had undertaken to improve the author's English, and one or two other minor articles were all that Mark accomplished. But meanwhile, at home, Henry Rogers had been working without stint to bring about an agreement between the American Publishing Company and the house of Harper, to the end that a collected edition of Mark Twain's works might be issued. Though the final contract was not completed until 1902, even the preliminary arrangements assured the author of an income of something like the scale on which he had lived before the crash. After spending the summer of 1900 at Dollis Hill, on the outskirts of London, the Clemenses sailed for America on October 14. Their decade of exile was over; they hoped to re-establish a home, and end their lives in their own country.

CHAPTER XVII

SUNSET

AMERICA gave Mark Twain a conqueror's welcome. None but the conqueror himself, and his wife, knew what scars he bore. They were in their homeland again, but they were still homeless. During the years of exile they had changed residence at least two or three times every year, until they both longed to be settled permanently. But not in Hartford. Livy frankly dreaded the thought of ever entering the old home again. "I feel," she wrote, "if we had gotten through the first three months all might be well, but consider the first night." And with her slowly failing strength she dreaded the responsibilities of that lavish establishment as much as she dreaded the memories it held. From the distance of London Mark had thought differently. "When we come home," he wrote to Twichell, "how shall we have billiard-nights again—with no Ned Bunce and no Henry Robinson? I believe I could not endure that. We must find another use for that room. Susy is gone, George is gone, Libby Hamersley, Ned Bunce, Henry Robinson. The friends are passing, one by one; our house, where such warm blood and such dear blood flowed so freely, is become a cemetery. But not in any repellent sense. Our dead are welcome there; their life made it beautiful, their death has hallowed it, we shall have them with us always, and there will be no parting." But when he returned, and revisited Hartford, he came round to Livy's feeling about it: "There was a pathetic pleasure in seeing Hartford and the house again; but I realize that if we ever enter the house again to live, our hearts will break. I am not sure that we shall ever be strong enough to endure that strain."

Accordingly, they did what they had done throughout their

282

European wanderings: rented, at 14 West Tenth Street, a furnished house for the winter. It quickly became the most famous private home in New York. America's greatest author was home again, and America, or its newspapers, made the most of it. In his daughter's words, "one could never begin to describe in words the atmosphere of adulation that swept across his threshold. Every day was like some great festive occasion. One felt that a large party was going on, and that by and by the guests would be leaving. But there was no leaving. More and more came. And the telephone rang so steadily that the butler got no time for other work. . . . It always puzzled me how Mark Twain could manage to have an opinion on every incident, accident, invention, or disease in the world." Nor were interviewers and visitors the whole of it. He was invited to eat dinners and make speeches until he was almost exhausted. After a time he formed the habit of staying away from the meal, and arriving just in time for the speechmaking, but even so the effort wore him down and he made resolutions—very imperfectly kept—to attend no more banquets.

Yet he found time to compose other things besides the speeches he delivered. No longer obliged to write for the market, he began to express himself on current affairs in writing, as he had been doing to the reporters. He had plenty of material. The American war against the Filipinos was in full swing, and the briefly allied nations of Europe had just captured Peking and extorted indemnities from China for the lives and property lost in the Boxer rebellion. Kitchener was ending the Boer War by methods of calculated brutality and terrorism; the first reports of the work in the Belgian Congo's heart of darkness were beginning to reach the world. On New Year's Eve, 1900, Mark Twain jotted down a greeting from the nineteenth to the twentieth century:

"I bring you the stately nation named Christendom, returning, bedraggled, besmirched, and dishonored, from pirate raids in Kiao Chou, Manchuria, South Africa, and the Philippines, with her soul full of meanness, her pocket full of boodle, and her mouth full of pious hypocrisies. Give her soap and towel, and hide the looking-glass."

From such a point of view, and with materials drawn from the newspapers, he composed "To the Person Sitting in Darkness," to which the *North American Review* gave leading place in its issue of February 1901. The supporting documents were a smug and self-congratulatory Christmas Eve editorial from the New York *Tribune,* against which he placed articles from the *Sun,* one of them describing the vice and crime of New York's lower East Side, and the other reporting that the American Board of Foreign Missions had collected, for loss of life and property in the Chinese rebellion, "national fines amounting to thirteen times the indemnity." At the time of the Spanish-American War Mark had fallen easily into the popular delusion that it was a war for righteousness, but its sequel in the Philippines had changed his mind, and now the missionaries' statement about China came to give the necessary release to the feelings about imperialism and exploitation which had been fermenting ever since his tour round the world. With one exception, to be considered later, the article was Mark's finest piece of invective. The abuses satirized in the *Yankee* had, after all, been far off and foreign; an American could afford to be smug about them. But here they lay on his own doorstep, and were given the blessing of the Christian churches of the country. Noah Brooks had said of the early days in California that he would rather have anyone else in the world down on him than Mark Twain. But the years had changed his invective from a bludgeon to an edged tool so sharp that at first its victims hardly knew they had been cut.

The article created a storm, of course. The church papers and the missionary societies ululated; the righteous outside the fold applauded. And then the missionary board extended its neck and handed Mark a hatchet. The reported amount of the indemnities, it was claimed, had been garbled in transmission. The Chinese had not been forced to pay thirteen times the amount of the damage; they had paid only one and one-third times. This fine distinction Mark fell upon like a football player dropping on the opponents' fumble.

"To Dr. Smith the 'thirteen-fold-extra' clearly stood for 'theft and extortion,' and he was right, distinctly right, indisputably right. He manifestly thinks that when it got scaled away down to a mere 'one-third' a little thing like that was something other than 'theft and extortion.' Why, only the board knows!

"I will try to explain this difficult problem so that the board can get an idea of it. If a pauper owes me a dollar and I catch him unprotected and make him pay me fourteen dollars thirteen of it is 'theft and extortion.' If I make him pay only one dollar thirty-three and a third cents the thirty-three and a third cents are 'theft and extortion' just the same." And he wound up his illustrations with a parable in the Lincolnian style of how in his youth he and a friend allegedly collected indemnities from Negroes who had stolen their watermelons. The suspected thieves had no ripe melons, so for the three stolen they collected four from other Negroes whose melons were ripe. They had a hard time explaining the matter to the magistrate, especially the fourth melon. That, they said, was the custom of the niggers—for the Board had been explaining that the amount of the indemnity was fixed according to Chinese custom.

"The justice forgot his dignity and descended to sarcasm.

" 'Custom of the niggers! Are our morals so inadequate that we have to borrow of niggers?' "

Noah Brooks was right.

After the rounds of banquets and speeches, and the clamor of his dispute with the missionaries, Mark and his family craved quiet and seclusion for a time. They found it for the summer of 1901 in a cottage at Saranac Lake. Mark Twain's last happy summer with his wife, it recalled the lost days at Quarry Farm. They lived outdoors most of the time, read no newspapers and relaxed. Jean, who had learned to type and was acting as her father's secretary, made friends with the red squirrels, and her father named them all Blennerhasset, after Burr's friend, for the blight had not yet killed the chestnut trees. He wrote as the spirit moved, but completed nothing for publication except *A Double-Barreled Detective Story*.

He wrote the twenty-five-thousand-word tale in a six-day burst of energy, and apparently sent it off to *Harper's Magazine* before it had time to cool. On its smaller scale, the story repeated the experience of *Pudd'nhead Wilson*. Two mutually contradictory themes had got mixed up in the writing, only this time Mark did not realize what he had done and consequently did not separate them in a drastic revision. His first intention was to write a parody of Sherlock Holmes, whose adventures he had first read years before in Joe Twichell's home. But he got off on the wrong foot. The story commenced as a grim revenger's tragedy, in which the parody had no lawful place; even the tragedy contained, in the bloodhound scent which was Archy's birthmark, an element perilously close to unintentional burlesque. The Sherlock Holmes business itself was heavy-handed, yet once more a minor and mainly unsuccessful effort of Mark's contained one of his best hits. He failed to make his major burlesque stick, but the paragraph which parodied the sappy nature descriptions of the late Victorian novelists deserved immortality.

"It was a crisp and spicy morning in early October. The lilacs and laburnums, lit with the glory-fires of autumn, hung burning and flashing in the upper air, a fairy bridge provided by kind Nature for the wingless wild things that have their homes in the tree-tops and would visit together; the larch and the pomegranate flung their purple and yellow flames in brilliant broad splashes along the slanting sweep of the woodland; the sensuous fragrance of innumerable deciduous flowers rose upon the swooning atmosphere; far in the empty sky a solitary oesophagus slept upon motionless wing; everywhere brooded stillness, serenity, and the peace of God."

To measure the distance Mark Twain had covered in mastering his art, one need only compare that paragraph, his last public hoax, with his first one, the Petrified Man of Gravelly Ford.

The absurdities were piled up with a cunning which wholly deceived the average reader. Had he not added the solitary oesophagus, few people would ever have noticed anything wrong. It has been said that the oesophagus is bad art, a return to Mark's earlier manner. Yet a hoax must not only take in the reader, but must let him know, too late, that he has been taken in. Even with the oesophagus to spring the trap, plenty of readers saw nothing else wrong with the paragraph, and so pestered the author with inquiries that he at last had to make public explanation. That paragraph, he said, had gathered in the guilty and the innocent alike, whereas he had been only fishing for the innocent—the innocent and confiding. No reference to the parody is complete, however, without honorable mention of the young woman who saw through it, and wrote to ask if the oesophagus was a kind of swallow.

West Tenth Street had proved too accessible as a New York home, so when the summer at Saranac ended the Clemenses took a large house at Riverdale-on-Hudson, just outside the limits of the greater city. Nevertheless, the winter was so full of public activity that Mark did little writing. After receiving an honorary Doctor of Letters from Yale, with Howells as fellow sufferer, he plunged into the municipal political campaign, where a fusion ticket was endeavoring to break the hold of Tammany Hall. It was a thoroughly characteristic Mark Twain proceeding. However loudly he might damn the human race, he was always trying to save it or portions of it by mental healing, by osteopathy, by plasmon or by opposing Tammany. Just as he never could remember, when someone had done him an injury, that the man was not, according to the gospel of Mark, accountable for his acts, so he never could remember for long at a time that the human race wasn't worth saving. He was caught in the fatalist's dilemma, though he seldom realized it. And yet, during this same winter, his deterministic theories furnished the basis for a piece of invective so devastating that his literary executor never dared to collect it.

The American imperialistic adventure in the Philippines,

which had been dragging along in a thickening stench of blood-shed and oppression, had culminated in the shabbiest act of treachery in American military annals—General Frederick Funston's capture of Aguinaldo. The country at large applauded; Mark Twain sat down in a cold fury and said what he thought. No exaggeration was necessary. He began by relating the facts, as reported by Funston himself:

"Some of the customs of war are not pleasant to the civilian; but ages upon ages of training have reconciled us to them as being justifiable. . . . Every detail of Funston's scheme—but one—has been employed in war in the past and stands acquitted of blame by history. By the custom of war, it is permissible . . . for a Brigadier-General (if he be of the sort that can so choose) to persuade or bribe a courier to betray his trust; to remove the badges of his honorable rank and disguise himself; to lie, to practise treachery, to forge; to associate with himself persons properly fitted by training and instinct for the work; to accept of courteous welcome, and assassinate the welcomers while their hands are still warm from the friendly handshake. . . .

"But there is one detail which is new, absolutely new. It has never been resorted to before in any age of the world, in any country, among any people, savage or civilized. . . . When a man is exhausted by hunger to the point where he is 'too weak to move,' he has a right to make supplication to his enemy to save his failing life; but if he take so much as one taste of that food—which is holy, by the precept of all ages and all nations— *he is barred from lifting his hand against that enemy for that time.*

"It was left for a Brigadier-General of Volunteers in the American army to put shame upon a custom which even the degraded Spanish friars had respected. *We promoted him for it. . . .*"

Mark then related in detail how Funston and his followers, after being fed and sheltered by Aguinaldo, attacked and murdered some of the guard, and kidnapped the Filipino leader.

No one, Funston least of all, had denied any of these facts. And then Mark's indignation reached a climax, which had it been penned by Swift or Voltaire would be in all the textbooks.

"These being the facts, we come now to the question, is Funston to blame? I think not. And for that reason I think too much is being made of this matter. He did not make his own disposition, It was born with him. It chose his ideals for him, he did not choose them. It chose the kind of society It liked, the kind of comrades It preferred, and imposed them upon him, rejecting the other kinds; he could not help this. . . . Its moral sense, if It had any, was color-blind, but this was no fault of Funston's, and he is not chargeable with the results; It had a native predilection for unsavory conduct, but it would be in the last degree unfair to hold Funston to blame for the outcome of his infirmity; as clearly unfair as it would be to blame him because his conscience leaked out through one of his pores when he was little—a thing which he could not help, and he couldn't have raised it, anyway. . . . If blame there was, and guilt, and treachery, and baseness, they are not Funston's, but only Its; It has the noble gift of humor, and can make a banquet almost die with laughter when it has a funny incident to tell about. . . . With youthful glee It can see sink down in death the simple creatures who had answered Its fainting prayer for food, and without remorse It can note the reproachful look in their dimming eyes; but in fairness we must remember that this is only It, not Funston; by proxy, in the person of Its born servant, It can do Its strange work, and practise Its ingratitudes and amazing treacheries, while wearing the uniform of the American soldier, and marching under the authority of the American flag. And It—not Funston—comes home now, to teach us children what Patriotism is! Surely It ought to know. . . ."

Scorn and righteousness anger were never more richly vocalized. Yet even here the continuity of Mark Twain's imagery appears. Back in his days on the Buffalo *Express* he had advised some mean citizens to varnish their hides, lest their souls leak out through a pore. Then the image itself contented him, as adequately stating his thought; now, the image was slipped into a subordinate place. A lifetime of practise in finding the exact word bore final fruit in the essay, and the mechanistic philosophy of *What Is Man?* justified itself for once. It is hard to imagine how the excoriation of Funston could have been made more scathing than by the irony of exculpating him on the ground that not he but his innate disposition was to blame. Mark Twain had not, as he fondly believed, formulated a complete philosophy, but he had forged a superb satiric tool. People who have accused him of moral cowardice must somehow have overlooked this essay, beside the earlier clash with the missionaries. To attack the character of a popular military hero in the hour of his triumph called for courage.

But the year was not wholly given to such serious work as attacking Tammany and General Funston. There were two trips in Henry Rogers' palatial yacht, one in August 1901 to Nova Scotia, and the other in the following April to the West Indies. Another guest was Tom Reed, late Speaker of the House of Representatives, whom Mark, in the comic log he kept for the edification of the party, dubbed the Reformed Statesman. Twichell was invited, but could not go; to let him know what he had missed, Mark wrote, "we had a noble good time in the yacht. We caught a Chinee missionary and drowned him." Actually they spent the time in endless games of draw poker, and endless chaff. When Mark, for instance, mentioned his own snoring, "Mr. Rogers said it infused him so with comfortableness that he tried to keep himself awake by turning over and over in bed, so as to get more of it. Rice said it was not a coarse and ignorant snore. Colonel Payne said he was always sorry when night was over and he knew he had to wait all day before he could have some more; and Tom Reed said the reason he moved down into the coal bunkers was because it was even sweeter there, where he could get a perspective on it. This is very different from the way I am treated at home, where there is no appreciation of what a person does."

In the spring of 1902, also, the University of Missouri at last

awoke to the fact that the state had produced a distinguished
man of letters to whom Yale had given two degrees. He was
invited to Commencement at Columbia, to receive an LL.D.
The old haunts held so many dead that Mark had never expected
to revisit them, but he could not refuse this honor, and the trip
became a reunion of survivors. He was met in St. Louis by his
old chief, Horace Bixby, and found Beck Jolly and one or two
other old-timers still on deck. He spent five days in Hannibal,
pursued by news photographers, and meeting the children and
grandchildren of the boys and girls who had been his play-
mates. John Briggs, John RoBards, and one or two others were
still alive; with Helen Kercheval Garth he visited John Garth's
grave, and his heart echoed the unanswerable question Susy had
asked so long ago, "What is it all for?" And out of the past
came a wizened little man, Jimmy McDaniel, and Mark shook
hands in age with the boy to whom he had first told the tale of
Jim Wolf and the cats. Then as he waited for the train which
was to take him away from Hannibal for the last time, another
ghost appeared in the crowd—Tom Nash, with whom Sam
Clemens had been almost drowned when the ice broke up as
they were skating a half century before. Tom, stone-deaf from
the scarlet fever which had followed his icy immersion, gestured
toward the crowd at the station, and bellowed, in a deaf man's
confidential whisper, "Same damn fools, Sam!" For the author
of *Huckleberry Finn,* Hannibal could have given no more
fitting valediction.

Glowing with the memory of his royal progress, its demon-
strations of popular affection for the time overruling the many
reminders of mortality, Mark returned East for what promised
to be a happy summer. They had taken "a wide, low cottage in
a pine grove" at York Harbor, Maine, only forty minutes away
from the Howells' summer home at Kittery Point. Livy's
health was frailer than ever, but the friends saw each other
often. "We used," Howells said, "to sit at a corner of the
veranda farthest away from Mrs. Clemens's window, where we
could read our manuscripts to each other, and tell our stories,

and laugh our hearts out without disturbing her." Besides the usual grist of unfinished or rejected articles Mark wrote two stories in the earlier part of the summer. One of these, "The Belated Russian Passport," was a mere skit, an ostensible tragedy given a sudden comedy twist at the end. It was the sort of thing O. Henry was doing in those years with greater technical competence. The other, "Was It Heaven? or Hell?," went for its ending not to O. Henry but to Frank Stockton; its theme, however, had no relation to Stockton. The conflict of religious and moral codes with human affections was worked out in an allegory which turned out to be unconscious prophecy.

On the sixth anniversary of the day on which Susy was to have sailed for England Livy was wakened by a violent heart attack. She had severe palpitations, could not breathe, and believed herself dying. A doctor, hurriedly summoned, relieved the worst symptoms, but ordered absolute rest and quiet. Nurses were brought in, Sue Crane came from Elmira, and Clara took charge of the household, while her father, barred from the sickroom, wandered forlornly about the house and, in pathetic hope that the report of it might brighten the patient, pinned notices on the trees warning the birds not to sing too loudly under Livy's window. He corrected and mailed the two manuscripts he had completed, but otherwise could do no work. Livy comforted herself with the reflection that her seclusion at least saved her from hearing anything more about the damned human race for a while—a flash of comment which shows that she was human, after all.

The weeks dragged on, samples of the twenty-month vigil ahead. "We are a drifting ship without a captain. We survive by accident," Mark wrote in his notebook. It was two months before Livy could be moved, even on a stretcher. Henry Rogers offered his yacht to bring her home to Riverdale, but when at last, on October 15, the journey was possible they dared not risk the sea voyage, and brought the patient through by rail in a specially chartered invalid coach. The family hoped she was making progress, after she got home, but it was discouragingly slow. All her husband could do was to write little notes to her, two or three times a day, from which all bad news and violent opinions were carefully excluded. When his publishers gave him a dinner in honor of his sixty-seventh birthday he included a eulogy of Livy in his speech, but not until December 30 was he able to record, "Saw Livy five minutes by the watch— the first time in more than three months. A splendid five minutes." And also a five minutes which included prodigies in the way of withholding facts.

"Was It Heaven? or Hell?" appeared in the Christmas number of *Harper's Magazine*. Two days before Christmas Jean developed pneumonia. For nearly a week her life flickered, with nurses and doctors in constant attendance. No word of all this was allowed to reach the mother. Clara was the only member of the family admitted to the sickroom, and Livy regularly questioned Clara as to Jean's doings. Clara had to lie steadily and inspiredly for weeks, inventing amusements and activities for Jean, and giving circumstantial accounts of them. Even in the midst of his anxiety Mark delighted in the fact that the only member of the family with a reputation for always telling the exact truth should be forbidden to tell it to the one person to whom she found it hardest to lie. And every day Clara had to give her father detailed reports of all the lies she had told, so that he could furnish confirmation in the little notes he sent in.

As spring came on the invalid began to mend, and the doctors held out hope that in a milder climate she might regain a measure of health. Remembering their happy days in the Villa Viviani, they made plans to rent a Florentine villa for the coming winter. The previous summer they had bought a house at Tarrytown, intending to make it their home when the Riverdale lease was out. But now they realized that the dream would probably never be fulfilled; they put the house on the market, and Mark told Howells that they would in all likelihood spend the rest of their lives in Florence. By the first of July Livy was well enough to be moved to Elmira, where they bathed themselves for the last time in the peace and beauty of Quarry

Farm. Livy kept in the open air as much as possible, and was taken out often in the carriage or a wheel chair. "In the matter of superintending everything and everybody," her husband told Twichell, "[she] has resumed business at the old stand."

He himself did a little work in the old study where his best books had been written, but completed nothing except "A Dog's Tale"—written primarily to please Jean, who was horrified by reports of animal vivisection. His older writings, however, at last became an agreeable source of revenue in this year. The long negotiations which Henry Rogers had been conducting were satisfactorily ended at last: all Mark's books were transferred to Harper's, the final contract being signed on October 22, only two days before the family sailed for Italy. It assured the author of a minimum income of $25,000 a year from his collected works, and actually the receipts were frequently double the guaranteed sum. Mark Twain was free from financial worry at last, and the latent superstition of his Hannibal boyhood revived in the attention he gave in his notes to a prediction, made by Cheiro the palmist in 1895, that in his sixty-eighth year Mark would become suddenly rich. The prophecy came true with only thirty-nine days to spare, and its fulfillment, together with Livy's apparent slow improvement in health, set him lightheartedly on the voyage to Italy.

Livy bore the journey well, and the family soon settled into the routine of life in the Villa Quarto. It had its drawbacks. The villa was a huge Renaissance barn, built for Cosimo de Medici and infested by its current owner, the American wife of an Italian count, who for a time made the Clemens' life ingeniously uncomfortable. Once, when Mark found that the outer gates had been locked, preventing the entrance of the doctor, he lavishly cursed, not the person who had locked them, but Cosimo, who had built the place. In spite of annoyances, however, he was able to write. He had left New York under a half promise to furnish the Harper magazines with several articles. "Magazining," he told Twichell at the beginning of January, "is difficult work because every third page represents two pages that you have put in the fire; (because you are nearly sure to *start* wrong twice) and so when you have finished an article and are willing to let it go to print it represents only 10 cents a word instead of 30. But this time I had the curious (and unprecedented) luck to start right in each case. I turned out 37,000 words in 25 working days; and the reason I think I started right every time is, that not only have I approved and accepted the several articles, but the court of last resort (Livy) has done the same."

During this winter and spring he turned his attention seriously to composing fragments of his autobiography. It was not a new project. As long ago as when he was planning *The Gilded Age* he had written a fragment about the Tennessee land, and in the middle '80's he had set down in detail the story of his part in the publishing of the Grant *Memoirs*. He had written other fragments in Vienna in 1898, but now he was sure that he had hit upon the right way to do it: "Start at no particular time of your life; wander at your free will all over your life; talk only about the thing which interests you for the moment; drop it the moment its interest threatens to pale, and turn your talk upon the new and more interesting thing that has intruded itself into your mind meantime. Also, make the narrative a combined Diary and Autobiography. In this way you have the vivid things of the present to make a contrast with memories of like things in the past, and these contrasts have a charm which is all their own. No talent is required to make a Combined Diary and Autobiography interesting."

In fact, he was merely formulating the method by which the earlier fragments had been written. In these Florentine chapters he illustrated the theory by ranging from descriptions, made with all the loving detail of perfect hatred, of the architectural and decorative abominations of the Villa Quarto to characteristically inaccurate memories of the writing of the *The Innocents Abroad*, and thence to reminiscences of Robert Louis Stevenson, Thomas Bailey Aldrich and Henry H. Rogers. He did not intend that any of this material should appear in his lifetime. Howells wrote, "I'd like, immensely, to read your autobiography. You always rather bewildered me by your veracity, and I fancy you may tell the truth about yourself. But *all* of it? The black truth which we all know of ourselves in our hearts, or only the whity-brown truth of the pericardium, or the nice whitened truth of the shirt-front? Even *you* won't tell the black heart's-truth. The man who could do it would be famed to the last day the sun shone." And Mark replied:

"Yes, I set up the safeguards, in the first day's dictating;— taking this position: that an autobiography is the truest of all books; for while it inevitably consists mainly of extinctions of the truth, with hardly an instance of plain straight truth, the remorseless truth *is* there, between the lines, where the author is raking dust upon it, the result being that the reader knows the author in spite of his wily diligences."

But after all the dictations did not get very far. Livy seemed at times to improve, rallying from a two-day bout of rheumatic pains to plan a sojourn in Egypt for the coming winter, though the family knew in their hearts that she could not be moved for months, if ever. "But it comforts us to let on that we think otherwise, and these pretensions help to keep hope alive in her." All bad news had still to be kept from her. In May, acknowledging a letter from Twichell, he gave a glimpse of their loving deceptions:

"You've done a wonder, Joe: you've written a letter that can be sent in to Livy. . . . You *did* whirl in a P.S. that wouldn't do, but you wrote it on a margin of a page in such a way that I was able to clip off the margin clear across both pages, and now Livy won't perceive that the sheet isn't the same size it used to was. It was about Aldrich's son, and I came near forgetting to remove it. It should have been written on a loose strip and enclosed. The son died on the 5th of March and Aldrich wrote me on the night before that his minutes were numbered. On the 18th Livy asked after that patient, and I was prepared, and able to give her a grateful surprise by telling her 'the Aldriches are no longer uneasy about him.' "

There were moments of hope, but they had learned to distrust them. In May Katie Leary announced that Mrs. Clemens was really and truly better—had felt it herself, and said so. "There—it is heartwarming, it is splendid, it is sublime," said Mark, in the same letter to Twichell just quoted. "Let us enjoy it, let us make the most of it today—and bet not a farthing on tomorrow. The tomorrows have nothing for us. Too many times they have breathed the word of promise to our ear and broken it to our hope. We take no tomorrow's word any more." Only two days after those words were written he told R. W. Gilder that "after twenty months of bed-ridden solitude and bodily misery she all of a sudden ceases to be a pallid shrunken shadow, and looks bright and young and pretty. She remains what she always was, the most wonderful creature of fortitude, patience, endurance and recuperative power that ever was. But, ah, dear, it won't last; this fiendish malady will play new treacheries upon her, and I shall go back to my prayers again— unutterable from any pulpit!" And before the letter was mailed he had to add a postscript fulfilling his forebodings: "I have just paid one of my pair of permitted two minutes visits per day to the sick room. And found what I have learned to expect—retrogression, and that pathetic something in the eye which betrays the secret of a waning hope."

Yet she seemed in no immediate danger, and her husband and daughters began searching the neighborhood of Florence for a really livable villa which they might purchase and settle down in. On June 5, Jean and her father inspected one which they thought might serve, and returned from their drive to be told that the patient had been better that afternoon than she had been for three months. Her husband's letter next day to Howells tells the rest:

"Last night at 9:20 I entered Mrs. Clemens's room to say the usual goodnight—and she was dead—tho' no one knew it. She had been cheerfully talking, a minute before. She was sitting up in bed—she had not lain down for months—and Katie and the nurse were supporting her. They supposed she had fainted, and they were holding the oxygen pipe to her mouth, expecting to revive her. I bent over her and looked in her face, and I think I spoke—I was surprised and troubled that she did not notice me. Then we understood, and our hearts broke. How poor we are today!

"But how thankful I am that her persecutions are ended. I would not call her back if I could.

"Today, treasured in her worn old Testament, I found a dear and gentle letter from you, dated Far Rockaway, Sept. 13, 1896, about our poor Susy's death. I am tired and old; I wish I were with Livy."

CHAPTER XVIII

EVENING

THE ending of their vigil left the survivors stunned. Clara, who had borne the largest share of strain in the long ordeal, was prostrated; her father strove desolately to plan what they must do. On June 7 he wrote to Gilder: "An hour ago the best heart that ever beat for me and mine went silent out of this house, and I am as one who wanders and has lost his way. She who is gone was our head, she was our hands. We are now trying to make plans—*we;* we who have never made a plan before, nor ever needed to. If she could speak to us she would make it all simple and easy with a word, and our perplexities would vanish away." He had at last suggested an arrangement at which the girls did not shake their heads; he asked Gilder to find them a quiet house near the Gilder summer place at Tyringham, in the Berkshires. But still there remained the task of breaking up the establishment at the Villa Quarto, and arranging for the return to America. The first available boat sailed on June 14, but it was the one they had come over in, and they could not face returning with Livy dead on a ship on which she had been alive. They waited until the twenty-sixth to get a different steamer.

Through the days and weeks that followed, Mark tormented himself with the disconsolate arithmetic of bereavement. "Think—in three hours it will be a week!" he wrote to Howells, "and soon a month; and by and by a year. How fast our dead fly from us." All through the homeward voyage his mind kept up the same round, recalling former journeys in Livy's company, reproaching himself for his sins of negligence and ignorance against her. "In my life there have been 68 Junes—but how vague and colorless 67 of them are contrasted with the deep blackness of this one," he wrote in his notebook; and again, "I cannot reproduce Livy's face in my mind's eye—I was never in my life able to reproduce a face. It is a curious infirmity—and now at last I realize that it is a calamity." But the pilgrimage ended at last, and on July 14 Joe Twichell conducted Livy's funeral in the old Elmira home where he had performed the marriage ceremony thirty-four years before, and she was laid to rest beside her children.

But the disasters of the year were not finished. No sooner had they removed to the summer place at Lee which the Gilders had found for them than Clara had a complete nervous breakdown. She was taken back to New York to rest under a doctor's care, and ultimately had to enter a sanitarium for a year of rest and recuperation. While her elder sister was still in New York Jean went on a moonlight ride with a party of young folks. Her horse took fright, collided with a trolley car, and was killed. Jean was picked up unconscious, badly bruised, and with a broken tendon in her ankle. The state of her father's mind can be inferred from his subsequent action. He telephoned Clara's doctor to keep the newspapers away from her until he could come and break the news gently himself. When he reached New York what he actually did was to thrust into Clara's hand a newspaper containing a highly colored account of the accident, which he then proceeded to relate in his most feeling and dramatically impressive way. Plainly, he was so beside himself with grief and anxiety that he did not realize what he might be doing to his daughter's nerves, for this was the same man who only a week before had hurriedly extinguished a fire in his bedroom because he remembered that there was a brood of swifts in the chimney.

On September 1 Pamela Moffett died—the third death in the family that year, for Mollie, Orion's widow, had died in January, and her death had been one of the many things concealed from Livy. But life had to go on, and in the fall he rented a house at 21 Fifth Avenue, and brought the old familiar things from Hartford to furnish it. With Jean and Katie Leary as the

only members of his diminished family he lived for the first
months in what, for him, was almost complete seclusion. He
wrote but little—an article on copyright, and diatribes against
the Tsar and King Leopold of the Belgians were the only manuscripts completed and passed for print, the last named as a contribution to the fund for the relief of the natives of the Congo.
The presidential campaign of that fall moved him only to
nausea. "Oh, dear! get out of that sewer—party politics," he
told Joe Twichell, for Theodore Roosevelt the politician he
detested, though he never failed to yield to the magnetism of the
man. In this connection he added a postscript to the letter to
Twichell which revealed the weakness of his "philosophy" as
a guide to life: "I wish I could learn to remember that it is
unjust and dishonorable to put blame upon the human race for
any of its acts."

In time the wound of Livy's death closed, but it never healed.
Mark Twain went out into society again, but there was an empty
place in life. At home, he solaced himself in his loneliness with
a glorified player piano, an Aeolian orchestrelle. But people
were necessary to him, and when the summer of 1905 came he
took a house at Dublin, New Hampshire, where a colony of
artists and literary people included Thomas Wentworth Hig-
ginson, Raphael Pumpelly, and Abbott Thayer, whose wife,
then Emma Beach, had been a member of the *Quaker City*
party in the far past. Here he labored at a characteristically
impossible literary stunt, the story called *3000 Years Among the
Microbes,* and wrote *Eve's Diary* as a companion piece for the
Adam skit of a dozen years before. Its last line, supposedly
added by Adam after Eve's death, is Livy's epitaph: "Where-
soever she was, *there* was Eden." He also wrote *A Horse's Tale,*
at the request of Minnie Maddern Fiske, who was conducting a
crusade against bullfighting, as two summers before he had
written *A Dog's Tale* to please Jean.

The summer restored his strength and his zest for life, however, and again he was full of comments on world affairs. He
disliked the settlement of the Russo-Japanese war, because he

thought that had it been allowed to go on a revolution would have overthrown the Russian monarchy, and he retained enough nineteenth-century American optimism to believe that the destruction of a monarchy meant the end of tyranny. But he withheld his most vitriolic comments, as he continued to withhold "The War Prayer" and his many criticisms of the God of the Old Testament. Yet it was probably not Livy's dead hand which checked him. His estimate of what would shock the public was formed before he ever knew Livy; like his philosophy, it had its roots in the Presbyterian Sunday school of Hannibal. He never in his life wrote anything more scathing than the "Defence of General Funston" and the controversy with the missionaries; he published them, and the heavens did not fall. But it flattered him to believe that he was full of thoughts so devastating that the world could not take them.

With the return in the fall to 21 Fifth Avenue Mark Twain's life resumed its public character. Indeed, he may be said, during the next three years or so, to have had no private life. The heart of the old home was gone, and though Clara assumed some of the duties of social and literary supervision which had been Livy's, her father lived in a constantly thickening atmosphere of adulation and even sycophancy. The procession of pilgrims and reporters to his doors seldom was interrupted for long. Some of the pilgrims came with axes to grind; some came out of genuine admiration, but either way the cumulative effect was not altogether wholesome.

Public acclaim reached a climax on December 5, 1905, at a dinner given in honor of Mark's seventieth birthday. Most of the surviving friends of other days were there—Howells, Twichell, Brander Matthews, Henry Rogers—along with most of the leading authors and editors of the day. And the speech in which Mark Twain made his acknowledgments and took his farewell marked the summit of his power as a public speaker. His daughter, watching him run up and down stairs on the day of the banquet, had thought to herself, "Father is younger now than I have ever felt." But the speech had age for its theme, and after playing along with pleasant jests about Florida, Missouri, about smoking, about morals, closed with a couple of paragraphs of pure eloquence and beauty which none but the most expert of artists could have trusted himself to repeat with steady voice. No better example exists of Mark Twain's consummate mastery of the art of words:

"Threescore years and ten!

"It is the Scriptural statute of limitations. After that, you owe no active duties; for you the strenuous life is over. You are a time-expired man, to use Kipling's military phrase: You have served your term, well or less well, and you are mustered out. You are become an honorary member of the republic, you are emancipated, compulsions are not for you, nor any bugle call but 'lights out.' You pay the time-worn duty bills if you choose, or decline if you prefer—and without prejudice—for they are not legally collectable.

"The previous-engagement plea, which in forty years has cost you so many twinges, you can lay aside forever; on this side of the grave you will never need it again. If you shrink at thought of night, and winter, and the late home-coming from the banquet and the lights and the laughter through the deserted streets—a desolation which would not remind you now, as for a generation it did, that your friends are sleeping, and you must creep in a-tiptoe and not disturb them, but would only remind you that you need not tiptoe, you can never disturb them more—if you shrink at thought of these things, you need only reply, 'Your invitation honors me, and pleases me because you still keep me in your remembrance, but I am seventy; seventy, and would nestle in the chimney corner, and smoke my pipe, and take my rest, wishing you well in all affection, and that when you in your turn shall arrive at pier No. 70 you may step aboard your waiting ship with a reconciled spirit, and lay your course toward the sinking sun with a contented heart."

Probably at some time during this winter, if he had not done it earlier, Mark Twain wrote the unforgettable closing chapter of *The Mysterious Stranger*—a chapter which he later could not remember having written. It was his testament of bitterness; like Malaspina in hell, he shook impotent but defiant fists at Heaven, and cried out, "That to you, O God!" "There is no God, no universe, no human race, no earthly life, no heaven, no hell. It is all a dream—a grotesque and foolish dream. Nothing exists but you. And you are but a *thought*—a vagrant thought, a useless thought, a homeless thought, wandering forlorn among the empty eternities!"

Certainly during this winter he was still in the mood of the story. Less than three weeks after the seventieth birthday dinner, he concluded a speech before the Society of Illustrators with a memory of Jack Van Nostrand of the *Quaker City* party. Jack, dead of consumption in his twenties, "had seen all there was to see in the world that was worth the trouble of living in it; he had seen all of this world that is valuable; he had seen all of this world that was illusion, and illusion is the only valuable thing in it. He had arrived at the point where presently the illusions would cease and he would have entered upon the realities of life, and God help the man that has arrived at that point." Again in the same mood, probably during the same month, he wrote a little essay on Old Age which ended with the picture of life's pilgrim at the close of his journey: "Whiteheaded, the temple empty, the idols broken, the worshipers in their graves, nothing left but You, a remnant, a tradition, belated fag-end of a foolish dream, a dream that was so ingeniously dreamed that it seemed real all the time; nothing left but You, center of a snowy desolation, perched on the ice-summit, gazing out over the stages of that long trek and asking Yourself, 'Would you do it again if you had the chance?' " And at the beginning of 1905 he had written in his notebook, "Sixty years ago optimist and fool were not synonymous terms. This is a greater change than that wrought by science and invention. It is the mightiest change that was ever wrought in the world in any sixty years since creation." He had come a long way from the dominant moods of Hannibal and Virginia City.

The first week in January 1906 Mark Twain took the decisive step of engaging an official biographer. Albert Bigelow Paine, who had begun life as an itinerant photographer in Kansas, was in his middle forties in 1906. After marrying a small-town heiress, he soon abandoned the photographic business for a literary career in the East, beginning work on the editorial staffs of *Harper's Young People* and *St. Nicholas,* and writing books for children. Apart from a couple of casual meetings, he had first come to Mark Twain's attention as the biographer of Mark's old friend, Thomas Nast, the cartoonist. At a Players Club dinner on January 3, a friend told Paine that he ought to write Mark's life. Gathering his courage, Paine made an appointment to call on the sixth and broached the proposal. Mark was in a receptive mood. He told Paine of the autobiographical fragments he had written, and added that he hoped his daughters would some day collect his letters, but said that no arrangements had been made for a detailed biography. Then he asked, "When would you like to begin?" Three days later they were at work.

Paine engaged an expert stenographer, and Mark zestfully resumed the autobiographical dictations, which he continued at intervals for more than two years. He followed the planless plan he had defined at Florence, and at times dreamed that his was going to be the greatest and frankest autobiography ever written. But it came out differently. For forty years Mark Twain had been a public speaker and an author; during those years he had constantly used episodes in his own life as foundations on which to build anecdotes and parables. The factual truth of the result did not concern him; it was the literary effect which he wanted. By the time the work with Paine began the old habit was too strong to be broken. He was not writing history; he was talking to an audience, even though the audience consisted only of Paine and Miss Hobby. Instinctively, unconsciously, he shaped his utterances for their effect. Mark Twain the literary person did the talking, not the Samuel Clemens who had lived the events on which the utterances were founded. Add to this instinctive distortion the fact that as he grew older Mark's memory, always unreliable, reshaped events out of all semblance to reality, and it is easy to see why the *Autobiography* is wholly unreliable as fact.

Paine was the first to discover this weakness. "It was not for several weeks that I began to realize that these marvelous reminiscences bore only an atmospheric relation to history; that they were aspects of biography rather than its veritable narrative, and built largely—sometimes wholly—from an imagination that, with age, had dominated memory, creating details, even reversing them, yet with a perfect sincerity of purpose on the part of the narrator to set down the literal and unvarnished truth. It was his constant effort to be frank and faithful to fact, to record, to confess, and to condemn without stint. If you wanted to know the worst of Mark Twain you had only to ask him for it. He would give it, to the last syllable—worse than the worst, for his imagination would magnify it and adorn it with new iniquities, and if he gave it again, or a dozen times, he would improve upon it each time, until the thread of history was almost impossible to trace through the marvel of that fabric; and he would do the same for another person just as willingly. Those vividly real personalities that he marched and countermarched before us were the most convincing creatures in the world, the most entertaining, the most excruciatingly humorous, or wicked, or tragic; but, alas, they were not always safe to include in a record that must bear a certain semblance to history. They often disagreed in their performance, and even in their characters, with the documents in the next room, as I learned by and by when those records, disentangled, began to rebuild the structure of the years. His gift of dramatization had been exercised too long to be discarded now."

But the biography might have been wholly inaccurate and still have remained consistently interesting reading, had Mark's old tendency to elaborate on trivialities not obtruded itself, and had he confined himself more closely to his own experiences. But too often he centered his remarks on some item in the day's news which looked big at the time but which had in it nothing capable of survival except in a fossil state. Strangely little of his inner life and thought and feeling entered the *Autobiography;* for those, the reader must go to *Tom Sawyer, Huck Finn,* and *The Mysterious Stranger.* The nearest he came to really personal emotion was in what he said of Livy and Susy, and even there he usually gave character studies of his lost ones rather than revelations of his own feelings towards them.

Still another habit of the past also reappeared—his readiness to think of his work primarily in terms of quantity. In June 1906, after he had returned to Dublin for the summer, he reported to Howells the progress made in the first six months:

"I find that I have been at it, off and on, nearly two hours a day for 155 days, since Jan. 9. To be exact, I've dictated 75 hours in 80 days, and loafed 75 days. I've added 60,000 words in the month that I've been here; which indicates that I've dictated during 20 days of that time—40 hours, at an average of 1500 words an hour. It's a plenty, and I am satisfied.

"There's a good deal of 'fat.' I've dictated (from Jan. 9) 210,000 words, and the 'fat' adds about 50,000 more. The 'fat' is old pigeon-holed things, which I or editors didn't das't to print"—among them, the perennial Captain Stormfield, and at a later date his obeisance to that critical marijuana or patent medicine, the Baconian theory. And he concluded the report with the cheerful announcement, "Tomorrow I mean to dictate a chapter which will get my heirs and assigns burnt alive if they venture to print it this side of 2006 A.D.—which I judge they won't. There'll be a lot of such chapters if I live three or four years longer. The edition of A.D. 2006 will make a stir when it comes out. . . ."

The chapter in question is still unpublished, but Paine attests that it was one of several which dealt with the orthodox conceptions of God, and therefore merely another illustration of Mark's delusion that his theological ideas were excessively shocking. He and Howells liked to expatiate on the possibilities of the *Autobiography.* "As we talked it over the scheme enlarged itself in our riotous fancy. We said it should be not only

a book, it should be a library, not only a library, but a literature. It should make good the world's loss through Omar's
barbarity at Alexandria; there was no image so grotesque, so
extravagant that we did not play with it."* Yet there were other
times when Mark thought of the work merely as a refuge from
boredom, or as a means whereby his heirs might extend his
copyrights by distributing fragments of it among his books
and reissuing them thus when the copyrights ran out.

The most publicized, because the most public, of Mark's acts
after he reached Pier 70 was his decision thenceforth always to
dress in white. The reason why most men would have avoided
so distinguishing themselves—that it would make them conspicuous—was not operative with Mark. That was why he did
it. Nevertheless, underlying the love of display, he had a
passionate love of cleanliness. Ten years before, in India, he
had written of the high-caste Hindu's attitude toward Euro-
peans: "The upper castes regard us as the dirty peoples. Dirty
is the right word; it accurately describes what the Hindu thinks
of us. Of course we must be disgusting objects to him; of course
we often turn his stomach. He washes his garments *every day;*
we come into his presence in coat, vest and breeches that have
never been in the wash since they left the tailor's hands; they
are stale with ancient sweat, tobacco smoke and so on. No doubt
he says 'Ugh!' and retches; but his feelings are not allowed to
show outside, for he is a courteous being."

But still, of course, the Tom Sawyer instinct that as a boy had
enlisted him in the Temperance Cadets because of their gaudy
regalia was strong in him. Indeed, the crumbling away of his
home life had left him with little except the sense of public
acclaim to serve as a bulkhead between him and the edge of
nothing. He liked to walk on Fifth Avenue when the crowds
were coming out of church, to see people recognize him and turn
to look again. He ceased to go to Dublin after the second summer because he was lonely there. In December 1906, when he
went to Washington to lobby in behalf of a new copyright bill,

---

*From *My Mark Twain* by William Dean Howells. Copyright 1910 by
Harper & Bros., 1938 by Mildred Howells and John Mead Howells.

Paine, who accompanied him, was self-conscious about appearing in the wake of the white clothes. At the Willard Hotel the biographer steered his illustrious employer to a side entrance of the dining room without passing through "Peacock Alley." Finding himself at the side door, Mark asked, "Isn't there another entrance to this place?" When Paine admitted that there was Mark took him back upstairs and down again by the great staircase into the main lobby, where he could enjoy the sensation of the crowd's immediate recognition.

To this same Washington expedition belongs one of the most picturesque bits of Mark's objurgation which has been allowed to reach print. The cream for his breakfast coffee was served in a gourd-shaped jug with a very narrow neck. "Seizing it with a jerk, he slopped an unnecessary amount of the contents into his coffee, and a good deal into the tray. He banged down the pitcher and glared at it helplessly. 'That hell-fired thing,' he said, 'one might as well try to pour milk out of a womb!' And a moment later, 'I get so damned short of profanity at a time like this.' "

His temper after Pier 70 was just as volcanic as it had been in earlier years. In the fall of 1906 Mrs. Rogers gave him a billiard table, and he gleefully resumed the game which he had seldom played since the Hartford home was broken up. As the chief interest in Mark's life billiards supplanted the autobiographical dictations, and one of Paine's primary duties became that of resident billiardist. It was an arduous assignment. Mark's nervous energy had not abated; he could play all afternoon and all evening—sometimes into the small hours of the morning—until his partner reeled with fatigue. "He played always at high pressure," says Paine. "Now and then, in periods of adversity, he would fly into a perfect passion with things in general. But, in the end, it was a sham battle, and he saw the uselessness and humor of it, even in the moment of his climax. Once, when he found it impossible to make any of his favorite shots, he became more and more restive, the lightning became vividly picturesque as the clouds blackened. Finally, with a regular thunder-blast, he seized the cue with both hands and literally mowed the balls across the table. . . . I do not recall his exact remarks during the performance; I was chiefly concerned in getting out of the way, and those sublime utterances were lost. I gathered up the balls and we went on playing as if nothing had happened, only he was very gentle and sweet, like the sun on the meadows after the storm has passed by. After a little he said:

" 'This is a most amusing game. When you play badly it amuses me, and when I play badly and lose my temper it certainly must amuse you.' "

In these years Paine and the staff formed the habit of referring to Mark as "the King"—a title perhaps originated by Howells at the seventieth birthday dinner, when he introduced the guest of honor with the words, "I will not say, 'O King, live forever!' but 'O King, live as long as you like!' " It was symbolic of the atmosphere which surrounded him. When S. J. Woolf came to paint his portrait, early in 1906, he found the humorist defended by a fiercely efficient secretary, "haughty to strangers and subservient to Mr. Clemens and his family. She gave the impression that he could not be left alone, and all the time I worked she sat guarding him and laughing at his remarks before he finished making them. One of her functions, apparently, was to show appreciation of his humor, which at that time was not always in evidence." Clara and Jean were often absent through illness, and Clara, besides, was developing as a concert singer and made extensive tours. Late in 1907, moreover, Jean was sent to a sanitarium for nearly two years, in the hope that her malady might yield to a long course of treatment. Mark spent his seventy-first birthday wholly alone except for Paine, for even his secretary was ill.

The winter and spring of 1907 brought a complete interruption of the autobiographical dictations. During the winter Mark and Twichell revisited Bermuda for the first time since 1877, and shortly afterward Paine was dispatched on a long tour of the Mississippi and the West Coast to interview the few surviving friends of Mark's youth—John Briggs, Horace Bixby,

Steve Gillis and Joe Goodman among them. Then in April came the offer of an honorary degree from Oxford. To Moberly Bell of the London *Times,* one of the chief movers in obtaining the offer, he wrote, "Although I wouldn't cross an ocean again for the price of the ship that carried me, I am glad to do it for an Oxford degree." He sailed for England on June 8, forty years to the day from the time the *Quaker City* had anchored all night in the Lower Bay because it was blowing too hard outside.

The four weeks he spent in England were a round of public and private honors such as England has rarely paid to a private citizen of another country. From the moment the dockers at Tilbury cheered him as he came down the gangplank until a swarm of reporters and autograph hunters pursued him aboard ship for the return voyage, he had seldom an idle or a private minute. The dockers' cheers, incidently, later inspired one of the finest flights of fiction in the *Autobiography,* in which he hailed the stevedores as men of his own class—a claim which would have curdled the Virginian blood of John Marshall Clemens and Jane Lampton. What with royal garden parties, dinners from the staff of *Punch,* and visits from all the great men and women of the kingdom, even the Oxford degree and the historical pageant which followed the Encaenia that year almost faded into insignificance. The constant round of activity would have worn down the average man of half Mark Twain's age, yet he seemed to thrive on it, and not only returned all the calls that were paid him, but hunted up all surviving friends, including the lowly, whom he had known on his earlier visits to England.

This same year of 1907, the climax of his public honors, was also the last year in which he did any notable amount of publishing. In the previous year he had bought a small farm at Redding, Connecticut. Paine had suggested the investment, for the biographer had acquired an old farmhouse as a country home, and his enthusiasm about the scenery and the cheapness of the land inspired Mark to buy. Then George Harvey persuaded Mark to allow selected passages from the *Autobiography* to be published in the *North American Review,* and with the payment received for these Mark commissioned John Howells, son of his old friend, to build a house on the Redding property. Also in the fall of 1906 he printed two hundred and fifty copies of *What Is Man?* for private distribution among his friends.

During 1907 the serial publication of the *Autobiography* continued, and at long last he permitted Harper's to make a little book of *Captain Stormfield's Visit to Heaven.* The work which Mark had held back for thirty years, because he thought it would shock the public, created a mild ripple of amusement and that was all. Harper's also brought out the various articles on Christian Science in book form, and the earnings from these two books also went into the new house. But Mark took no direct interest in the building. Clara visited the site before work started, and paid other visits of inspection from time to time, but her father refused, saying, "I don't want to see it until the cat is purring on the hearth." He had spent the remainder of the summer of 1907 at Tuxedo Park, and during the winter returned again to Bermuda for the relief of the bronchitis which had become his regular winter visitant. Not until the middle of June 1908 was the new house completely finished and furnished, and Mark Twain moved into his last home.

The old friends were dropping away rapidly, now. E. C. Stedman, whom Mark had known for thirty-five years, had died in January 1908; Aldrich was gone, too, and a few weeks after the move to Stormfield Mark Twain made the long trip in hot weather to Portsmouth, New Hampshire, where the old Aldrich home was being dedicated as memorial to the poet. His tribute to Aldrich was one of his last formal public speeches; subsequently, in an account of the ceremonies which he dictated for his autobiography, he squared accounts for that occasion nearly four decades before when Mrs. Aldrich, thinking him drunk, had refused to invite him to dinner. Much as he had loved Aldrich as man and wit, he had no illusions about the importance of Aldrich's work: "his prose was diffuse, self-conscious, and barren of distinction," and his few first-rate poems appealed only to a limited audience. The Memorial he considered a folly, created by the vanity of the widow—"A strange and vanity-devoured, detestable woman! I do not believe I could ever learn to like her, except on a raft at sea with no other provisions in sight."

In his increasing loneliness he found his greatest happiness in the company of children, little girls for choice. As he said, he had arrived at a grandfather's age without having any grandchildren, so he had to adopt some. As far back as 1902 he had organized a private club of young girls, with one member from each country and himself as Member at Large for the Human Race. "One of my members," he told Hélène Picard, newly elected Member for France, "is a Princess of a royal house, another is the daughter of a village bookseller on the continent of Europe. For the only qualification for Membership is intellect and spirit of good will; other distinctions, hereditary or acquired, do not count." And on his later visits to Bermuda he organized the Angel-fish. "To be an Angel-fish one must be a girl, and one must be young, and one must have won Mr. Clemens's heart," Elizabeth Wallace explained. With them he played the games of serious pretending which children love; to them he told his most amusing stories; their occasional visits brightened his days at Stormfield.

For Stormfield, though he loved the beauty of the house and the countryside, was lonely, and growing lonelier. On August 1, 1908, came the news of the death by drowning of his nearest male relative, Samuel E. Moffett, Pamela's son, a brilliant man of whom his uncle had been fond and proud. Mark Twain attended the funeral, and on his return suffered the first overt attack of the heart disease which ultimately killed him. His mood, and his own diagnosis of the attack of dizziness which had come upon him, he put into a letter to Sue Crane:

"I came back here in bad shape, and had a bilious collapse, but I am all right again, though the doctor from New York has given peremptory orders that I am not to stir from here before frost. O fortunate Sam Moffett! fortunate Livy Clemens!

doubly fortunate Susy! Those swords go through and through my heart, but there is never a moment that I am not glad, for the sake of the dead, that they have escaped."

Though he spoke so casually of his own condition his actions showed that he was conscious of failing powers. He ceased the dictations which had continued, with interruptions, for nearly two and a half years. The *Autobiography* had reached a bulk of about half a million words, but he made no effort to unite its heterogeneous fragments into a consecutive narrative; it was laid aside for good. He had reached in fact the time he had spoken of, almost three years before, when he would nestle in the chimney corner, and smoke his pipe, and read his book, and take his rest.

CHAPTER XIX

THE DARK

It was not in Mark Twain's nature, however, to be wholly idle for any length of time. Though he had originally planned to use Stormfield only in the summers, returning to New York for the winters, the charm of the place had so taken him that 21 Fifth Avenue was closed and Redding became his sole home. He found some of the company he craved by interesting himself in the affairs of the village, holding an occasional open house for his neighbors, and once arranging a benefit concert to raise funds for a community library. Old friends and new, from Howells down to Helen Allen and Margaret Blackmer, two of the Bermuda "Angel-fish," visited him; Clara was with him in the intervals of her professional and social engagements, and in the spring of 1909 Jean returned from her sanitarium exile, apparently much improved in health.

Though he had laid aside the *Autobiography,* he still wrote when the mood served, and added new fragments to his store of unfinished articles—mainly on the now hackneyed theme of gibes at traditional Christian theology. But during the winter of 1908-1909 he finished the long essay, published as a separate volume, "Is Shakespeare Dead?" The immediate stimulus was a Baconian tract, *The Shakespeare Problem Restated,* by George Greenwood. A specious logic in the Baconian thesis appealed to that side of Mark's mind which had always been a ready prey to the vendors of patent medicines and plausible inventions. It was characteristic that the argument of Greenwood's which bore most weight with Mark was Shakespeare's alleged familiarity with the fine points of law—that is, an argument on which he had to take the special pleader's word, since he had no intimate knowledge of his own by which he could verify Greenwood's contentions. When the book was published in April it caused some talk, and there were critics who thought it merely another of Mark's legpulls. It might have been better if it had been.

At the beginning of April he went to Norfolk, Virginia, as Henry Rogers' guest, to attend the ceremonies at the opening of the Virginian Railway, and took advantage of the opportunity to pay public tribute to Rogers for his help in the period of bankruptcy. It was his last meeting with that loyal friend. On May 20 Mark went down from Redding to New York for a business consultation with Rogers. Clara, then in the city, met him at the train with the news that Rogers had died suddenly in the night. Of course reporters were there too, as Mark Twain remembered seven months later:

"When Clara met me at the station in New York and told me Mr. Rogers had died suddenly that morning, my thought was, Oh, favorite of fortune—fortunate all his long and lovely life—fortunate to his latest moment! The reporters said there were tears of sorrow in my eyes. True—but they were for *me*, not for him. He had suffered no loss. All the fortunes he had ever made before were poverty compared with this one."

A couple of weeks after Rogers' death, Mark Twain went to Baltimore to attend the graduation of Frances Nunnally, one of his adopted granddaughters. It was just two years after he had sailed to receive his Oxford degree, and forty-two years since the start of the *Quaker City* excursion. In Baltimore he suffered the first definite attack of the angina which the dizziness that beset him in the previous August had foreshadowed. He rallied quickly, however, and at the commencement of St. Timothy's School spoke briefly for the last time in public, advising the girls not to smoke—to excess; not to drink—to excess; not to marry—to excess. Had he planned it, he could not have had a happier farewell to the platform, for an audience of young girls always delighted him, and brought out his most charming traits.

As summer wore on at Stormfield the heart attacks became more frequent, but he did not let them interfere with his interest in life and billiards. Paine was almost constantly in attendance, and a house guest during most of the summer was Ossip Gabrilowitsch, who was recuperating from a series of painful operations. The Clemenses had first met him in Vienna, when Clara was studying with Leschetizky; before this summer ended, he and Clara were engaged.

The engagement was announced after the concert, on September 21, for the benefit of the Redding Library, and the marriage followed only a fortnight later, for Gabrilowitsch was booked for an all-winter concert tour in Europe. The wedding was held at Stormfield, with Twichell to perform the ceremony, the bride's father resplendent in his Oxford gown over his white clothes, and Jean, apparently radiant with health, as the only bridesmaid. In the statement which he prepared for the press, Mark Twain said that the marriage pleased him "fully as much as any marriage could please me or any other father. There are two or three solemn things in life and a happy marriage is one of them, for the terrors are all to come." What he meant by his last phrase, a letter written on the marriage of a clergyman friend in the previous year explains:

"Marriage—yes, it *is* the supreme felicity of life, I concede it. And it is also the supreme tragedy of life. The deeper the love the surer the tragedy. And the more disconsolating when it comes.

"And so I congratulate you. Not perfunctorily, not lukewarmly, but with a fervency and fire that no word in the dictionary is strong enough to convey. And in the same breath and with the same depth and sincerity, I grieve for you. Not for both of you, and not for the one that shall go first, but for the one that is fated to be left behind. For that one there is no recompense—for that one no recompense is possible."

And two months later he wrote, "When Clara went away . . . to live in Europe, it was hard, but I could bear it, for I had

Jean left. I said *we* would be a family. We said we would be close comrades and happy—just we two."

In the third week in November Mark Twain took Paine with him for a month's holiday in Bermuda. Though the eve of his departure was saddened by the news of the sudden deaths of two more of his old friends, Richard Watson Gilder and William M. Laffan, the peace and mildness of the islands seemed to benefit him. The attacks of angina were less frequent and less severe, and besides talking endlessly on his favorite topics of astronomy and theology Mark completed the last article he ever wrote for publication—"The Turning-Point in My Life," prepared at the invitation of the editor of *Harper's Bazaar*. Though as autobiography the article was more picturesquely inaccurate than was usual, even with Mark Twain, it had unique value as his final appraisal of the significance of his career. "To me, the most important feature of my life is its literary feature. I have been professionally literary something more than forty years." And he used the essay as an opportunity to restate his favorite philosophy, that a man is made what he is by Circumstances working on his temperament— when Circumstance blew a fifty-dollar bill into his hands in Keokuk, "Circumstance furnished the capital, and my temperament told me what to do with it.

"By temperament I was the kind of person that *does* things. Does them, and reflects afterward. So I started for the Amazon without reflecting and without asking any questions. That was more than fifty years ago. In all that time my temperament has not changed, by even a shade. I have been punished many and many a time, and bitterly, for doing things and reflecting afterward, but these tortures have been of no value to me. I still do the thing commanded by Circumstance and Temperament, and reflect afterward. Always violently. When I am reflecting, on these occasions, even deaf persons can hear me think."

And so, tracing his youthful career as printer, pilot, miner, journalist and lecturer, he explained how the last-named activity had furnished him with the means to make the *Quaker City* excursion. And since that led to his being asked to write a book, and so established him at last as a member of the literary guild, "I can say with truth that the reason I am in the literary profession is because I had the measles when I was twelve years old.

"Now what interests me, as regards these details, is not the details themselves, but the fact that none of them was foreseen by me, none of them was planned by me, I was the author of none of them. Circumstance, working in harness with my temperament, created them all and compelled them all. I often offered help, and with the best intentions, but it was rejected—as a rule, uncourteously. I could never plan a thing and get it to come out the way I planned it. It came out some other way—some way I had not counted on."

However inaccurate the autobiographical statements, however much one may disagree with Mark Twain's determinism, one thing is plain from this summary of his career. As he looked back he was convinced that he had always done the thing that fitted his temperament—in other words, he had been a humorist because his nature required it. Not even in the loneliness and bitterness of his old age did it ever occur to him that he was a thwarted Swift or Juvenal. He had been the thing he was meant to be, and all in all he had enjoyed being it.

Mark Twain decided to spend the holidays at home, and when he reached New York, on December 20, Jean was waiting to greet him at the dock. With all the eagerness of the family temperament Jean, on re-entering her home, had burdened herself with duties—housekeeping, managing the little farm and acting, as at Florence and Saranac, as her father's secretary. To both her father and Paine it seemed that she was doing more than was good for her health, and on the afternoon of December 23 her father told her the plans he had made while in Bermuda to lighten her duties. They would get a housekeeper, and have Paine do her share of the secretarial work:

"No—she wasn't willing. She had been making plans herself. The matter ended in a compromise. I submitted. I always did.

She wouldn't audit the bills and let Paine fill out the checks—she would continue to attend to that herself. Also, she would continue to be housekeeper, and let Katy assist. Also, she would continue to answer the letters of personal friends for me. Such was the compromise. Both of us called it by that name, though I was not able to see where any formidable change had been made."

She was busy with her preparations for Christmas, and at dinnertime that night there came a telephone inquiry about her father's health. It had been reported that he had returned from Bermuda in a dying condition. When the question came from the Associated Press he scribbled a reply, and Jean telephoned it to the press:

"I hear the newspapers say I am dying. The charge is not true. I would not do such a thing at my time of life. I am be having as good as I can. Merry Christmas to everybody!"

After dinner father and daughter strolled hand in hand from the table to the library, and went upstairs together at nine. "At my door Jean said, 'I can't kiss you good night, father; I have a cold, and you could catch it.' I bent and kissed her hand. She was moved—I saw it in her eyes—and she impulsively kissed my hand in return. Then with the usual gay 'Sleep well, dear!' from both, we parted."

Next morning she was found dead in her bathroom. The shock of a cold plunge had brought on an epileptic seizure and heart failure. Dazed, at first, with the shock of the news, the father even then recognized the death as a release for the girl, for he had dreaded what might happen to her were she left alone in the world. He told Paine the story of their last evening together, and sent a cable to Clara, breaking the news and forbidding her to come home. Then, when relating the story had brought the relief of tears, he went to his room and began to write. "Has any one," he said, "ever tried to put upon paper all the little happenings connected with a dear one—happenings of the twenty-four hours preceding the sudden and unexpected death of that dear one? Would a book contain them? Would two books contain them? I think not. They pour into the mind in a flood. They are little things that have always been happening every day, and were always so unimportant and easily forgetable before—but now! Now, how different! how precious they are, how dear, how unforgetable, how pathetic, how sacred, how clothed with dignity!"

All that day, and at intervals during the next two, he continued to write, setting down all the details of their last hours together, calling the roll of his dead, and from time to time slipping into Jean's room to take another look at the dead face, so like Livy's in its dark and chiseled beauty. In his state of health it would have been dangerous for him to go to Elmira for the funeral, but he felt that he could not have gone in any case. "I saw her mother buried. I said I would never endure that horror again; that I would never again look into the grave of any one dear to me." So it was Katie Leary, and Jean's cousin, Jervis Langdon, who accompanied the body to Elmira for burial beside her mother and sister. In his desolation the father asked, "Why did I build this house, two years ago? To shelter this vast emptiness? How foolish I was! But I shall stay in it. The spirits of the dead hallow a house, for me." And he added, "There are no words to express how grateful I am that she did not meet her fate in the hands of strangers, but in the loving shelter of her own home." Always, too, his thoughts came back to the theme he had so often expressed before:

"Would I bring her back to life if I could do it? I would not. If a word would do it, I would beg for strength to withhold the word. And I would have the strength; I am sure of it. In her loss I am almost bankrupt, and my life is a bitterness, but I am content: for she has been enriched with the most precious of all gifts—that gift which makes all other gifts mean and poor—death."

On the evening of Christmas Day, in a driving snowstorm such as Jean had always loved, her body was borne away, and her father was left alone in the home from which love and death had within three months taken the last of his family. The next afternoon, at the hour of the funeral, he returned to his writing to picture briefly the library in the Langdon homestead: "Jean's coffin stands where her mother and I stood, forty years ago, and were married; and where Susy's coffin stood thirteen years ago; where her mother's coffin stood five years and a half ago; and where mine will stand after a little time." Then, when the funeral was over, he recorded his dream of how he and Jean would by themselves be a family. "It was in my mind when she received me at the door last Tuesday evening. We were together; *we were a family!* the dream had come true—oh, precisely true, contentedly true, satisfyingly true! and remained true two whole days."

That evening he handed his manuscript to Paine, saying, "It is the end of my autobiography. I shall never write any more." Yet next day he added a couple of brief paragraphs, which he subsequently discarded, the first presumably because it merely reiterated the idea of failure to appreciate Jean's true value, which he had already sufficiently expressed, the other because its self-analysis had no place in the elegiac theme. Nevertheless, as his final summary of his own temperament, underscoring in his grief the thoughts lightheartedly stated in "The Turning-Point of My Life," it has a value of its own:

"Shall I ever be cheerful again, happy again? Yes. And soon. For I know my temperament. And I know that the temperament is *master of the man,* and that he is its fettered and helpless slave and must in all things do as it commands. A man's temperament is born in him, and no circumstances can ever change it. My temperament has never allowed my spirits to remain depressed long at a time. That was a feature of Jean's temperament, too. She inherited it from me. I think she got the rest of it from her mother."

And two days later he wrote to Clara, "I am so glad she is out of it and safe—safe! I am not melancholy; I shall never be melancholy again, I think." During the ensuing days and evenings he talked freely, as ever, with Paine, until January 4, when he left Stormfield with the intention of spending the rest of the winter in Bermuda. That evening, in New York, he had his last chat with Howells; the next day, with his butler as his only attendant, he sailed.

He stayed at Bay House, Hamilton, with his friends the Allens, parents of Helen the Angel-fish. For the first month or two he was peaceful and happy, and well enough to go on occasional picnics and to play clock golf with Woodrow Wilson. There wasn't a fault in the life, he wrote—"good times, good home, tranquil contentment all day and every day without a break." Though he raged when a professional pianist insisted on coming to play for him, he could still jest and indulge in pure nonsense, as when he solemnly took Helen Allen's written receipt for two dollars and forty cents, in return for her promise to believe everything he said thereafter. But as the weeks passed Paine noticed that he was dictating nearly all his letters, and on March 25 he wrote that he was planning to return to Stormfield in four weeks, and gave the first hint of the seriousness of his condition. He might have to return sooner if his breast pain did not mend. He added:

"I don't want to die here, for this is an unkind place for a person in that condition. I should have to lie in the undertaker's cellar until the ship would remove me and it is dark down there and unpleasant.

"The Colliers will meet me on the pier, and I may stay with them a week or two before going home. It all depends on the breast pain. I don't want to die there. I am growing more and more particular about the place."

Three days later he announced that if he was able to travel he would start sooner than he had first intended, and the same mail brought Paine a letter from Mr. Allen, warning him that Mark Twain's condition was regarded by the doctors as critical. Paine sailed at once, and found that the reports were true. He immediately cabled Clara, and took charge of the arrangements for returning to New York. Mark Twain had several severe attacks of angina during the days that followed, and the trip home, begun on April 12, was a forty-eight-hour nightmare. The dying man could scarcely breathe; he could not lie down, and even opiates gave him only fitful snatches of sleep. "We'll never make it," he said, and when Paine urged that they must, on Clara's account, he gasped, "It's a losing race; no ship can outsail death." And he added, during an interval when the pain and breathlessness held off, "When I seem to be dying I don't want to be stimulated back to life. I want to be made comfortable to go." He showed, Paine recorded, "not a vestige of hesitation; no grasping at straws, no suggestion of dread." He did not waver in the face of the dark, nor clutch in his weakness at the shadows of a faith which he had lost in the days of his strength.

When they got out of the Gulf Stream the cold northern air revived him and brought sleep, so that he was able to make the rest of the trip, from New York to Redding, with less difficulty than had been thought possible. For two or three days he seemed to rally in the peace of Stormfield, and when Clara arrived on the morning of April 17 he was ready to talk and spent no words on complaints about his illness. He spoke about finances, and doubted whether the sale of his books would continue long after his death. "Except for a gray look in his face his appearance was about as usual, and for several hours he filled his conversation with the same vivacity as of yore." The pains were not so severe, but his breathing became more difficult, and his attention wandered, though from time to time he would try to read a few paragraphs of his favorite Carlyle and Suetonius.

With the abating of the angina pains the doctors had withdrawn the morphine which had eased his homeward journey, but when drowsiness overcame him the borders between the worlds of dreams and of waking sometimes blurred. "This is a peculiar kind of disease," he told Paine. "It does not invite you to read; it does not invite you to be read to; it does not invite you to talk, nor to enjoy any of the usual sick-room methods of treatment. What kind of a disease is *that?* Some kinds of sicknesses have pleasant features about them. You can read and smoke and have only to lie still."

On the nineteenth Paine brought Clara her father's request that she sing for him. She made an inarticulate response, but she could not refuse his last request. She faced the ordeal, and somehow found heart and voice to render three of the Scottish songs he had always cared for. Father and daughter both thought that this might be their last meeting, and he said good-by, but he lingered for two days more. On the morning of Thursday, April 21, his mind was still clear, though he did not care to talk. He dozed off as Clara was sitting by his bedside. "Suddenly he opened his eyes, took my hand, and looked steadily into my face. Faintly he murmured, 'Goodbye dear, if we meet——' " Then he sank into the coma that possessed him until he died, at sunset. He had come into the world with Halley's comet, in 1835; he had gone out of it, as he had more than once declared he would, with Halley's comet in 1910.

It was left for Howells, almost the last survivor of the friends of Mark Twain's golden noon, to say the perfect word in the letter of sympathy he wrote to Clara:

"I found Mr. Paine's telegram when I came in late last night; and suddenly your father was set apart from all other men in a strange majesty. Death had touched his familiar image into historic grandeur."

ACKNOWLEDGMENTS AND SOURCES

ACKNOWLEDGMENTS

THE chief problem in writing a reasonably brief life of Mark Twain is one of selection from the wealth of material available. The primary source is, naturally, Mark's own works, though as I have explained, perhaps too often, these—even contemporary letters—are seldom to be trusted as pure history. In fact, after one has spent months in seeking the skeleton of truth behind some of Mark's more picturesque draperies, it is a relief to come to a tale like that of Livy's effort to cure her husband of swearing. No witnesses were present then, and the biographer can relish a good story, well told, without having to ask if it really happened that way. (Incidently, in quoting from the *Autobiography* I have wherever possible used the text which Mark Twain himself passed for publication in the *North American Review*, and not the text as revised and expurgated by Albert Bigelow Paine.) The difficulties in dealing even with the best testimony have been enough to deter me from adding to my troubles, and the reader's, by endeavoring to unearth grains of possible truth from the garbled memories of C. C. Goodwin and the out-and-out lies of Bill Gillis and Ab Grimes. And since I am neither a mind reader nor a psychoanalyst, I have not sought to reveal hidden springs of action which may once have been known to Mark Twain and to God, but which now are known only to the latter.

The only complete, full-length life of Mark Twain is Albert Bigelow Paine's official biography. For my purposes this is unsatisfactory. To begin with, Paine undertook to tell everything, with the result that Mark's literary career is submerged in a welter of other matters. Moreover, Paine was neither a critic nor a literary historian. Greatly as he admired Mark Twain's books, he was capable neither of analyzing them nor of relating them to the literary traditions from which they grew. He made little effort, if any, to trace Mark Twain in Nevada and California through the files of contemporary newspapers. For all the earlier career, indeed, Paine relied too much on the *Autobiography*, even though he had learned by experience that Mark had so creative a memory that it was unwise to accept any statement as literal unless it could be confirmed from other sources. On the other hand, Paine had the inestimable advantage of intimate, day-by-day association with the humorist during the last four years of his life, and had access to a vast store of documents, some of which have since disappeared and none of which was available to other investigators while Paine lived. No student can go far without Paine, but his work demands constant supplement and correction from other sources.

First among these is Clara Clemens' *My Father, Mark Twain*. The humorist's daughter printed a copious selection from her father's love letters and other intimate documents which Paine had hesitated to use; as a picture of the Clemens family life the volume has the same finality as Paine's memorabilia of the closing years. After Mark Twain's death, many of his surviving friends and acquaintances wrote about him at greater or less length. Howells' *My Mark Twain* is by all odds the best of these memorabilia.

In recent years many studies of special phases of Mark Twain's life and work have been made. Most of his significant contributions—with the glaring exception of the *Quaker City* letters—to the California newspapers and magazines have been reprinted. A group of Chicago enthusiasts have published a periodical leaflet called *The Twainian* in which, along with much information about misprints in first editions, they have settled such useful facts as the dates of Sam Clemens' pilot's license, and of his sister's wedding. (The latter makes possible for the first time an approximately accurate dating of the episode of Jim Wolf and the cats.) But though the great valley, from Minneapolis to the sea, bristles with colleges and universities, no historian, literary or otherwise, has yet thought it worth while to write a detailed history of Mississippi steamboating. Such a book might do for Mark Twain's years as a pilot what Miss Minnie Brashear's *Mark Twain, Son of Missouri* has done for his boyhood and Mr. Ivan Benson's *Mark Twain's Western Years* has done for his literary apprenticeship. These latter works bring together a mass of information nowhere else available, and on innumerable details replace myth and conjecture with fact. My indebtedness to them is profound.

So, too, is my indebtedness to the work of Bernard DeVoto, Walter Blair, George R. Stewart, Franklin Meine, Franklin Walker, Fred Lorch, Theodore Hornberger, Edward Wagenknecht and other specialists. To Professor Willis Wager I owe thanks for the use of a summary of the results of his collation of the manuscript of *Life on the Mississippi,* and Professor Ernest E. Leisy has been most helpful in answering questions on the material included in his forthcoming edition of the Quintus Curtius Snodgrass letters. Besides the work of these real scholars, there is, of course, a vast amount of Mark Twain "criticism." I have read some of it. My dissent from certain of its basic theses will, I hope, be plain to the specialist without hindering the pleasure of the ordinary reader.

Perhaps I should add that this book was complete in manuscript before *Mark Twain at Work* appeared. Mr. DeVoto's admirable study has enabled me to correct a number of factual statements, but in several instances my own examination of the evidence had already led me to the same conclusions, and even to some of the same imagery which Mr. DeVoto has used. Outside of graduate seminars in literature it is fairly well understood that two people can reach the same result independently, but if I do not mention the matter here Mr. DeVoto is certain to be identified as the "source" of some of my chapter titles.

For my own investigations I owe thanks to the American Council of Learned Societies for a grant which made possible my collation of the original manuscript of *Huckleberry Finn* and my obtaining photostats of the *Quaker City* letters in the *Alta California,* of the Fairbanks correspondence in the Huntington Library, and of numerous uncollected writings of Mark Twain and of the California humorists. Librarians all over the country have answered questions for me; if I here single out for special mention Mr. Alexander Galt of the Buffalo Public Library, and Mr. H. I. Priestley of the Bancroft Library, Berkeley, California, it is not that I am the less grateful to the many others. I also owe thanks to Mrs. Louise Conn McGregor for her secretarial aid, to Mr. Hiram Haydn for interposing at the right time and in the right place, and to Mr. Carl Melinat and other members of the reference staff of Western Reserve University Library for obtaining inter-library loans and for verifying numberless details. Whatever errors remain in the book are mine.

Finally, I owe thanks to copyright owners. Miss Mildred Howells has permitted me to quote from *The Life in Letters of William Dean Howells* and from *My Mark Twain* (Copyright, 1910, by Harper and Brothers; Copyright, 1938, by Mildred Howells and John Mead Howells). Messrs. Harper and Brothers have consented to my quoting from Clara Clemens' *My Father: Mark Twain*, from A. B. Paine's *Mark Twain: A Biography*, and from *Mark Twain's Autobiography, Speeches, Letters* and *Notebooks, Europe and Elsewhere, A Connecticut Yankee in King Arthur's Court* and other copyright books. And I am especially grateful to Messrs. Jervis Langdon and Charles T. Lark, Trustees of the Estate of Samuel L. Clemens and President and Secretary, respectively, of the Mark Twain Company, for allowing me to quote from Mark Twain's unpublished letters to Mrs. A. W. Fairbanks and from the uncollected "Defence of General Funston."

A number of my facts and ideas and a few paragraphs of my text I have previously published in the form of articles in several magazines and university journals.

The hitherto unpublished portrait of Mark Twain which serves as frontispiece is contributed by the kindness of Professor Ernest F. Amy of Ohio Wesleyan University.

DeLancey Ferguson

SOURCES

EXHAUSTIVE bibliographies of material relating to Mark Twain and his times will be found in several of the works listed below, notably in those of Walter Blair, Ivan Benson, Bernard DeVoto, and Edward Wagenknecht. My own list which follows includes only titles on which I have actually drawn in my text—books and articles which contain primary source material. The uncollected writings of Mark Twain himself will be found fully listed in Merle Johnson's *Bibliography of the Work of Mark Twain* (New York: Harper and Brothers, 1935); I have named only those titles which I have used.

Aldrich, Mrs. Thomas Bailey. *Crowding Memories*. Boston: Houghton Mifflin Co., 1920.

Anon. [Moses S. Beach?] "The Quaker City Pilgrimage," New York *Herald*, 21 November, 1867.

Bellamy, Gladys C. "Mark Twain's Indebtedness to John Phoenix," *American Literature*, Vol. XIII (1941), pp. 29*ff*.

Bennett, Arnold. *The Journal of Arnold Bennett*. New York: Viking Press, 1933.

Benson, Ivan. *Mark Twain's Western Years*. Stanford University Press, 1938.

Blair, Walter. "Mark Twain, New York Correspondent," *American Literature*, Vol. XI (1939), pp. 247*ff*.

———. *Native American Humor*. New York: American Book Co., 1937.

Brashear, Minnie M. *Mark Twain, Son of Missouri*. University of North Carolina Press, 1934.

Brooks, Van Wyck. *The Ordeal of Mark Twain*. New York: E. P. Dutton & Co., 1920. "Revised" ed., 1933.

Clemens, Clara. *My Father, Mark Twain*. New York: Harper and Brothers, 1931.

Davis, Sam P. (Ed.). *History of Nevada*. Reno and Los Angeles: The Elms Publishing Co., 1913.

DeCasseres, Benjamin. *When Huck Finn Went Highbrow*. New York: Thomas F. Madigan, 1934.

De Quille, Dan (William Wright). *History of the Big Bonanza*. Hartford: American Publishing Co., 1876.

Derby, George Horatio. *Phoenixiana*. New York: D. Appleton & Co., 12th ed., 1879.

DeVoto, Bernard. *Mark Twain at Work*. Harvard University Press, 1942.

———. *Mark Twain's America*. Boston: Little, Brown & Co., 1932.

Eastman, Max. "Mark Twain's Elmira," *Harper's Magazine*, May, 1938.

Ewer, Ferdinand C. "The Eventful Nights of August 20th and 21st," *The Pioneer*, San Francisco, September and October, 1854.

———. Letter in New York *Herald*, 12 March, 1855.

Ferguson, DeLancey. "The Case for Mark Twain's Wife," *University of Toronto Quarterly*, Vol. IX (1939), pp. 9*ff.*

———. "Huck Finn A-Borning," *Colophon*, new series, Vol. III, No. 2.

———. "Mark Twain's Comstock Duel: The Birth of a Legend," *American Literature*, Vol. XIV (1942), pp. 66*ff.*

———. "The Petrified Truth," *Colophon*, new series, Vol. II, No. 2.

———. "The Uncollected Portions of Mark Twain's *Autobiography*," *American Literature*, Vol. VIII (1936), pp. 37*ff.*

Gates, William B. "Mark Twain to his English Publishers," *American Literature*, Vol. XI (1939), pp. 78*ff.*

Goodwin, C. C. *As I Remember Them*. Salt Lake City, 1913.

Greenslet, Ferris. *Thomas Bailey Aldrich*. Boston: Houghton Mifflin Co., 1908.

Hannibal *Courier-Post*, Mark Twain Centennial Edition, 6 March, 1935.

Harris, Julia Collier. *Life and Letters of Joel Chandler Harris*. Boston: Houghton Mifflin Co., 1918.

Howells, Mildred. *Life in Letters of William Dean Howells*. Garden City, N. Y.: Doubleday, Doran & Co., 1928.

Howells, William Dean. *My Mark Twain*. New York: Harper and Brothers, 1910.

Hutcherson, Dudley R. "Mark Twain as a Pilot," *American Literature*, Vol. XII (1940), pp. 353*ff.*

Kipling, Rudyard. *From Sea to Sea*. New York: Doubleday & McClure Co., 1899.

Lawton, Mary. *A Lifetime with Mark Twain*. New York: Harcourt, Brace & Co., 1925.

Leisy, Ernest E. "Mark Twain & Isaiah Sellers," *American Literature*, Vol. XIII (1942), pp. 398*ff.*

———. "Mark Twain's Part in *The Gilded Age*," *American Literature*, Vol. VIII (1937), pp. 445*ff*.

Lorch, Fred W. "Lecture Trips & Visits of Mark Twain in Iowa," *Iowa Journal of History and Politics*, Vol. XXVII (1929), pp. 507*ff*.

———. "Mark Twain in Iowa," *Iowa Journal of History and Politics*, Vol. XXVII (1929), pp. 408*ff*.

———. "A Mark Twain Letter," *Iowa Journal of History and Politics*, Vol. XXVIII (1930), pp. 268*ff*.

———. "Mark Twain and the 'Campaign that Failed,'" *American Literature*, Vol. XII (1941), pp. 454*ff*.

———. "Mark Twain's Early Nevada Letters," *American Literature*, Vol. X (1939), pp. 486*ff*.

———. "Mark Twain's Orphanage Lecture," *American Literature*, Vol. VII (1936), pp. 452*ff*.

———. "Mark Twain's Trip to Humboldt in 1861," *American Literature*, Vol. X (1938), pp. 343*ff*.

———. "Molly Clemens's Notebook" [and other articles], *The Palimpsest*, Vol. X (1929), pp. 353*ff*.

———. "A Note on Tom Blankenship," *American Literature*, Vol. XII (1940), pp. 351*ff*.

Lyman, George D. *The Saga of the Comstock Lode*. New York: Charles Scribners' Sons, 1934.

Mark Twain Quarterly, The, Webster Groves, Mo., 1936 *ff*.

Meine, Franklin J. (Ed.). *Tall Tales of the Southwest*. New York: Alfred A. Knopf, 1930.

Paine, Albert Bigelow. *Mark Twain: A Biography*. New York: Harper and Brothers, 1912.

Powell, Lawrence C. "An Unpublished Mark Twain Letter," *American Literature*, Vol. XII (1942), pp. 405*ff*.

Richardson, Lyon N. "Men of Letters and the Hayes Administration," *New England Quarterly*, Vol. XV (1942), pp. 110*ff*.

Schultz, John Richie. "New Letters of Mark Twain," *American Literature*, Vol. VIII (1936), pp. 47*ff*.

Seitz, Don C. *Artemus Ward*. New York: Harper and Brothers, 1919.

Stewart, George E. *Bret Harte, Argonaut and Exile*. Boston: Houghton Mifflin Co., 1931.

Stewart, George R. *John Phoenix, Esq.* New York: Henry Holt & Co., 1937.

Stewart, William M. *Reminiscences*. New York, Neale Publishing Co., 1908.

Twain, Mark.

The uniform collected edition of Mark Twain's works is published by Harper and Brothers, New York, and comprises 21 volumes. Also published by Harpers, but not in the uniform edition, are the *Letters* (2 vols., 1917), *Autobiography* (2 vols., 1924), *Speeches* (1910), *Notebooks* (1935) and *Mark Twain in Eruption* (1940). The following titles have appeared under other publishers' imprints:

————. *The Curious Republic of Gondour.* New York: Boni & Liveright, 1919.

————. *Letters from the Sandwich Islands written for the Sacramento Union,* Ed. G. Ezra Dane. Stanford University Press, 1938.

————. *Mark Twain's Letters in the Muscatine Journal,* Ed. Edgar M. Branch. Chicago: Mark Twain Association of America, 1942.

————. *Mark Twain's Letters to Will Bowen,* Ed. Theodore Hornberger. Austin: University of Texas Press, 1941.

———— . *Mark Twain's Travels with Mr. Brown,* Ed. Franklin Walker and G. Ezra Dane. New York: Alfred A. Knopf, 1940.

————. *Republican Letters,* Ed. Cyril Clemens. Webster Groves, Mo., 1941.

————. *Sketches of the Sixties, by Bret Harte and Mark Twain.* San Francisco: J. Howell, 1926.

————. *The Washoe Giant in San Francisco,* Ed. Franklin Walker. San Francisco: G. Fields, 1938.

————. Uncollected writings:

"Chapters from My Autobiography," *North American Review,* September, 1906—December, 1907. About one-fifth of this material is still uncollected; the collected portions were frequently revised by A. B. Paine.

"A Defence of General Funston," *North American Review,* May, 1902.

"How I Escaped Being Killed in a Duel," *Tom Hood's Comic Annual,* London, 1873.

Letter to the Editor of *The Spectator,* London, 1872.

"Memoranda," *Galaxy* (N. Y.), January-December, 1870. Only partly collected.

"The Holy Land Excursion," 53 letters in the *Alta California* (San Francisco), between August 25, 1867, and May 17, 1868.

"The Mediterranean Excursion," letters in New York *Tribune,* July 30, September 6, September 19, October 25, November 2, November 9, 1867.

"The Quaker City Pilgrimage," letter in New York *Herald*, 20 November, 1867.
————. Unpublished writings:
More than 100 letters to Mrs. A. W. Fairbanks, Huntington Library.
Twainian, The. Chicago: Mark Twain Society, 1939 *ff.*
Underhill, Irving S. "Diamonds in the Rough. Being the Story of Another Book that Mark Twain Never Wrote," *Colophon*, Pt. XIII (1933).
Vogelback, Arthur L. "The Publication and Reception of *Huckleberry Finn* in America," *American Literature*, Vol. XI (1939), pp. 260*ff.*
Wagenknecht, Edward. *Mark Twain: The Man and his Work.* Yale University Press, 1935.
Waggoner, Hyatt Howe. "Science in the Thought of Mark Twain," *American Literature*, Vol. VIII (1937), pp. 357*ff.*
Walker, Franklin. "An Influence from San Francisco on Mark Twain's *The Gilded Age*," *American Literature*, Vol. VIII (1936), pp. 63*ff.*
————. *San Francisco's Literary Frontier.* New York: Alfred A. Knopf, 1939.
Wallace, Elizabeth. *Mark Twain and the Happy Island.* Chicago: A. C. McClurg & Co., 1913.
Warfel, Harry R. "George W. Cable Amends a Mark Twain Plot," *American Literature*, Vol. VI (1934), pp. 328*ff.*
White, Frank Marshall. "Mark Twain as a Newspaper Reporter," *Outlook* (N. Y.), December 24, 1910.
Woolf, S. J. *Here Am I.* New York: Random House, 1941.

INDEX

INDEX

Abdul-Aziz, Sultan, 123
Abelard, 121
Abolition, MT and, 42-43
Academy of Design, New York, 118
Adair Co., Ky., 16
Adam's Diary, 255
Addison, Joseph, 27
Adolph, Father, 280
Adventures of Captain Simon Suggs (J. J. Hooper), 27
Adventures of Huckleberry Finn, The, see *Huckleberry Finn*
Adventures of Tom Sawyer, The, see *Tom Sawyer*
Age of Reason, The (Paine), 48
Aguinaldo, Emilio, 288-289
Ahab, Captain, 53
Ah Sin, 186-187
Aix-les-Bains, MT at, 248
Ajax, S.S., 106-108
Albert, Prince, 41
Alcott, Bronson, 229
Aldrich, Charles, 296
Aldrich, Lilian Woodman (Mrs. T. B.), 165-166, 312-313
Aldrich, Thomas Bailey, 89-90, 98, 164, 165-166, 178-179, 182, 186, 190, 195, 295, 296, death of, 312
Alexander II, Tsar, 124-125, 146
Alexander the Great, 90
Alexandria, MT in, 136
Allen, Helen, 315, 323
"All Kinds of Ships," 250
Alta California, 81, 105, 112, 115-126, 134-136
Amazon River, 45-46, 48, 50, 318
Ament, Joseph P., 33-35, 253
America, S.S., 116
American Board of Foreign Missions, 284-285
American Claimant, The, 216, 246, 250, 253
American Publishing Co., 130-131, 133-134, 203-204, 263, 281
Andalusia, MT in, 126
Angel-fish, 313, 315
Angels Camp, 102-103
Appomattox, Battle of, 232
Architecture, MT's knowledge of, 124
Arles, MT in, 248
Army of the Tennessee, Reunion of, 196

Arnold, Matthew, 166, 238, 246
Art, on the frontier, 28-29; MT's knowledge of, 118, 124, 194
Athens, MT in, 125
A. T. Lacey, steamboat, 52
Atlantic Monthly, 146, 174-175, 177-178, 180, 182, 185, 188, 201, 209, 212, 229; dinner, MT's speech at, 189-191, 196, 202
Austen, Jane, 207, 268
Australia, MT in, 263, 266
Autobiography, MT's, 33, 35, 41, 95, 97, 135, 139, 150, 153-154, 187, 218, 311; writing of, 295-296, 305-308, 314, 315; publication of, 311
Autocrat of the Breakfast Table, The, 106
Azores, MT in, 136

Baalbec, MT at, 137
"Babies, The," MT's speech on, 196-197
Babson, Roger, 278
"Baby Bell" (Aldrich), 90
Baconian Theory, 213, 307, 315-316
Baden-Baden, MT in, 193
Bailey, Tom, 182
Baker, Jim, 102, 200
Balaam's Ass, 188
Ballou, Mr., 72, 199
Baltimore, MT in, 316
Bankruptcy, MT's, 259-260, 265, 271
"Barbara Allen," 28
"Barbara Frietchie," 190
Barnum, Phineas T., 206
Barr, Robert, 240
Barrett, Dr., 16
Barstow, William H., 74, 75, 78
Bates, Edward, 64
Battles and Leaders of the Civil War, The, 231
Bauman, Nikolaus, 24
Bayreuth, MT at, 248
Beach, Emma, 120, 133, 301
Beach, Moses E., 120, 127, 133
Beadle's Dime Novels, 92
Beard, Dan, 242
Beecher, Henry Ward, 116, 133, 141
Beecher, Thomas K., 142, 149
Beerbohm, Max, 199
"Belated Russian Passport, The," 292
Bell, Moberly, 311

341